MW00526403

Procyon
Canis Minor

onoceros

Pollux

Castor

Gemini

Alhena

Betelgeuse

itak
nilam

Orion
Bellatrix

Alnath
Ceres

Auriga

HAWAIKI RISING

HAWAIKI RISING

Hōkūle'a, Nainoa Thompson, and the
Hawaiian Renaissance

SAM LOW

University of Hawai'i Press
Honolulu

First published by Island Heritage Publishing
Reprint edition published by University of Hawai'i Press 2018

Printed in the United States of America
23 22 21 20 19 18   6 5 4 3 2

A record of the Cataloging-in-Publication data can be found at the Library
of Congress Website:
http://catalog.loc.gov/

University of Hawai'i Press books are printed on acid-free
paper and meet the guidelines for permanence and
durability of the Council on Library Resources.

Designed by Nan Bacon and Tara Kenny

This book is dedicated to the memory of

Eddie Aikau
Myron "Pinky" Thompson
Mau Piailug
and the
'Ohana Wa'a

Special Thanks to:

Papa Ola Lōkahi

for a grant to assist with the writing and the distribution
of free copies to educational institutions throughout the
Hawaiian Islands.

CONTENTS

FOREWORD

By Nainoa Thompson

G rowing up in Hawai'i in the nineteen sixties, I found my Hawaiian culture ebbing away. I had never seen an authentic *hula*, attended a traditional ceremony and seldom heard our language spoken. It was a confusing time for me and I felt lost between worlds that seemed in conflict. All that changed one night when Herb Kane introduced me to the stars and explained how my ancestors had used them to find their way across a vast ocean to settle all of Polynesia. At that moment, my vision of my ancestry became timeless and alive in those same stars.

Our canoe, *Hōkūle'a*, and our dreams have now carried us over one hundred and fifty thousand miles of ocean, following in the wake of our ancestors who discovered and settled Polynesia. It has been a process of finding ourselves not only as Hawaiians, as native to these islands, but also as native to planet Earth. On all of our voyages, we have been guided by the wisdom of our elders, our *kūpuna*. Among them is my father, Myron "Pinky" Thompson, who understood that voyaging is a process in which we are guided by values that are universal. "Before our ancestors set out to find a new island," my father told me, "they had to have a vision of that island over the horizon. They made a plan for achieving that vision. They prepared themselves physically and mentally and were willing to experiment, to try new things. They took risks. And on the voyage they bound each other with *aloha* so they could together overcome those risks and achieve their vision. You find these same values throughout the world," he said, "seeking, planning, experimenting, taking risks, and caring for each other. The same principles that we used in the past, are the ones that we use today and that we will use into the future. No matter what race we are or what culture we carry, these are values that work for us all."

Hōkūle'a embodies the *mana*, the spiritual power and wisdom, of all who have sailed aboard her or laid their caring hands on her. Our great teacher, Mau Piailug, taught us to travel always with *seram*, with the light. He taught us that

Nainoa Thompson steering *Hōkūle'a*

voyaging aboard *Hōkūle'a* was a *kuleana*, both a privilege and a responsibility: that a voyager sets out to discover new worlds and new values, and to bring them home to nourish the spirit of his people. As we continue to explore new sea-paths, we celebrate the founders of our voyaging society, Herb Kane, Ben Finney, and Tommy Holmes, whose tenacious pursuit of their vision of an ancient canoe traveling ancestral sea paths gave birth to *Hōkūle'a*. We follow the guiding stars that Will Kyselka helped us discover by his constant encouragement and support. As we raise new islands and new lands from the sea, we realize the dream of Eddie Aikau, who gave his life for his vision of seeing Tahitian mountains rising from the distant horizon. And we are inspired by the wisdom given to us by astronaut Lacy Veach who, from his vantage point in space, taught us to see our world holistically so that we might know that we are all one and that we might *mālama*, care for, our planet so that Earth may sustain all human life. As we sail on into the future all these people and many, many more—our *kūpuna*—sail with us.

The vision of *Hōkūle'a* was conceived in 1973, so the publishing of this book marks the 40th anniversary of her creation. Sam Low, the author, has sailed with us. He has been a documenter on four voyages, written numerous articles and now, after ten years of work, has finished *Hawaiki Rising*. This book is an important part of our *'ōlelo*, our history, and it contains the *mana* of all those who helped create and sail *Hōkūle'a*.

I hope that *Hawaiki Rising* may inspire not only Hawaiian children, but all children, to pursue their dreams. In that pursuit my father's teaching may assist them. "Success is ninety percent in the preparation for it," he told me. Fear of failure is the constant companion of dreamers and it hindered me in my early life. It was not until, after completing my first voyage aboard *Hōkūle'a* as navigator in 1980, that I learned that fear was not my enemy, but my ally because it goaded me to prepare for success. When we made landfall after thirty-one days at sea, I realized that all dreams are achievable, but only by hard and constant work.

PREFACE

The title of this book, *Hawaiki Rising*, has *kaona* or multiple meanings. It is the name of the mythic homeland of the Polynesian people. It refers to the nautical concept of raising land from the sea as when a mariner says, "we raised O'ahu," meaning he saw the Hawaiian island rise above the horizon as he approached it from the ocean. More personally, it refers to the dream of the legendary Hawaiian waterman, Eddie Aikau, of seeing Tahiti rise from the sea on a voyage aboard the Hawaiian canoe, *Hōkūle'a*. It also evokes the legend of the Hawaiian demigod Maui, who created the Hawaiian Islands by pulling them from the sea with his magical fish hook, *mānai-a-ka-lani*. And finally it celebrates the raising of the Hawaiian consciousness in their great seafaring heritage—and their pride in it—by voyaging aboard *Hōkūle'a* in the wake of their ancestors.

As much as possible, I have attempted to present this story of *Hōkūle'a's* creation, her voyages and her deep meaning in the words of those who created her, sailed aboard her, or in other ways joined with her.

Most quotations in this book are taken from interviews I conducted. Some of them may have been corrected for grammar or edited to make them more succinct, but every effort has been taken to keep them accurate to the intended meaning of the speaker. A few quotations have come from interviews conducted by John Kruse and Keani Reiner after the 1976 voyage to Tahiti. Conversations have been reconstructed from interviews, log books and writing by crewmembers. Descriptions of life aboard *Hōkūle'a* have been taken from statements made by the crew as well as from my own experience sailing aboard the canoe.

Mistakes of any kind are solely my fault.

Sam Low – April, 2013.

INTRODUCTION

"Bring her down!"

With this command from the navigator, my watchmates and I threw our weight against the steering paddle to bring our vessel off the wind. We are aboard a sailing craft the likes of which have not been seen for centuries. She is called *Hōkūle'a*—star of joy—and she is a replica of canoes that once carried Polynesian explorers to discover and settle thousands of islands in a vast watery domain known as the Polynesian Triangle.

For twenty-one days we had sailed through storms and uneasy calms and now we were nearing our destination. Our navigator, Nainoa Thompson, had guided us here without compass, sextant, or chart by signs that only he could read—the paths and shapes of constellations, the curl of ocean swells, the winds. It is an ancient art, practiced for millennia before the "discovery" of Polynesia by European explorers.

Our voyage took us northeast from Tahiti for twenty-four hundred miles until today when Nainoa ordered us to steer directly west. Running with the trade wind, a gossamer mist wafted over the canoe, parting ahead and reforming behind us as we continued on.

Except for catnaps, Nainoa had been on watch the entire voyage, willing himself back to a time when his Polynesian ancestors sailed across similar expanses of ocean. Now, having observed signs invisible to the rest of us, he was certain that the island of Hawai'i lay directly in our path.

"The mist to the north and south moves," he told me, "but ahead of us it seems to stall. It sits there like a constant fog. That makes me think there's land ahead."

There was also the wind. For a time it held steady from astern and we sailed wing-on-wing—one sail to port and one to starboard—then the wind shifted southeast making it hard to fill our sails without changing course. For those of us manning the sweep it was an annoyance. For Nainoa, it was another land sign.

"The trade winds cannot rise over the high slopes of Mauna Kea so when they encounter the volcano they split to flow around it. One branch blows southwest

Hōkūle'a at sea

down the Puna coast, the other flows southeast along the Hāmākua coast. When the wind veered southeasterly, it was an indication we are north of Hilo."

As the sun descended, Nainoa observed a slight shift in the density and the color of the sky ahead.

"To the left I see a brightness on the horizon. Looking to the right it's dark, until farther right it becomes light again. Where it's dark, there is land breaking the rays of the sunset."

To demonstrate, Nainoa joined his two open palms to form a "V", one hand pointing to the opening on the left, the other to the opening on the right.

"You can triangulate our position like this," he said. "My left hand points to the opening to the south, my right hand to the opening to the north. Where my two hands join is where we are. I think we're to the northeast of Hilo, maybe twenty to twenty-five miles away from the Hāmākua Coast."

None of us can see these signs. We do not doubt they exist, but to predict our position within a few miles after such a long voyage seemed impossible. We tacked the canoe to starboard. The Hāmākua Coast, if it was there, was invisible in the darkening mist.

Slowly, by a latent instinct, we became aware that something large lay to port. We felt it—a kind of pressure. The feeling drew us to the rail, where we stood peering into the darkness. Then, the clouds began to lift, and we saw the twinkling lights of Hilo on our beam.

Speaking for all of us, Nainoa said simply, "We're home."

✧ ✧ ✧ ✧ ✧

My voyage aboard *Hōkūle'a* began improbably with a 1964 visit to the Peabody Museum in New Haven. In the cloistered stacks of the museum's library, I spread out notes for a term paper on Polynesian archaeology. Wandering the stacks, I pulled down an intriguing title—*Canoes of Oceania*—a book filled with images of indigenous seagoing craft drawn by early European explorers. Here were sleek sailing vessels from islands sprawled across an immense ocean—from Tonga east across four thousand miles to Easter Island, north three thousand miles to Hawai'i and south fifteen hundred to New Zealand. Some looked like creations from an alien planet; others like strange insects—but it was obvious they were all capable of fast voyages over stormy seas. It was a revelation.

As a young boy, I had read *Kon Tiki,* Thor Heyerdahl's account of his 1947 voyage from Peru deep into Polynesian waters aboard a balsa raft. For a hundred and one days, Heyerdahl and his crew drifted with the prevailing winds and currents on a forty-three hundred mile voyage to landfall on Raroia Island in the Tuamotus. With this voyage, he claimed to prove that Polynesia was settled by South American mariners who sailed craft so primitive they could neither be steered nor navigated.

Yet here in *Canoes of Oceania* were vessels that had sailed circles around the clumsy square-rigged ships of European explorers like Captain James Cook. Some of them were more than a hundred feet long. They spread fore-and-aft sails like those on modern yachts, capable of carrying them swiftly upwind. Heyerdahl thought Polynesians were hapless drifters—prisoners of nature's forces. But why, I wondered, would they have used clumsy rafts when they possessed such graceful and advanced sailing vessels? Something was wrong with Heyerdahl's theory.

For the next dozen years or so, this discovery slept in my imagination as I completed my undergraduate degree, served in the U.S. Navy—traveling to Hawai'i for the first time in 1964—and then finished a Ph.D. in anthropology and embarked on a career as a college professor and filmmaker. In 1976, I read a National Geographic article about new research that showed Polynesians had set out from Island Southeast Asia and ventured upwind—against the winds and currents—to Tonga, Fiji, and Samoa, arriving at about the time Troy was falling to the Greeks. They sailed onward, eventually populating all of Polynesia a thousand years or so after Christ was born and they voyaged in sleek seaworthy vessels like the ones in *Canoes of Oceania.* I also read about *Hōkūle'a,* a replica of such vessels, and her successful voyage from Hawai'i to Tahiti—carrying her crew 2400 miles in thirty-five days. Even more astonishing, she was navigated by Mau Piailug, a man from a tiny Micronesian Island who found his way as his ancestors always had, without charts or instruments, relying instead on a world of natural signs. I determined to make a film about this story and to tell it from the perspective of the scientists who had discovered the truth about ancient Polynesian explorers and men like Mau Piailug who continued to sail in the old way.

Author Sam Low with Mau Piailug—Satawal 1980

I spent two years traveling the Pacific with experienced archaeologists as guides, retracing steps taken by early Polynesian mariners. I sailed with Mau Piailug from his home island of Satawal. He told me how he navigated by the stars and by signs in the wind and waves using secret knowledge handed down from father to son over thousands of years. I spent time in Hawaiʻi with Nainoa Thompson who combined Mau's teachings with his own discoveries to reveal how ancient Polynesians may have guided their canoes. I began to feel a stirring in my blood. I am one-quarter Hawaiian, and three-quarters *haole*—descended from a Hawaiian *aliʻi* (a chief) and a New Englander who ventured to the islands in 1850 seeking wealth and bringing with him disease and an alien way of life. At first glance, this influx of outsiders seemed to have destroyed Hawaiian culture. But as I visited the islands more often, I discovered an astonishing revival of the Hawaiian language, poetry, dance, and all the other arts of indigenous life.

Hawaiian culture had not died. It had gone underground—waiting for a spark to ignite it. That spark was *Hōkūle'a*.

In 1995, I was invited to join a voyage from Tahiti to the Marquesas and on to Hawai'i as crew aboard an escort vessel, a modern sloop that ghosted in *Hōkūle'a's* wake. In 1999, I sailed aboard *Hōkūle'a* for the first time on a voyage from Mangareva to Rapa Nui (Easter Island); in 2000, I sailed on the canoe from Tahiti to Hawai'i and in 2007 I made the trip from Chuuk, in Micronesia, to Satawal, the homeland of Mau Piailug. From these experiences comes this book.

I have written it from the point of view of the crew who sailed aboard *Hōkūle'a* in the early period of her voyaging—from 1973 to 1980. This was a time of intense joy as Hawaiians took pride in the achievements of their ancestors, mixed with sadness and anger as they understood how their culture had nearly been destroyed. And it was during this time that Nainoa Thompson found his way not just among waves and stars, but back to the spiritual world of his ancestors. This book is the story of an astonishing revival of indigenous culture by voyagers who sailed deep into their ancestral past.

DISCOVERY AND DECLINE

Chapter One

O n the 17th of January, 1779, Captain James Cook piloted his ship *Resolution* into Kealakekua Bay on the island of Hawai'i. Steep cliffs ascended on three sides. Palm trees girded the shore. *Resolution* and her consort vessel *Discovery* had been at sea for almost a year as Cook explored the Northwest coast of America. He was glad to anchor in a place where he could refit his vessels and rest his men.

The Hawaiians had been watching the two great ships work their way up the coast and now they surrounded them in a large fleet of canoes. The beach thronged with women and children waving, clapping, and singing while others gathered in the trees and along the cliff tops ringing the bay. The din was overwhelming.

On two previous voyages, Cook had explored deep into the Pacific, visiting the islands of New Zealand, Tahiti, Tonga and Samoa and everywhere he recognized the same lilting tones of the Polynesian language. He was a sailor-scholar who surmised these far flung islanders shared a similar culture and he posed an intriguing question: "How shall we account for this Nation spreading itself so far over this Vast ocean?"

It was a fascinating puzzle. Beginning with Magellan in 1520, Europeans began to explore the Pacific aboard large ships guided by navigators equipped with the tools of the Enlightenment—charts, compasses, and other instruments— abetted by a scientific understanding of the cosmos revealed by astronomy. Yet almost every island was already inhabited by a people that appeared to be "primitive" with a "Stone Age" culture. How had these islanders managed to explore and settle this vast ocean? Where had they come from?

In 1595, when a Spanish expedition stumbled upon the Marquesas, the expedition's navigator, Pedro Fernandez de Quiros, surmised that a yet undiscovered continent—Terra Australis—must lie to the south, a highway

Captain Cook entering Kealakekua Bay

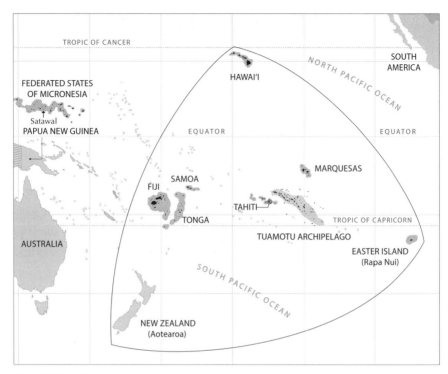

Map of Polynesia

upon which the Marquesan people had traveled to these remote islands. Julien Crozet proposed a similar theory—Polynesian islands were the remnant mountaintops of a sunken continent, a land bridge that allowed the natives to settle them without getting their feet wet. In 1722, when the Dutch navigator Jacob Roggeveen discovered tiny Easter Island some seventeen hundred miles from the nearest land, he proposed the inhabitants were the descendants of Adam.

Captain Cook knew differently. Throughout Polynesia he encountered large double canoes that sailed circles around his own ships. On his first voyage to Tahiti in 1769, he met Tupaia, a high priest and navigator who guided him through the Society Island chain. From memory, Tupaia described more than a hundred islands stretching from Tonga in the west to the Australs in the east—a distance of twelve hundred miles. Tupaia told Cook that navigators from Ra'iatea had sailed for twenty days or more aboard their large double canoes, called *pahi,* and in 1769 Cook had written in his log: "In these Pahee's ...these people sail in those seas from Island to island for several hundred Leagues (about 600 nautical miles), the Sun serving them for a compass by day and the Moon and stars by night. When this comes to be prov'd we Shall be no longer at a loss to know how these Islands lying in those Seas came to be people'd."[1]

For the next two centuries, the question of Polynesian origins was largely forgotten as those who followed in Cook's wake pursued a more practical question—how to profit from these new discoveries? Colonies sprouted everywhere, tended by German, British, French, Spanish and American overlords. In Hawai'i, a trickle of adventurers and beachcombers took up residence, followed soon by missionaries and by whalers on their way to the Pacific whaling grounds.

In the beginning, the newcomers, which the Hawaiians called *haole*—foreigners, or more generally white people—were content to be agents for their Hawaiian hosts: managing their ports; organizing the trade in sandalwood, hides, and meat; and tending small farms on land generously given to them. Land tenure at that time was basically feudal. The metes and bounds were kept by old men in their heads—men who also kept the genealogies of their princes. They were called *kāhuna*, "masters of knowledge," a word that also meant "priest." Title to the land (meaning the right to use it) resided always in the king or paramount chief, who apportioned it to a group of high ranked *ali'i* who, in turn, set aside small plots for the commoners, the *maka'āinana*. The death of a king was accompanied by some reshuffling of land, but the system worked smoothly enough for over a thousand years.

But the new *haole* residents, mostly American, were accustomed to owning land in freehold. Their ancestors had departed England for the New World precisely over this issue; they had experienced feudal tenure first-hand and wanted nothing of it. They hungered to own their land outright—to enjoy the "fruits of their labor" rather than toiling for the benefit of a landlord. Tied to this was the concept of "improving" the land, of investing their labor and money in it. But why would anyone risk this if title to the land was not secure? In 1839, under severe pressure from his missionary advisors and the growing *haole* population, King Kamehameha III proclaimed a Declaration of Rights, which established the basic property rights of both *haole* and Native Hawaiians—land could not be taken from them arbitrarily but only by "express provision of the laws." In 1840 the Kingdom of Hawai'i passed a constitution with further provisions for the guarantee of property rights.

It was hard for any western person to imagine how Hawaiians felt about the land. The *haole* who lived in Hawai'i were wanderers. They had departed their homes to seek new worlds. Most Hawaiians, on the other hand, had lived in a single place all their lives. They could recall stories about the land told by their fathers and grandfathers. And their *kāhuna* remembered stories that went back to the beginning of time, a hundred generations or more, all of them associated with particular events and people and places. And so the land had become layered with meaning that shaded into myth, no less powerful than if the events had happened yesterday. It was a Homeric topography which an Athenian might understand but which eluded most of the *haole*, although they prided themselves in their philosophical descent from the ancient Greeks. It was also a vision that was doomed.

The missionaries thought that freehold would create a nation of simple yeomen farmers like their own ancestors. The new Hawaiian society based on private property would elevate the common man, the *maka'āinana*, by releasing them from a life of servitude to the *ali'i*. But only a few years after the passing of the new constitution, the flaw in that vision was evident. "I am sorry to be obliged to say," wrote Missionary Edward Johnson from his station in Hanalei, Kaua'i, "that the people in this region have little confidence in what their rulers say about the security of lands. They are told in the Constitution, as published some seven years since, that they, (the people) should have secured to them the right of holding their own house-lots and the fruits of the earth that their own hands had planted and reared up. Well, now, in the face and eyes of this sentiment of the Constitution, some twenty families in the single valley of Hanalei, are stripped of the fruit their own hands had planted; and not only that, but are now, some of them, being literally driven from the spot where they have always lived and were born. They are told that the white man has paid their king dollars, and therefore they must be content with their lot."[2]

In 1850, Colonel Richard Bland Lee, Robert E. Lee's cousin, traveled to Hawai'i in search of fresh produce for military garrisons in California. In Waimea, on the Big Island, he observed the effects of privatizing the land first hand: "This valley was formerly thickly settled with villages of natives and abounded with numerous herds of horses, black cattle, sheep, goats and swine," he wrote, "and twenty years ago contained a population of perhaps twenty thousand natives, in the full enjoyment of health and plenty. At this time it presents the most forlorn and abject spectacle, more than nine tenths of the people having disappeared from the face of the earth, and the remaining tenth being the most abandoned, diseased and wretched beings that live. The fine lands of this valley are gradually falling into the possession of white men, principally from the United States, and large plantations and farms are being established which in the course of a few years will yield most of the products of the temperate and torrid zones."[3]

Haole newcomers brought with them not only new ideas, laws and religions, but also new diseases. On February 10th, 1853, smallpox broke out in Honolulu when an American Merchant ship appeared in the port flying a yellow quarantine flag. It was a single case and was treated successfully with vaccine and quarantine. But in May, two Hawaiian women fell sick, apparently stricken by contact with a recent arrival from California where the disease was raging. On the island of O'ahu, "Hawaiians fell sick everywhere. Some were abandoned and died alone; their bodies were left to rot. Others were buried where they lay, without coffins, in graves so shallow that wandering pigs and dogs could unearth them. Some native families nursed their sick at home, devotedly and uselessly, and carefully laid the dead under the dirt floors of their thatch huts or in their house yards, following their old burial practices and condemning themselves to follow the dead into the grave."[4]

The disease was carried to Kawaihae, a few miles from Waimea on the Big Island, where for a time the district was without vaccine, medicine, or a doctor. The local constables were tasked with burying the dead. They responded by running away. Panic prevailed. Church attendance soared as survivors prayed for deliverance, but each Sabbath showed the congregation diminished. Houses stood abandoned or burned. A yellow flag flew over most of those left standing.

In 1873, when Mark Twain visited the islands, a little less than a hundred years after Cook, he found the Hawaiian population dispirited and dying. "The natives of the islands number only about 50,000, and the whites about 3,000, chiefly Americans. According to Captain Cook the natives numbered 400,000 less than a hundred years ago. But the traders brought labor and fancy diseases— in other words, long, deliberate, infallible destruction; and the missionaries brought the means of grace and got them ready. So the two forces are working along harmoniously, and anybody who knows anything about figures can tell you exactly when the last kanaka will be in Abraham's bosom and his islands in the hands of the whites. It is the same as calculating an eclipse—if you get started right, you cannot miss it. For nearly a century the natives have been keeping up a ratio of about three births to five deaths, and you can see what that must result in. No doubt in fifty years a kanaka (native Hawaiian) will be a curiosity in his own land, and as an investment will be superior to a circus."[5]

The question was no longer where had the Polynesians come from, but would they survive into the next century?

REVIVAL

Chapter Two

In 1947, interest in the origins of the Polynesian people was rekindled when Thor Heyerdahl and six companions set out from Peru to sail into Polynesia. The prevailing Pacific winds and currents flow from east to west—from South America into the Pacific—so Heyerdahl surmised this vast ocean was settled by South Americans who drifted aboard primitive rafts. After a voyage of a hundred and one days, Heyerdahl fetched up on Raroia, a coral atoll in the Tuamotus. His account of the trip, *Kon Tiki*, was an international best seller and for laymen it settled the question once and for all. But scholars knew Heyerdahl was wrong— the Polynesians had come from the opposite direction, from Southeast Asia.

The evidence was overwhelming. Ethnobotanists traced plants introduced by the first settlers to their origins in Southeast Asia. Carbon 14 dates were earlier in the west and later in the east, indicating not only a route of migration but giving it a timetable. Archeologists discovered distinctive Lapitaware pottery in New Guinea and the Bismark Archipelago, and dated it to 1,650 BC. Four hundred years later, it appeared in the first Polynesian settlements in Fiji, Tonga, and Samoa, hundreds of miles to the east, carried there by seafaring explorers. Linguistic and genetic studies showed similar results. Polynesia had been settled by voyagers who sailed from west to east, against the winds and currents, eventually colonizing islands scattered across ten million square miles of ocean. How was this possible? How could a people without metal tools have built vessels capable of sailing against the wind and how could they have navigated such a vast extent of ocean without charts or instruments?

◇ ◇ ◇ ◇ ◇

In 1968, an imposingly tall part-Hawaiian named Herb Kawainui Kane was working in Chicago as a commercial artist on an advertising campaign that featured a giant vegetable man—the "Jolly Green Giant"—who presided over a mythical "Valley of Plenty." As he sketched the affable Goliath, Kane found himself distracted by other visions swirling in his head—images of large ocean-going Polynesian canoes.

Herb was born in Garrison Keillor's iconic American town—Lake Wobegon—to a Danish mother and Hawaiian-Chinese father. "My parents were on their way through Minnesota," he recalls, "and roads and cars being what they were in nineteen twenty-eight, and my mother being in a state of advanced maternity, she delivered in Stearns County Minnesota, which is the location that Garrison Keillor avers is Lake Wobegon."

Herb grew up in both Hawai'i and Wisconsin, the family moving back and forth. He finished high school and did a stint in the Navy. He then studied at the School of the Art Institute of Chicago. He took courses in anthropology at the University of Chicago, a hotbed of the discipline, and briefly considered a career in the field. He married, had kids and prospered. He bought a house in a little town called Glencoe on the shore of Lake Michigan "because they had a nice beach and a sailing club." He learned to race catamarans and crewed on a yacht from Maui to Honolulu. He traveled often to the islands where he befriended the famous anthropologist Kenneth Emory of the Bishop Museum.

Herb read the journals of Cook and other early explorers. He studied the drawings of canoes they published. "I saw that some of them were very clumsy. In those days, people were trained to draw headlands and distinct landforms in the Naval Academies for recognition purposes. It was a part of cartography but that did not make them artists—their drawings were all out of proportion. The figures on the canoes, the sails, were out of whack. So I wondered 'What did these damn things look like?' I got very curious and I started researching."

Herb's research took him to a famous book—*Canoes of Oceania*—reams of text and thousands of drawings, paintings and sketches of canoes gleaned from early European explorers by A. C. Haddon and James Hornell. Armed with a letter of introduction from Kenneth Emory, Herb sent queries to world famous museums. Responses poured into his Glencoe studio. He sat at his drafting board and redrew the canoes, smoothing their crude lines into seagoing shapes. "Having synthesized all these fragments into drawings, I was curious to see what they looked like on the sea with people on their decks." He began to

Painting of *Hōkūle'a* by Herb Kane

paint a series of illustrations that would inspire a stunning revival of interest in Polynesian origins and, more important, a search by Hawaiians themselves for their cultural roots.

Among Hawaiians today there's a notion that a call has gone out to their mainland brothers and sisters. "Come home," says the call, "we need you to help us reclaim our culture and our land." No one is keeping track, but in the last generation or so, thousands of Hawaiians have heeded the call. Herb was one of them. In 1970, this cultural awakening lured Herb back to Hawai'i where his canoe paintings were exhibited, and reproduced as prints and on postcards and calendars. Their enthusiastic reception reinforced Herb's curiosity—How did these canoes sail? Were they seaworthy? Could they carry large cargoes of people and goods? "What I really wanted to do was build one and take it out and find out. A lot of people didn't get it. They thought I was going to build a canoe as some kind of monument. They were rather appalled when I explained, 'No, this is something I want to take out and actually sail.' "

One of the few people who knew precisely what Herb had in mind was Ben Finney. Ben is a lean six foot three Californian with sandy hair and blue eyes. He grew up in San Diego surfing and diving for abalone. He learned to sail catamarans. He attended Berkeley where he "wandered from engineering, to humanities, to history to anthropology." It was the fifties and jobs were plentiful, so he was indulging his interests. Ben traveled to Hawai'i to surf and became fascinated by Polynesian culture. "My question was, how did they adapt so well to the sea? Everything I read in anthropology was about land people. The Polynesians were a sea people—how did they learn to use the ocean so well, to create this ocean-based way of life?"

At the University of Hawai'i, where Ben earned his undergraduate degree, he met Kenneth Emory, then the world's foremost authority on Polynesia, and folklorist Katherine Luomala who supervised his Master's thesis, "Surfing, the History of an Ancient Sport," which was published, rare for a scholarly treatise, and is now in its second edition. Luomala introduced him to a book called *The Ancient Voyagers of the Pacific*, by Andrew Sharp.

"I don't like this book and I want you to read it," Loumala told him.

Andrew Sharp had accepted the scholars' conclusion that Polynesia had been settled from Southeast Asia, but he could not accept Captain Cook's theory that Polynesians had been skilled navigators who found their way by sun, moon and stars. How would they have plotted their course without a map or have found their latitude and longitude without instruments? Sharp thought Polynesia was settled by castaways blown off course in storms. "On occasion," he wrote, "voluntary exiles, or exiles driven out to sea, were conveyed to other islands on one-way voyages in which precise navigation played no part."[6]

"I didn't believe it," Finney remembers. "Here are the Polynesians, sitting in the middle of this huge ocean and they've got these big canoes—the ones seen by Captain Cook on his voyages—so they must have sailed here. Sharp said flatly that you can't sail more than three hundred miles out of sight of land without instruments because of navigational errors. But you have Hawaiian legends of people going back and forth between a place called Kahiki which is arguably, but not necessarily, Tahiti. Was Polynesia settled by competent sailors on purposeful voyages of discovery, or by accident—by storm-tossed castaways? So the obvious idea occurred, 'Well, we have to rebuild an ancient canoe, relearn how to navigate and sail her on some of the legendary voyages.'"

In 1966, after earning a Ph.D. in anthropology at Harvard, Ben got a teaching job at the University of California in Santa Barbara. He was newly married. He had a few thousand dollars saved up. He still dreamed of building a big canoe to sail throughout Polynesia but he settled on a more prudent first step. Why not build a smaller canoe of the same type and test that? "There was a mold for a Hawaiian-shaped hull in California," he recalls. "I could plunk down five hundred dollars and put my labor in and end up with two hulls for a forty-foot double canoe." He developed the project under the non-profit umbrella of his university, recruited some students as labor, and launched the canoe within a year. Mary Kawena Pukui, famous Hawaiian scholar, named her *Nālehia*—"the skilled ones."

Ben received a grant from the National Science Foundation to find out how much energy was needed to paddle her. In 1971, he shipped *Nālehia* to Hawai'i where he conducted oxygen uptake tests, and discovered that paddling long distances would take more water and food than the canoe could possibly carry. Clearly, Polynesian explorers must have been skilled at harnessing the power of the wind.

Finney knew some surfers and canoe paddlers at the Waikīkī Surf Club—people like Rabbit Kekai and Nappy Napoleon, big names in those days. He enlisted them to sail aboard *Nālehia* and their fame soon attracted others. Among them was Andrew Miller, a young eighteen-year-old nicknamed "Hoss" because he was big and somewhat clumsy. Hoss had just graduated from high school and was having trouble finding a job. He became deeply involved in the canoe. He soaked up Ben's stories of his early ancestors. A few months after their first acquaintance, Ben met Hoss on the beach.

"Hey Ben, I got a job now," Hoss told him.

"Yeah, what?"

"Working for the telephone company."

"How did you get that?"

"Well, I went for the interview and I told them about the canoe project and I got so excited they said, 'Well, you are an enthusiastic guy, we'll hire you.'"

"It was a revelation," Ben remembers, "Look at what the canoe can do for Hawaiians. This project is not going to be another *Kon Tiki*—eight *haole* on a raft. It will help revive Hawaiian culture. We will make it a Hawaiian-Polynesian project and I will get my Hawaiian and Tahitian friends involved."

✧ ✧ ✧ ✧ ✧

Early in 1973, Ben Finney met with Herb Kane and Tommy Holmes, a famous island surfer and canoe paddler. "We started talking among ourselves," Ben recalls, "and we said, 'Let's do it. Let's build a big canoe and sail to Tahiti and back.'"

Their first task was to come up with a plan for the vessel. "We wanted a design that would be from the early period of Polynesian exploration," Herb recalls, "But how to choose the best design from all those drawings made by European explorers?" Herb's study of anthropology had introduced him to the "age-area" theory, which proposed that the cultural attributes most common and widespread in an area must be the most ancient. Imagine a stone tossed into a still pond. Where the stone hits is the source of a cultural invention—a canoe design, for example—and the ripples represent how the design radiates out over time. Innovation may occur at the source, producing more ripples, but the original early designs are distributed far and wide. Hence, those canoe designs that are the most widespread in an area are the earliest.

"I looked for hull and sail design features most widely distributed throughout Eastern or marginal Polynesia (including Hawai'i, the Marquesas, Tahiti, the Cook Islands, and New Zealand) when Europeans arrived," Herb recalls, "and I figured these were the most ancient because they must have been common features in the era of Polynesian exploration and settlement. To these features I added some distinctively Hawaiian stylistic elements—the *manu* (bow and stern pieces) and *'iako* (arched crossbeams)."

Ben agreed with Herb that their canoe would be modeled on the kind of canoe seen by Captain Cook, called a *pahi*, which had a curved vee-shaped bottom and rounded sides. The underwater vee shape would allow the canoe to sail to windward. The rounded sides would prevent her from plunging in swells. Given the distance between the predominant Pacific swells, Herb figured that sixty feet was a good size for the canoe.

Herb enlisted others to help. Kim Thompson, a naval architect, designed the bow and stern pieces—the *manu*. Rudy Choy, an expert naval architect who had designed modern catamarans and written a book about them, helped with the line drawings for the hulls. Building such a canoe as the ancient Polynesians once did—by carving it from a log—was a lost art so they decided to build her of cold-molded plywood covered with fiberglass. In all other respects the canoe was authentic—a "performance replica" designed to test the sea-keeping qualities of an ancient canoe.

"We needed to raise money," says Ben Finney, "so we decided to form a non-profit corporation—the Polynesian Voyaging Society."

"We set a three-year time table from 1973 to 1976 to do the whole project," says Herb, "the first year to raise money, the second to build the canoe, the third to learn how to sail her and make the trip." They named their canoe *Hōkūle'a*— Star of Joy—the Hawaiian name for the star Arcturus, which reaches its zenith directly over Hawai'i and was likely a navigational guide for ancient navigators seeking the islands.

The projected cost to build *Hōkūle'a* was a hundred thousand dollars, an enormous sum in 1973. To raise the funds, Ben Finney began writing grants to foundations known to fund anthropological research. The canoe was an exercise in "experimental archaeology," he wrote, a new field of study that tested ancient technologies by building something—a catapult, a fortification, a Roman chariot, a Polynesian canoe—and experimenting with it to see how it worked.

Tommy Holmes put the touch on his wealthy friends. Herb Kane began a grass roots effort—he printed thousands of posters to sell all over Hawai'i. One of those recruited to help sell them was Dr. Ben Young.

Like most Hawaiians, Ben came from a mixed ethnic heritage. His mother was born in China, his father was Hawaiian. Ben graduated from Roosevelt High School and went to Kentucky Christian College. He worked summers in the coal

Hōkūle'a

Type: *Wa'a Kaulua* (Double-Hulled Canoe)
Length Overall: 62' 4"
Beam: 17' 6"   **Draft:** 2' 6"
Displacement (fully loaded): 27,000 lbs.

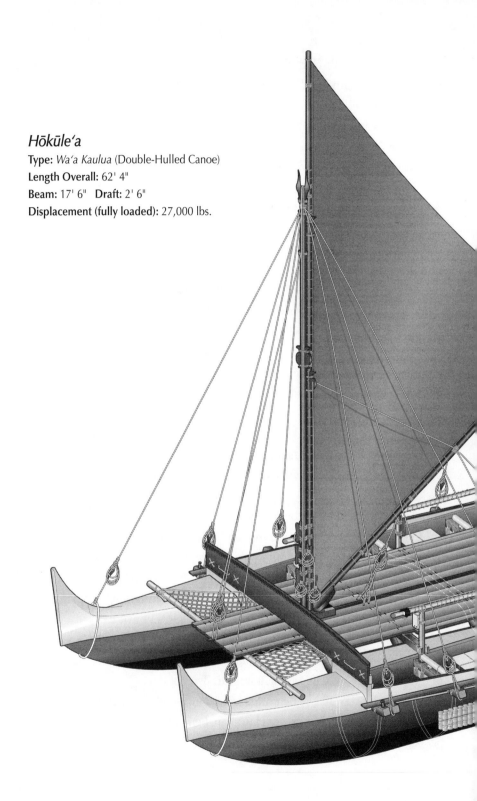

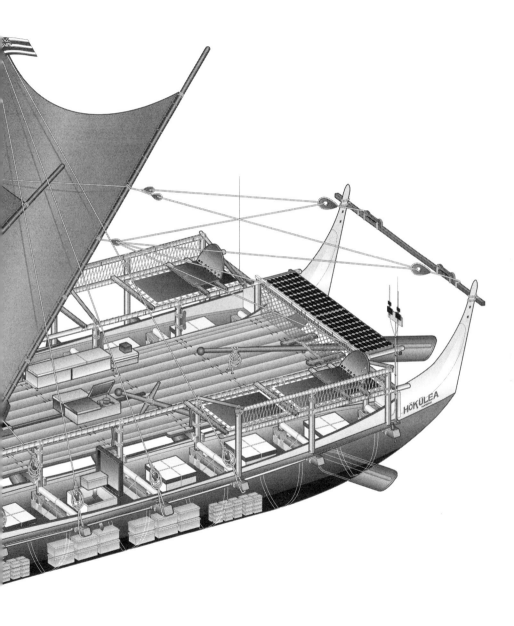

mines of Carter County, Kentucky. Two years later, he moved on to Milligan College in Tennessee and became interested in the culture of the region's hill folk. He played guitar and 'ukulele and learned old country folksongs. He studied to be a minister and worked as a student pastor in a small church in Blue Licks, Kentucky. He graduated with a degree in English. He studied for the ministry at Pepperdine, in California. He finished class work for a master's degree in church history but he found himself "bored to tears." He decided on a career in medicine. Ben had taken almost no science courses so he backtracked to study pre-med. He was married at the time. He took the medical admissions test and blanketed the country with applications. He was accepted with a scholarship into Howard University, a black medical school in Washington, D.C. "It was in the mid sixties, during the Watts riot, the era of black power. I went from the world of the poor south to the world of poor Afro-Americans," he recalls. Ben did public health work among migrant workers in New Jersey. Alongside them, he picked tomatoes and peppers in the summer and he wrote a report on the health of their children. He graduated with an MD and returned to Hawai'i where he completed his psychiatric residency. Through all of these studies, Ben had never had a course in Hawaiian history.

In 1973, Ben met Herb Kane at his home in Hawai'i Kai and learned of the plan to build *Hōkūle'a* and sail her to Tahiti. "Herb had an air about him of someone who really knew what he wanted to do," Ben remembers. "He was very determined. He was very well organized. When I heard of this project I thought, 'My god, what a wonderful opportunity—I can see where my ancestors came from.' " Ben volunteered to sell Herb's posters. "We went out to Holiday Mart, to Sears, and we set up booths and sold these crazy posters for a dollar each. You got to stop people. 'Hey, let me tell you about this project. It is so exciting. Here's a poster. This is going to be something you will love and appreciate years from now. Your dollar, or your five dollars or ten dollars will help buy lumber for this canoe.' And all of the proceeds we ploughed back into the Polynesian Voyaging Society."

Herb had been making the rounds of Hawaiian corporations and was getting nowhere until he received an invitation from Dr. Harold W. Kent, the president of Kamehameha Schools, to present the *Hōkūle'a* project at a meeting of the Social Sciences Society. The meeting was held in the executive dining room of the Dillingham Corporation. "Here's the president of Dillingham Corporation and his wife and they are welcoming everyone. Everyone has a suit and tie on except me," Herb remembers. Herb's presentation was limited to fifteen minutes. "Then the questions started. And the questions went on and on and on. These guys were the movers and shakers of Honolulu business and industry and the next day I got a call from the secretaries of three foundations: 'Mr. Kane, we would appreciate it if you could come by and see us.' " Suddenly the doors and the coffers were open.

❖ ❖ ❖ ❖ ❖

Herb traveled to each of the eight main Hawaiian islands to introduce the canoe and the upcoming voyage to Tahiti. Sam Ka'ai went to Maui Community College to listen to Herb's talk and when it was over, Sam stood up holding a copy of Honolulu Magazine and pointed to a picture of the canoe. He spoke to Herb in Hawaiian. Herb said, "Speak English please."

"We cannot participate in the making of your canoe because it's going to be in O'ahu, so maybe we can make some small part," Sam said. "In the picture, there are two *ki'i* (sculpted figures) on the *manu*—the two stern pieces of your canoe. Have they been made yet? If not, I will do it."

It was a busy meeting so Sam gave Herb his address and left. A few days later, a letter arrived from Herb: "If you come from a canoe family, please dream and make your own design for the *ki'i*."

Sam was brought up in Kaupō, an old district of Hawaiian homesteads in rural East Maui. Until 1938, there was no road to Kaupō. When they finally put one in, Sam's father and stepfather worked on it. His family raised pigs and cattle. They fished. They grew papaya, avocado, and peanuts. They made *'ōkolehao*, liquor distilled from *ti* root. "We grew our own food," Sam remembers, "so we didn't know there was a depression going on. We had little need for money. We made our own pipes for smoking. A pipe bought in a store was called 'a lazy man's pipe.' " Sam's father and grandfather made canoes. Sam continued in this tradition, although as a carver of fine sculpture. He used adzes, files and drills that came down to him from his ancestors. They were fashioned a century or two ago.

Sam carved two *ki'i*—a man and a woman. The female figure would be lashed to the port *manu*, the male *ki'i* to the starboard. Sam carved the male figure as a blind man reaching up to the heavens in supplication.

"This is an image of how we are after so many years of oppression," Sam explains. "Blind to our past, we reach up to grasp heaven one more time. The same stars are rising at the same time as they did for our forefathers for many, many generations. So if you lose your way—if you cannot find your way—remember that you once sailed on your mother's lap and you were never lost. The stars turned minute by minute, hour by hour, dawn and dusk and you always came home or your kind wouldn't be here. So you were never lost. This is an effigy of the *Hōkūle'a* experience—the *'ohana wa'a*, the family of the canoe. He is reaching above himself, beyond himself, to the story that has not changed, the forever and ever story, the *'ōlelo, 'ōlelo, 'ōlelo*—down the corridor of time—the *lei* of bones. He is showing that we are taking hold of the old story once again."

Male *ki'i* reaching to the heavens

NAINOA

Chapter Three

Herb Kane lived in a rented beach house in Kuli'ou'ou, a suburb to the east of Honolulu. A banyan tree spread its branches to the trade winds and a *hau* tree shaded the property. In the far distance, the ocean was creased where heavy swells met the outlying reef and an outrigger canoe was drawn up on the beach in front. To the left, a canal led into one of Hawai'i's largest and most ancient fish ponds, a place where the people of old once raised *'ama'ama* (mullet) and *awa* (milkfish) to supplement their diet. Now, the pond was being dredged into neat yacht basins and bulldozers were scraping the land into subdivisions. On the other side of the canal, the Hui Nalu Canoe Club launched their outriggers every afternoon to practice paddling. When the crews returned, they were weary and salt-encrusted so Herb invited them to use his outdoor shower. "It was just a short walk over the bridge and down my side of the canal," Herb remembers. "I got to know some of the crew that way. That's how I met Nainoa."

In 1974, when he first met Herb, Nainoa Thompson was twenty years old. He stood about five-foot ten. He was slender, obviously an athlete—a swimmer, canoe paddler, surfer, football player. Jet black hair extended below his ears. He had a gentle manner that suggested an unselfconscious humility. When addressing others, he looked them in the eye, listening intently in a way that encouraged conversation, but it was often difficult to get him to talk about himself. Some considered him a little shy.

One evening, Herb invited Nainoa and some others to his home for dinner. Nainoa remembers Herb's living room piled with books about Polynesian history, canoes and navigation, and his stories of the ancient navigators who had discovered Hawai'i. After dinner, Herb took his visitors out onto the terrace and pointed to stars that guided their ancestors to the islands. "He was the first person to introduce me to the heavens," Nainoa recalls. "I was fascinated that the stars had a pattern and that you could use them to guide you on the ocean.

Nainoa Thompson

All of a sudden, I realized that our ancestry is tied to the heavens and the ocean. My whole world as a Hawaiian became immense, timeless, without measurable distance. My interest in navigation and my ancestral history started right there, at that very moment."

"Nainoa was quiet and modest," Herb recalls. "There was nothing flashy about him that would make him stand out. But he was obviously a bright kid and that impressed me. Later, I got the Bishop Museum to donate the use of the planetarium and a bunch of us would gather there one night a week. We would run through the stars at different latitudes between here and Tahiti. It's dark and comfortable in there and you've got your head back and pretty soon guys would start snoring. But Nainoa would never fall asleep. He was always watching intently, so I knew we had a live one in that kid."

Nainoa was born on March 11ᵗʰ, 1953, in Queens Hospital in downtown Honolulu. He was brought home to the Niu Valley where his parents, Laura and Pinky, lived on land owned by Laura's father and mother, Charlie and Clorinda Lucas. Traveling the road from Honolulu in those days, the city limits were soon reached and the landscape rapidly became rural. Simple bungalows lined the beach and much of the land toward the mountains was uninhabited. The Lucas family owned six hundred acres in Niu. Charlie and Clorinda lived in a ranch house near the head of the valley surrounded by fruit trees. Cows grazed on the Lucas land and their milk was sold in local stores and delivered door-to-door. Living nearby was a short stocky Japanese man named Yoshio Kawano. Yoshi was a Nisei—a child born to a Japanese couple who had immigrated to Hawai'i. He lived with his wife Mioko in a simple twenty-four by twenty-foot house that the Lucas family had provided. When Nainoa's parents needed a babysitter, they would bring him to Yoshi and Mioko.

"I spent a lot of time with them," Nainoa recalls, "in that old dark brown wooden house in the valley." Nainoa remembers the metal roof and vinyl floor, the tiny kitchen and bedroom and particularly the *furo*, or Japanese bath—a simple cement box into which Yoshi poured water warmed by wood burned in a fire-pit. "Everything in the house was Japanese—the pictures on the wall, the decorations, the low table on the floor where you sat to eat. When you went into that house, you went into another culture. You slept in the Japanese way, ate in the Japanese way and bathed that way. It was a kind culture that held you and cared for you."

Yoshi spoke Japanese fluently but he also spoke good English. He had learned little of the Hawaiian language, which was understandable because so few spoke Hawaiian in those days, but he ingested a great deal of the Hawaiian culture. "He had an enormous love and respect for the Hawaiian land and people and, being a spiritual man himself, he learned about Hawaiian spiritual beliefs." The central ridge in the Niu Valley is called Kūlepeamoa, and it was here that Bishop Museum archeologists discovered a traditional Hawaiian temple or *heiau*. Many times, Yoshi saw spirits descend from the ridge. They appeared as dancing blue lights, a sight that some Hawaiians call the *menehune*—the little people. But Yoshi called them *'aumākua*—ancestral spirits.

Yoshi loved to fish and he made a point of taking Nainoa with him. He gave Nainoa his first fishing pole and taught him to catch *pāpio, weke, awa, ulua, kūmū,* and *'ama'ama* with it. They fished at night with torches and they speared octopus in reef holes. They encircled schools of fish with a gill net buoyed at the top and weighted at the bottom and tied to two poles. Yoshi gave much of the catch to neighbors. "He was a poor man in terms of financial wealth, but to me he was the richest man I knew. He defined wealth by what he could give away. He took care of people. He lived the old values, both Japanese and Hawaiian. He taught me to love the sea. I remember standing by the stream down at Hawai'i Kai, or going on the reef, or seeing a *kūmū*—a red fish—swimming in this narrow hole in the reef. I still know exactly where that is. There are connections to nature that need to be made while you're still young, and so Yoshi may have been my most important ocean teacher of all. I didn't know it then, and certainly he didn't either, but he was preparing me for my life."

Nainoa's grandmother on his father Pinky's side was Irmgard Luukia Kamuookalani Harbottle Perkins. Gardie, as she was called, grew up with her grandfather in a traditional Hawaiian thatch house near the now famous surfing beach of Makapu'u. Like many old-time Hawaiians, Gardie was clairvoyant. In 1944, she dreamed of her son Pinky who was then in France with the 44th infantry division. "She dreamt that Pinky was in his football uniform," Nainoa remembers, "and he wore a white carnation lei and he was coming in the back door of the house. The football uniform symbolized that Pinky was in a battle and the white carnation meant that he was wounded. Coming in the back door meant he was coming home." Shortly after Gardie's dream, the family received a telegram saying that Pinky had been seriously wounded and might not live. "No," said Gardie, "he will recover and he will come home. That is the meaning of the dream."

Gardie received her clairvoyance from her grandfather. "Gardie and her grandfather lived on the beach," Nainoa recalls, "and one day without saying anything he collected all the chickens and he put them in a cave in a cliff above the ocean. Then he got her and they all went into the cave. Then a tsunami came and washed away the house. That was in the early 1900s."

When Gardie was seven years old, in 1893, the Hawaiian Queen was deposed by *haole* sugar planters intent on annexing Hawai'i to the United States to get favorable treatment for their exported sugar. During her lifetime, Hawaiian religious practices were banned, the language was forbidden in schools and *haole* bought up most of the land—divorcing Hawaiians from both their roots and their ability to make a living. The culture was dying.

"Gardie would talk story and I would sit there," Nainoa says. "She would talk about living with her grandfather and her whole being would light up—she would become young. Then her conversation might switch and she would say that when she was in school she would be beaten by the teachers with sticks if she spoke Hawaiian, or danced the *hula*, and her whole being, physically and spiritually would change."

Nainoa was sent to a private school, Punahou, where he experienced *haole*-Hawaiian friction for the first time. On his first day of school, he fought with a *haole* kid who pushed his way into line in front of him. He detected a subtle expectation that *haole* students would perform well and Hawaiians would lag behind. Grades, class standing and SAT tests were taken seriously at Punahou, and Nainoa rebelled. He was afraid of not doing well and thereby confirming the diminished expectations of his teachers. He didn't like competing against his friends. He considered it "unHawaiian." "The whole notion of achievement and success was defined by values that did not mean shit to me," he recalls. "I did not care about being better than my friends. But the system did. Our society taught native Hawaiians to be dumb, lazy, and unproductive. All the reasons are there. Just go back a couple hundred years and look at what happened to Hawaiians. But when I was growing up our institutions—especially in education—they just did not care."

Nainoa did poorly in social studies and English, but he excelled in math and science. He was good at recognizing spatial relationships. Playing football, he knew intuitively where each player was on the field and made quick judgments about where the ball was going and where he should be to make the tackle. He excelled on defense because he could quickly analyze what was going on and call the defensive plays. When Nainoa was stimulated, he was meticulous. He convinced his Punahou teammates to stay after school to analyze their opponents' game films and helped lead them to victory over teams that were expected to beat them easily.

Nainoa was always the smallest boy on the football team. When he tried out for Pop Warner football, he put fishing weights in his pockets, ate bananas, and drank water to make the eighty-five pound minimum weight. With all that, he was still too light but was accepted anyway. At Punahou, in spiked shoes and helmet, he stood five-foot seven. The other players towered over him. He was among the last to make the team as a freshman — but by his senior year he was captain because, as he admits, "It was inspiring how much I could beat up on myself. I played defense so I could whack somebody." Pinky remembers games where he had to look away when he saw his boy rushing at a lumbering fullback. "I had tremendous intensity as a kid," Nainoa says. "I was angry. But anger is a powerful driving emotion. When I played football, I released all that anger."

Many times while growing up in the Niu Valley, Nainoa felt disoriented, vaguely uneasy. The feeling usually came at night and when it was particularly bad, he would run a few miles through darkened streets to a cliff above the ocean. Behind him Kūlepeamoa Ridge rose up against the darkness. Beneath him, waves sucked at the polished lava. He felt their strength, heedless to his own turmoil. Then he dove straight out, reaching for the horizon, bending at the last second to release his anger and confusion in the sweeping swell. He stroked out. The bottom sloped away until he reached the curl at the reef's end and was beyond it — in the deep ocean. There were sharks in those waters. Whitetip sharks. Tiger sharks. Makos. "You can't see anything under you. I was swimming outside there in the deep. Swimming at night and cliff diving was all about the same damn thing. If I went to the cliff's edge, I had to dive, because if I walked away from it I was a coward. I was trying to understand my place in the larger society where Hawaiians were considered second-rate. I had a tough time dealing with that. The ocean gave me peace. I was uncomfortable with who I was in that society so the ocean was my special place where I could be by myself. It wasn't just the ocean. It was being alone. That's when I was really happy. "

THE STAR OF JOY

Chapter Four

Late in 1974, sufficient funds had been raised to begin building *Hōkūle'a* and a place in Honolulu's seaport, Pier 40, was set aside for the project by the Dillingham Corporation. Warren Seaman lofted the lines and began work on the hulls, then boatwrights Curt Ashford, and Malcolm Waldron took over, assisted by Tommy Heen, Calvin Coito, and many volunteers. One of the first to join the labor force was John Kruse.

John had served a tour in Long Bin, Viet Nam, with the 90th Replacement Company in support of the First Air Cavalry. He hauled fuel up to Na Trang in helicopters. "That was one of the best times in my life," he remembers, "even though it was shitty. I was young. I didn't know any better." Shortly after his return from Viet Nam, John heard that *Hōkūle'a* was being built so he went down to Pier 40 where he saw the canoe's frames being laid up. He had worked for a time in a Chris Craft boatyard in Costa Mesa, California, so he ended up fiberglassing *Hōkūle'a's* hulls. "The canoe was like a magnet," John recalls. "I saw people come to work on her and they just got hooked. You got thrown the bait and ate it and it went down into your *na'au* (gut) and you were stuck."

Marion Lyman-Mersereau had recently graduated from college. Returning to Hawai'i, her brother Dave invited her to sail on *New World*, a maxi-yacht competing in the annual Labor Day sailboat race from Lahaina to Honolulu. Herb Kane was aboard. "I remember being up on the bowsprit and Herb telling me about his background—about his family in Waipi'o, going to Chicago, becoming a commercial artist and being drawn by his roots to come back and do all this research on Polynesian voyaging and building *Hōkūle'a*. The more he talked the more fascinated I got. I said, 'How can I be a part of this?' "

"The canoe is in frame at Dillingham shipyard," Herb told her.

"I don't know anything about building canoes."

"Well, just go down there and volunteer your time."

Marion Lyman-Mersereau

"I knew I had to get my foot in the door," Marion recalls. "They had a shop and the shipwright handed me this board and says 'Watch your fingers and cut along this line' and I was doing the whole deal. I had never done any manual labor where you are actually seeing things made. I cut holes. I had three older brothers and I liked being around men—working with the guys. I was a tomboy, one of the guys. We had so much fun."

Marion's brother, Dave Lyman, was living on the Big Island in the small town of Volcano when he attended a lecture by Herb Kane at U.H. Hilo. "I was fascinated," he remembers. "I wanted to know more." Dave was an accomplished sailor. He graduated from California Maritime School in 1965 with a Third Mate's license. Then he shipped aboard commercial vessels for part of the year and raced TransPac the rest. He made four trips on yachts from the mainland to Hawai'i, including three TransPac races. He became a proficient delivery

Dave Lyman and Bruce Blankenfeld

skipper, bringing yachts across the Pacific. He progressed through the ranks to Chief Mate and by the age of twenty-eight he had earned his Master's license. Herb's talk set the hook. In 1974, Dave moved to O'ahu and began working as a Honolulu harbor pilot. He found his sister working on the canoe so he began to volunteer his labor as well.

Hōkūle'a rose slowly from her birthing place. Her skeleton appeared, suggesting a shape not seen for many centuries. Then her flesh — a sheathing of marine plywood laid crosswise, one layer, another, then another. The canoe swelled from her keel to her waist, narrowing toward her gunwales — muscled with promise. For the men and women who labored over her she seemed almost alive.

There was no lack of volunteers even though much of the work was stygian, requiring the workers to climb into the hulls and lay on fiberglass and foul-smelling resin. When the resin had hardened, they went back in to sand it, emerging from their labor covered with fiberglass dust. As the hulls took shape, Wright Bowman laminated a dozen or so pieces of oak to make ʻiako, elegantly shaped cross beams that spanned the hulls. Five miles of rope lashings were employed to fasten the ʻiako to the twin hulls. A deck was laid over the crossbeams. Masts and spars were fashioned. Sails were sewn from canvas. Some sails, as an experiment, were hand-woven from pliable *hala* (pandanus) leaves in the traditional manner. Almost nonstop the work went on. Many of the men and women who labored over the canoe slept right beside her—in converted shipping containers. "They made a huge sacrifice," says Ben Young. "They were down at the wharf day in and day out—sanding, hammering—doing the gut work to build *Hōkūleʻa*."

◇ ◇ ◇ ◇ ◇

In the Fall of 1974, Nainoa Thompson entered Willamette College in Salem, Oregon. Salem sits in a flat basin—sixty miles wide and two hundred long—carved by the Willamette River over eons. It is gently rolling prairie with hills rising to the west, east and south—treed with white oak, broadleaf maple, and Douglas fir. All he remembers now of his academic curricula is an astronomy course taught by a professor with a foot-long gray beard, an intense man, passionate about the stars. "He was consumed with his science—a kind of nutty professor. I learned a lot from him." The professor expected his students to study a book entitled *The Stars* and to observe the sky until they could identify the major constellations and first magnitude stars. *The Stars* was written by H. A. Rey—author of the famous series of children's books *Curious George*.

Salem's lights bounced off cloud layers captured by the enfolding hills, obscuring all but the brightest stars, so Nainoa spent a lot of time on a hilltop above Salem's luminous penumbra. "In the hills outside town, the air was cold and dry. The stars were crystal clear. I was shocked there were so many. In Salem I could pick out the bright stars in the Big Dipper easily because all the other dim stars were washed away by the city lights but up on the hillsides it was more difficult to find the constellation in all that clarity."

At the semester's end, the professor led his class to that hilltop and quizzed them—separately—on the names of the stars and constellations as they wheeled overhead. "We were in this big field with pine trees all around us. It was beautiful. We spent the whole night until he had tested each student one at a time. That was the first time that I learned the stars in an organized way." Nainoa aced the exam. He spent one semester at Willamette, returning home for Christmas. That spring, he drove a dump truck to earn money and went to Dillingham shipyard to help finish building *Hōkūle'a*.

❖ ❖ ❖ ❖ ❖

Kiki Hugho was born in Kailua on O'ahu's north shore and spent every weekend he can remember on the water. When he was seven, his father built him a canoe of corrugated steel roofing folded like a taco and attached to two-by-fours bow and stern. It was caulked with roofing tar. With this vessel, Kiki fished on Kaneohe Bay with nets and a glass box that allowed him to look underwater. He learned to play slack key guitar from his uncle Joe Kamaka and his friends from Waiāhole Valley. When he was in the seventh grade, he began steering racing canoes for Waikīkī Surf Club under the watchful eye of Nappy Napoleon and Blue Makua—legendary watermen. In school he was always the class artist, painting murals for Easter, Christmas, and Thanksgiving. He studied mechanical drawing. His teachers still remember his rendering of a 327-cubic-inch Chevrolet engine in three dimensions, complete with wiring and four-barrel carburetor. When he was eighteen, he went on a scholarship to Whittier College in Southern California. He paddled for the Huntington Canoe Club for nine years—competing every year in the Catalina race in seat six—steering the canoe. As his art improved, Kiki moved into professional sign painting. He met a sign painter named Kenny Youngblood and got into painting drag racers owned by celebrity racers —Don Prudhome, The Snake, and Paul Mongoose. His hand lettering was elegant. His rendition of a Champion spark plug made other sponsors' mouths water. Kiki augmented his earnings by playing guitar in studio sessions. He learned some Hawaiian by listening to Gabby Pahinui, the Cazimaro brothers, and other groups beginning to play and sing authentic Hawaiian folk music. Kiki also learned to drive a semi—hauling loads all over America. Every other Monday, he found himself at Hunt's Point in Brooklyn, New York. He traveled up and down the Eastern seaboard. He delivered loads to Chelsea, Massachusetts, across the Mystic River from Boston. He traveled frequently to Bangor, Maine. He went to Connecticut, Rhode Island, Pennsylvania—then out west to Seattle via Toronto and down to Mexico. Finishing a delivery in Saugatuck, Michigan, he gathered up his box of paints and painted names on boats in dry-dock. At truck stops outside Los Angeles or Chicago or Boston he would paint designs on his own rig until other drivers came up and said, "Hey, can you do that on my truck?" He was making good money. He was enjoying life. But something kept drawing Kiki back to Hawai'i. When he returned in 1975, his brother, Kimo Hugho, was deeply involved with *Hōkūle'a*. When Kiki landed at Honolulu International Airport on March 5th, Kimo picked him up and filled him in on the canoe. It would be launched three days later.

"My brother took me out to Kualoa," Kiki remembers. "The canoe was sitting on the beach right there. I'm thinking, 'Man, am I glad to be home.' As a young guy, growing up in the islands, my tradition was go paddle a canoe. I never thought, How did we get this canoe? How did we get here? So when I first saw *Hōkūle'a* my first thought was, 'Wow, this is a voyaging canoe and this is a key to our past. I want to be a part of this.' At the same time on the radio they were playing this song by Country Comfort—Waimānalo Blues. What a perfect scene—to be sitting there, back in Hawai'i, a Hawaiian canoe in front of me and Hawaiian music on the radio. 'Yeah man, am I glad to be at home.' "

❖ ❖ ❖ ❖ ❖

In ancient times, each of the Hawaiian islands was divided into districts known as *ahupua'a* that usually extended up a deep valley from the ocean to a mountain peak. *Ahupua'a* were pie-shaped, with the crust along the shore and the pointed end in the mountains where the ridges joined. In the Hawaiian scheme of things, *ahupua'a* were a natural way to divide the land because it was so easily defined—a valley and its shoreline. It was also natural in a larger sense because it contained all the resources that its residents needed. Water cascaded in spectacular falls from the mountain peaks, gathered in deep pools and abraded its way through lava to form streams and rivers that Hawaiians channeled into their *taro* fields. The temperature gradient from shore to mountain peak enabled the cultivation of numerous crops such as *taro* in the lowland heat and sweet potatoes in the cool uplands. Farm settlements dotted the uplands and villages were established along the shore where seafood was plentiful and canoes could be easily drawn up. The *ahupua'a* was not just an ecologically viable land division—it was a map of political and social power. Each was the territory of a chief. Under him (or her) the land was divided into property cared for by *konohiki* (overseers) who supervised the work of commoners, or *maka'āinana*, who actually farmed the land.

Kualoa State Beach Park, where *Hōkūle'a* rested on her launching day, March 8th, 1975, is at the border of two such *ahupua'a*—Kualoa and Hakipu'u. There is a broad expanse of beach below the peak of Kānehoalani and the broad cliffs of Mo'okapuoHāloa. The place was chosen for the launching because it was the home two famous voyaging chiefs—La'amaikahiki and Kaha'i.

A voyaging canoe had not been launched in Hawai'i for more than eight centuries. Two thousand people attended the event. *Hōkūle'a* was decorated with a feather pennant and *lei* of *maile, 'ie'ie* and Tahitian *ti*. The crew seated themselves in a circle on the beach. Ka'upena Wong, a famous Hawaiian chanter, sprinkled seawater from a coconut shell in a ceremony to purify the canoe and crew. An offering was placed on a coconut-leaf platter and taken to the canoe by Ka'upena who performed a chant:

Ua pa'a ka wa'a
The canoe is finished,

A e ho'olana 'ia aku ana i ke kai
Ready to be launched onto the sea,

'O kona 'āina ia e huli ai i ka loa'a a me ka waiwai.
Its home where it will seek gain and wealth;

E nānā pono loa 'oukou
Watch over it carefully

E maka'ala i na pūko'a, nā pu'u pōhaku o kahi laupapa
Be alert for coral beds and stone outcroppings of the reefs,

Nā nalu, nā 'ale o ka moana.
For the waves and the swells of the ocean.

Ho'oholo no 'oukou i ka wa'a ma kahi hohonu o ke kai,
Guide the canoe over the depths of the sea,

I hele ai ka wa'a a nalukai,
Let the canoe ride over the waves of the sea,

A 'āpulu, a ulu ka limu pakaiea, a kaniko'oko'o.
Till it is worn out, overgrown with *limu*, and aged.

'Āmama, ua noa.
The *kapu* is lifted, it is removed.

"The day the canoe was launched," Nainoa remembers, "was the first Hawaiian cultural ceremony that I had ever been to. Everybody was dressed in *malo*. It was the first time I had heard such chants. I did not understand the language. I could see what we were doing but I did not understand why we were doing it. What was the significance of the ceremonies? It was a brand new experience for me as a Hawaiian. These were ancient traditions that were not valued in modern Hawai'i. This was a rebirth of all that."

After the chant, the crew manned ropes to launch the canoe. A path of banana stumps had been laid on the beach for *Hōkūle'a* to slide over.

"*E Ho'omākaukau*—Get ready," Ka'upena Wong ordered.

"We all lined up to pull the canoe," Nainoa remembers, "and I thought, 'This is not going to work. The canoe is just going to sit there. This is going to be a huge struggle.' "

Ka'upena began the hauling chant:

Kīauau, kīauau
Haul, haul

Hukiauau, hukiauau
Pull on, pull on

Koauau, koauau
Draw on, draw on

Ho'omālō he kaula
Keep the rope taut

Moku a he kaula.
Keep the rope in position.

"The canoe just rocketed," says Nainoa. "Once she turned down and slid on the banana stumps she took off. I was pushing the back *'iako* and I ran to the water's edge. When I got in the water, I hauled myself up on one of the *'iako* and got on board. I looked around. Everyone was in the water cheering and some of the Voyaging Society leaders were on deck but in the hulls there was not a single soul. For that one moment it was just *Hōkūle'a* and me."

MAU PIAILUG

Chapter Five

Among the tall muscular Hawaiians at the launching ceremonies was a man smaller in stature with darker skin and cropped curly black hair. He was a newcomer, having flown in from Micronesia on the very day of the launching, but from the way the crew treated him, even a casual observer could perceive that he was regarded with a kind of awe. His name was Pius Mau Piailug. He would navigate *Hōkūle'a* to Tahiti in the ancient way—without chart, compass or sextant—finding land instead by a world of natural signs.

Mau's home was on Satawal, a tiny coral island, one of many that stretch like a string of pearls across the Pacific from Yap Island in the west to Pohnpei Island in the east—the Caroline Islands of Micronesia. Here Mau lived very much as his ancestors did. He harvested *taro* from a garden behind his house. He gathered breadfruit and coconut from his trees. He bathed every day in a freshwater pond, surrounded always by the beat of surf on the encircling reef.

Along Satawal's sheltered shore, outrigger canoes were drawn up beneath lofty houses roofed with palm fronds and open on all sides. These vessels were called *wa'a serak*. Their design was ancient, the result of a thousand years of evolution, yet they were surprisingly modern looking. Narrow hulls were shaped like airfoils so that water flowing over them tended to lift them to windward, making them extremely efficient—and fast. They were fashioned with materials that Satawal provided—breadfruit planks for the hull, coconut husks and breadfruit sap for caulking to keep the water out, and sennit rope fashioned from coconut to hold the planks together. Satawal's isolation, and that of the other Caroline islands, had resulted in the preservation of a seafaring life that was unknown elsewhere. Mau and a handful of sailors still practiced an ancient way of navigating handed down by generations of their ancestors.

Mau's grandfather was a famous *pwo*—a man who had learned the technical art of navigating, passed his initiation and mastered the spiritual arts. It was an

Mau Piailug on Satawal

informal but rigorous course of study that took place on the beach where he watched for signs of weather with his master and learned the stars, and on a canoe where he learned to steer by large swells stirred by steady trade winds and evanescent ones motivated by brief storms. The teaching continued in a canoe house by lantern light where the master unrolled a woven pandanus mat and laid out a star compass, thirty-two brilliant white lumps of coral in a circle to represent the rising and setting of stars. It was a world of words but no writing. All knowledge was conveyed orally by the "talk of navigation" or by the "talk of the sea." Everything was committed to memory. Mau's grandfather chanted as he pointed to the star houses, *"Tana Mailap,"* he began, due east—the rising of Mailap—a star western navigators call Altair. *"Tana Paiiur,"* he continued, *"Tan Uliol, Tana Sarapul, Tana Tumur, Tana Mesaru, Talup, Machemeias, Wuliwiliup,"* pointing to stars equally spaced from east to south, one quadrant of a compass defined by stars. It was a beginning lesson called *paafu*—"numbering the stars"— and it conveyed a way of finding direction that Arabs crossing the great empty spaces of the Sahara might have found familiar and that Polynesians must have used in the great days of open-ocean voyaging. As he spoke, the master's voice

Mau Piailug teaching the star compass

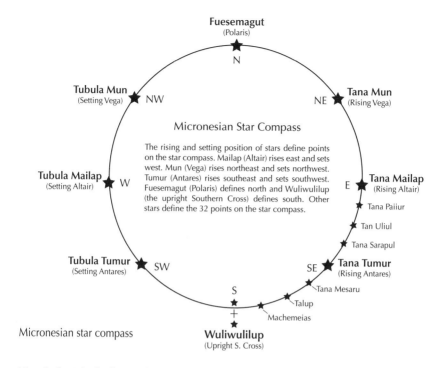

Fuesemagut
(Polaris)

N

Tubula Mun
(Setting Vega)   NW

Tana Mun
NE   (Rising Vega)

Micronesian Star Compass

The rising and setting position of stars define points
on the star compass. Mailap (Altair) rises east and sets
west. Mun (Vega) rises northeast and sets northwest.
Tubula Mailap   Tumur (Antares) rises southeast and sets southwest.   Tana Mailap
(Setting Altair)   W   Fuesemagut (Polaris) defines north and Wuliwulilup   E   (Rising Altair)
(the upright Southern Cross) defines south. Other
stars define the 32 points on the star compass.

Tana Paiiur

Tan Uliul

Tana Sarapul

Tubula Tumur
(Setting Antares)   SW

Tana Tumur
SE   (Rising Antares)

S

Tana Mesaru

Talup

Machemeias

Micronesian star compass   Wuliwulilup
(Upright S. Cross)

blended with the beat of swells against the island's reef and the clacking of palm
fronds overhead. When his grandfather completed one quadrant of the compass,
Mau would repeat the chant. Then on around the circle until each star house
had been recalled. Then came *aroom*, reciting the reciprocals of the star houses;
then *wofanu*, the sailing directions to hundreds of islands. Then came *fu taur*, the
alignment of stars with island landmarks to find a passage through the encircling
reef. Then he learned *etak*, how to dead reckon his position by imagining his
canoe in the center of the star compass and islands sliding by on each side under
star paths—a unique Micronesian mental system of triangulation. These are only
a few of the lessons that were passed on verbally in a cycle of repetition that
stretched back hundreds of generations.

Anthropologists distinguish between the status a person receives by
his birth and the kind that he earns by his individual talents. Most societies,
even those rigidly divided into various inherited ranks, provide some way of
motivating and rewarding personal achievement. The Aztecs, the Maya and the
Pueblo dwellers of the American Southwest recognized the abilities of warriors.
Pueblo dwellers also appreciated the ability to entertain and so they gave rank

Mau making a model of his canoe

to clowns, and the ability to philosophize, so they provided yet another rank for those who thought and spoke well. On Satawal, three chiefs regulate the island's affairs. They have the power of placing a *kapu* (as Hawaiians would call it) on various activities. They can ban fishing or harvesting breadfruit, for example, to preserve food stocks. The chiefs are born into their rank. They are the descendants of island dynasties. But their power ends at Satawal's fringing reef where that of the navigator begins. "At sea, I am the chief," Mau once explained. "To be a *palu* (navigator) you must have three qualities: *pwerra, maumau* and *reipy* (fierceness, strength and wisdom). …if you are not fierce, you are not a *palu:* you will be afraid of the sea, of storms, or reefs; afraid of whales, sharks; afraid of losing your way—you are not a navigator. With fierceness you will not die, for you will face all danger …that is a *palu:* a *palu* is a man. On the canoe I am above the chief. He has to do what I say."[7]

In Hawai'i, Mau said little and accomplished much. When *Hōkūle'a's* booms broke under the strain of sailing, he took out an adze and carved new ones. The booms were curved, so he fashioned graceful scarph joints and joined three pieces of *hau* with rope lashings. He did the same for the gaffs when they broke. When there was nothing to do, he sat quietly and carved a scale model of his canoe complete with rigging and sails—a work of art so perfect it could have graced a museum display case.

Nainoa tried to make sense of a man who could navigate a canoe across thousands of miles of ocean without a chart or a compass. "No one really knew how it was done, so it kind of got into this mystical realm out of our own ignorance. He could do things that none of us could. He was a miracle man." Nainoa didn't know what to say to Mau so he said nothing.

Another crewmember, Shorty Bertelmann, was equally mesmerized. "I watched Mau as he worked and how he used an adze with such precision. I had never seen that before." Shorty was from the Big Island. He had been born into a *paniolo* (cowboy) family and he knew how to ride and rope cattle. He was likewise a fisherman and a surfer. He is a lean man, graceful, almost delicate. His face is composed of angular planes; his glance is gentle yet intense. "There was something about Mau that I could see right away," Shorty recalls. "He was not like a normal man—he knew things that no one else knew." Shorty spent as much time as he could sitting next to Mau. Asking few questions, he tried to learn Mau's skills by repeating them. "I just spent a day with him trying to help him when I could, and another day and another and after a while it seemed like he welcomed me to be with him, and I was surprised because I never thought that a man like him would pay any attention to a person like me." Shorty learned how to hold an adze and how to swing it gently but with sufficient force to reveal shapes hidden in wood. "The way that I learned from Mau was by watching what he did and trying to understand how he did it—by figuring it out for myself and then asking him if that was the right way. You don't just go up and ask him to teach you. It's not a classroom with handouts and lectures."

Mau watched the crew carefully and he judged them silently. He looked for the nascent qualities that would serve a man well at sea. He looked for *pwerra, maumau,* and *reipy.* He respected stillness in a man, humility accompanied by knowledge. He looked for a willingness to learn. And he waited. In Satawal, a master does not proselytize. His students come to him, driven by their innate curiosity. Those who display talent and discipline become his apprentices. Among all the men and women who surrounded him, only two stood out in this way—Nainoa Thompson and Shorty Bertelmann. "When I look at them," Mau recalls, "I'm thinking good guys because they like learn. I am not asking them. They come to me and they want to learn. They ask questions. I am strong for teaching them because their talk to me is good. That's why I decided to teach them."

❖❖❖❖❖

After *Hōkūle'a* was launched, crew members assembled at Kualoa Park for weekend training sails.

"We went out on the bay," says Kiki Hugho, "I was proud and honored to be on the canoe. Is this how our ancestors did it back then? They had to be fascinating people to figure out how to navigate and build a vessel to withstand a long ocean voyage—and you got to consider those who never made it. There must have been hundreds of canoes that went down. We had modern materials— modern everything—to try and reenact this whole thing. It gave me a sense of pride to say I am part of this. To step back in time. To figure out how they did it. It started a resurgence in me to want to learn my culture."

Hawaiians had always been a sea people. Their race had explored and settled ten million square miles of ocean. Even after long distance voyaging stopped, they continued to sail and paddle smaller canoes to visit other islands and to fish. As their lands were taken by *haole* planters, farmers, and ranchers, Hawaiians focused even more on the ocean. They could still swim. They could still surf and paddle canoes. They could dive into reef holes and spear fish. As tourism grew in Hawai'i, hotels sprouted on the verge of white sand beaches. Waikīkī became a Mecca of water sports and almost everyone wanted to ride an outrigger down a sloping swell, learn to surf, and have their picture taken with a muscular beachboy—a term used only by the tourists. The term most of these ocean athletes preferred was waterman. It was a curious existence, this treading between an ancient heritage and an artificial romance created by chambers of commerce. But it was a decent living and it provided an opportunity to be in the sun and surf all day long and perhaps enjoy a moment cuddling a mainland *wahine* in the evening. Among the watermen who showed up to sail *Hōkūle'a* were a group of famous Hawaiian surfers and canoe paddlers: Clifford Ah Mow, Boogie Kalama, Buffalo Keaulana, Kimo Hugho and Dukie Kauhulu. They had a flair for drama. Pictures taken aboard *Hōkūle'a* show them in the forefront— steering the canoe, muscles bulging with effort, their heads adorned with crowns of *maile,* a Hawaiian vine that grows on the sides of mountains. These men seemed to be the natural inheritors of ancient seafaring glories. They knew how to steer and paddle a canoe and surf them in huge waves. Had they not, after all, continued the traditions of the sea?

"These guys were great paddlers, swimmers, surfers, body surfers," says Dave Lyman. "A lot of them were lifeguards. They were predominately Hawaiians. It was my first chance to meet Buffalo Keaulana, who I had heard a lot about, seeing him on the canoe, watching him steer, seeing him sail. I was very impressed by what a super good man he was on the water."

"Buffalo Keaulana was just so instinctual," Nainoa remembers. "I was very impressed by his confident handling of the canoe. He would catch waves coming into Kualoa and he would hold the canoe right on the wave and bring it in and place us right on the mooring buoy."

◇ ◇ ◇ ◇ ◇

Hōkūleʻa immediately proved the sea-going savvy of her ancient designers. Dave Lyman was impressed by the way the canoe seemed to track through the water without slipping to leeward, a result of the semi-vee shape Herb had given her twin hulls. He studied her crab claw sails, puzzling over their shape. The sails' upside-down shape, he observed, put a lot of area higher off the water than a modern Marconi rig "which is good in light airs because when the wind is calm you're going to have much less wind on the surface than you're going to find fifteen or twenty feet above the surface and so that helps quite a bit." *Hōkūleʻa's* sails are attached to wooden booms and gaffs so the leading edge of the sail which addresses the wind—the luff as it is called by sailors—is held firmly in place to make it a more efficient airfoil. Captain Cook's vessels were powered mainly by square sails which worked best in winds from astern, but they also carried "fore and aft sails" like *Hōkūleʻa's* to help them power into the wind. These were hauled aloft on rope stays that sagged under the wind's pressure and lost their aerodynamic efficiency. The Polynesian rig allowed voyaging canoes to point higher into the wind, Dave noted, "because the sail was made fast to a stick or spar and had an absolutely straight leading edge which is much more efficient." It was an improvement noted by Sir Joseph Banks, who sailed with

Cook. "With these sails, their canoes go at a very good rate," Banks wrote, "and lie very near the wind, probably on account of their sails being bordered with wood, which makes them stand better than any bow-lines could possibly do." [8]

"What's really interesting," says Dave Lyman, "is when you look at the newest, most modern boat the headsails are bent onto a solid rod headstay rather than a wire (or rope as in Cook's time). And the reason is because it stays straighter and makes for a more efficient airfoil." *Hōkūle'a's* rig, it turned out, had preceded the most modern design by centuries.

Sailing aboard *Hōkūle'a* thrilled the crew. Her fulsome shape and her sharp bows allowed her to slice cleanly through steep swells. Where other vessels might hobbyhorse—a tendency to bob and plunge—she continued straight on. Like all catamarans she did not heel much in stiff winds, providing a level platform for her crew to work on. With the wind behind her, she easily accelerated to ten knots, producing rooster tails in her wake, vibrating with what those aboard interpreted as a kind of joy. With the wind abeam, she leaned slightly and took off, leaving the stiletto mountains of Kualoa and Hakipu'u sinking in the distance. As she sliced through the swells, she seemed alive—channeling tons of water between her hulls as her ancient designers had intended.

"I FEEL MY ANCESTORS ALL AROUND ME"

Chapter Six

Herb Kane and Ben Finney wanted to accomplish the same thing—to build a canoe and sail her—but they had arrived at that goal by different routes. Ben had created *Hōkūle'a* primarily as a scientific experiment. Could Hawaiians have sailed double-hulled canoes to Tahiti and back? Could they have navigated without instruments? And might such a voyage prove Thor Heyerdahl and his raft theory wrong once and for all? Herb, on the other hand, was a "returned Hawaiian"—a person of Polynesian ancestry who had grown up in the Midwest—so he was doubly susceptible to view *Hōkūle'a* as a vehicle for Polynesian cultural rebirth. He was reborn too! His ethnic identity as part Danish—part Chinese receded as his Hawaiian identity advanced. Now he found himself at the center of a full-scale renaissance of Hawaiian values. It was intoxicating. And it led him to see the voyage as primarily a stimulus for cultural rebirth.

"I was interested in what effect the canoe might have on what was then beginning to be called the Hawaiian Renaissance," Herb recalls. "I saw the canoe as the central artifact of the old culture because everything in Hawaiian culture was related to the canoe in some way. Our ancestors had to get here by canoe. The foods that were transported by canoes had to be prepared in certain ways so they could be carried on long voyages. Songs and dances involved voyaging or canoes as themes. The canoe was the center of the old culture—the heart of a culture that was still beating—and I thought that if we could rebuild that central artifact, bring it back to life and put it to hard use, this would send out ripples of energy and reawaken a lot of related cultural components around it."

Herb considered the Tahiti trip an important part of the canoe's mission—but it was more important to find out if the canoe was accepted by the Hawaiian people. "If Hawaiians accepted *Hōkūle'a*, we would go to Tahiti—but we would not go if they did not accept it because I felt then it would be just a stunt. It would not have any real meaning." The only way to find out what Hawaiians thought, Herb figured, was to sail *Hōkūleʻa* to each of the islands and see how they reacted to her.

✧ ✧ ✧ ✧ ✧

Nainoa Thompson was among the crew when the canoe set sail from Oʻahu for Maui. "We left Kāneʻohe Bay and tacked around Mōkapu heading south. We sailed a whole day, we tacked, and finally the wind was light enough that we got south and into the lee of Lānaʻi. The next day, we approached the coast of Maui."

Sam Kaʻai lived on Maui and for months he had been preparing for *Hōkūleʻa's* arrival. Perhaps better said, he had been preparing for it all his life. In addition to his ability as a sculptor—Sam had created *Hōkūleʻa's* two *kiʻi*—he had learned many of the more practical arts at the knees of his elders. Sam learned to make fish hooks of various kinds of bone and to make fish line from the bark of the *ʻolonā* plant by stripping it, washing it, drying it, and then twisting it into cordage. Sam made an *ʻahu lāʻī*—a rain cape—by creating a net of *ʻolonā* fibers and then tying *ti* leaves to it. He did not speak Hawaiian fluently—but he spent considerable time memorizing specific chants, including those used to welcome voyagers from sea. Now, as *Hōkūleʻa* approached land, Sam stood facing the canoe, dressed in his rain cape, and raised his voice to the ancient gods.

"It was the first time I had sailed on any vessel, let alone *Hōkūleʻa*," Nainoa recalls. "And it was the first time I had seen such a greeting. There was a crowd of two hundred people. I remember being shy and not wanting to go ashore."

Sam assembled the crew in a circle on the beach. He had prepared a ritual drink of *ʻawa* made from a plant the earliest voyagers had brought to Hawaiʻi. The plant was sacred to both Kāne—the god who gave life—and to Kanaloa— the god of the sea. Sam gave each crewmember a cup of *ʻawa* from a large carved bowl and when they had finished drinking, he rose to speak.

"There is an ancient murmur," he told them. "It is a voice on the wind that some hear and some don't. If we heed this murmur we will make it a living song. The murmur is a distant memory, a feeling that Hawaiians have that we are all one. Yet today when we gather together everybody seems to be different. It's because there are songs that we have neglected to sing. You have to know the songs of birth and the songs of *pule oʻo*, coming of age, and the songs of *kuleana*, of work, and the songs of joy and the songs of places—the songs of mountains and of shore, of rivers and of water to drink. The songs are memories and if you put them aside for foreign songs then you forget who you are and where you came from. There is darkness in some places, but now a light is rising. *Ke ku'au ea ka lani*—this is the real light rising to heaven. The stars are in the heavens. Sun and moon are in the heavens. They are the guides to islands. The islands are on the Earth but their signs are seen in the heavens. Mau looks for the navigational star—for *hōkū'ula*. All the paths to islands are kept on the face of *Wākea*—the sky father."

"*Hōkūle'a* is an altar that we raise up again," Sam continued. "She is the *ahu o ka moana*—the altar of the sea. You who have been chosen as the crew are the *'ohana wa'a*—the family of the canoe. You will be the gifts to the gods. You will go down the sea trail, down the *lei* of bones, down the whispers. We are from Hawai'i *ahi*—from Hawai'i of the flame. You will sail to Hawaiki—the homeland."

"That's the first time I met Sam," Nainoa recalls. "He was spiritually powerful. He spoke to us and he made sense of the deeper purpose of the canoe. He sees the world differently. He rises above western logic. He made sense of what only my instincts could feel. There was a lot of stuff going on inside me about being Hawaiian and a part of *Hōkūle'a* that I could not understand. But Sam could. I remember that sandy hot morning on the beach—it deepened my desire to be a part of *Hōkūle'a*."

◇ ◇ ◇ ◇ ◇

Herb Kane returned to the Big Island, leaving Kimo Hugho and Tommy Holmes in charge. Sam helped find the best people on Maui to train for the crew. "I went around to see people who I thought should be on the canoe. I went all the way to Hāna and got Sam Kalalau. I asked Snake Ah Hee."

Hōkūle'a's appearance off the beach near Lahaina had taken Snake completely by surprise. He vaguely remembered reading something about the canoe in the newspaper but didn't connect the article with the apparition that ghosted along the shore. "One morning I just happened to drive to Lahaina town and out of nowhere I see this canoe come right into the shallows," Snake recalls. "It was early in the morning. I could hardly see it. I could just see the outline. I stopped my truck and just looked. What is this? They came right close to shore so I walked out and I saw Sam Ka'ai who was there for the canoe's arrival. I had to go to work, but I couldn't forget what I had seen."

Snake was born on March 18th, 1946 in Lahaina, Maui. "When I grew up it was kind of a hard time. There were jobs but the money was really little. When I went to school we didn't have enough money to buy lunch, so I came home. Dried fish, rice, or *poi* was my staple." Snake lived for a time with his great grandfather in a house on the ocean outside town. "We were a fishing family. We had nets and canoes and ever since I was a small kid my dad took me fishing. I learned how to find the fish, how the current moves, how to steer a canoe using Japanese oars. He taught me to get lobster without a spear. You have to be gentle, have a good hand, or you spoil the lobster's hole. If you do it right you can come back in a few days and there will be another lobster there."

The main street of Lahaina is now a tourist mall rimmed by hotels, diving

Snake Ah Hee aboard *Hōkūle'a*

establishments, travel agencies, bars, and joints of all kinds. Beyond the town stretches a vast expanse of mid-rise hotels. But when Snake grew up, Lahaina was still a sleepy village with only a hint of the tourist trades that would eventually overwhelm it. The beach, where the hotels now sit, was divided into fishing grounds that were the property of local families. "Each family had their own fishing ground," Snake recalls. "No one else can come into that area unless you have permission." Most weekends, Snake's extended family gathered at the beach to fish in the traditional way, called *hukilau*, using a net they carried out to sea. Long ropes tied to the ends of the net were led back to the beach. *Lau* (leaves) were fastened to the ropes to scare the fish into the net as they *huki* (pulled it in). "Every weekend the whole family—aunties and uncles—they always met down at the beach. You don't sell the fish, it all goes to the family."

Following ancient Hawaiian tradition, Snake's family shared the catch with their elders. "Whatever fish we caught we used to take to my great grandmother. If we don't offer the fish to her, maybe we won't catch any more fish. It's the old way that I learned from my grandparents. All those little things. I got to appreciate all the old ways. I was told a lot of stories, like the one about my grandma's mom. When she was *hāpai*—pregnant—she went into the ocean and she gave birth in the water and it turned into a fish. So my grandmother told my mother, 'You have a brother that lives in the ocean.' There are a lot of stories like that."

A few days after Snake had seen the canoe, Sam Ka'ai notified him that he had been chosen to train for her crew.

"We trained for I don't know how many weekends," Snake recalls. "I never missed one training day. I thought about how the Polynesians traveled from far away to Hawai'i and now we're going to do it the way they did it. It was an honor. I just wanted to be on the canoe—to keep on going. I was selected to take the canoe to the Big Island."

Herb's strategy was to sail among the islands as a kind of shakedown and to allow crew members from every island to try out for the voyage to Tahiti. "We would train a crew on one island, anyone who showed up," Herb recalls, "and then we would select a crew of a dozen or so men and sail to the next island. Then those guys would go home and we would start the process again. We would wind up with guys who were trained on the job, so theoretically we could select a crew for the trip to Tahiti who would represent the whole island chain. We were also introducing the canoe to the different islands and we were taking it through rougher water than I would expect on the voyage because the waters in the channels between the islands are rougher than anything between here and Tahiti. So it was a good shakedown."

The sail from Maui to the Big Island required *Hōkūle'a* to navigate the 'Alenuihāhā channel where prevailing northeast trade winds funnel between the two islands, producing high winds and dramatic seas. "We left Maui at eleven o'clock at night and went into the channel and we got our *'ōkole* (butt) kicked," Snake remembers.

As *Hōkūle'a* reached the midpoint of the 'Alenuihāhā Channel, she encountered extreme seas. With the wind astern, she was going fast and spray flew over the bows, drenching her sails and crew. "We just kind of held on," Snake recalls. "The spray was going right over the sail, we were going so fast. We lost the Zodiac rubber boat. We lost all the life jackets we had in the bow where the nets are. But we never lost anybody off the canoe. That was the roughest sail I ever did in my life. But it was training for us. It was a challenge. If *Hōkūle'a* could go into that kind of weather she could handle anything. I felt the canoe calling to me going through that wild sail in the channel. When we got to the Big Island some people said 'I don't want to go to Tahiti' but I said 'If you call me I'm ready. I will be glad to be chosen. I will go not just for myself but for you guys too.'"

Herb was pleased with the canoe's performance but he was even more pleased that Hawaiians seemed to immediately take to her.

"We came into Hōnaunau Bay and dropped the hook and the next day people started coming and coming and coming," Herb Recalls. "I thought the island was going to tilt. You could not see a rock. It was all solid people. They weren't doing anything. They weren't waving. They were just sitting there looking at the canoe. There was some kind of communication going on between the canoe and the people. It was wild. It went on for a couple of days. The faces would change but the crowd was still there. Wherever we went it was that way. That's what told me everything was all right."

The crew noticed it too, a kind of reverence emanating from the crowds that gathered to greet *Hōkūle'a*. Billy Richards got on board at Hōnaunau and he remembers the crowd's reaction as a kind of stunned silence, as if they were in the presence of—as he calls it—"the spaceship of our ancestors." "Hōkūleʻa evoked something deep in people everywhere we went," Billy recalls. "It was interesting—the Hōnaunau people were coming to picnic, bringing their families down. We asked them to come on the canoe and—no—it was just enough for them to see it."

When Hōkūleʻa sailed into Hōnaunau she fulfilled a prophecy that had been given to Aunty Clara, a respected Hawaiian elder. "One day," her grandfather told her, "you will see a Hawaiian double canoe sail into the bay." And so it was. Every day during the canoe's visit to Hōnaunau, Aunty Clara showed up with Boy, her pet pig, to sit on the same rock and gaze out at the canoe. "Aunty Clara was one of the local fixtures at Hōnaunau," Herb remembers. "She was stunned. She was excited. She must sail with us. I wasn't prepared to take an 80-year-old woman on board but she was not to be denied. So when we sailed up along the coast to Kailua Kona she went with us, and she kept up a historical commentary all the way, pointing out different things along the shore."

The canoe arrived in Kailua on the morning of a big canoe race. "We were coming around the point by Kamakahonu," John Kruse remembers, "and everybody just stopped racing. They were going around a turn and they saw this big canoe and they just stopped the whole race. They were in awe. They put their paddles up like in a salute."

When Hōkūleʻa docked in Kailua, Tava Taupu was working at the Kona Village Hotel, carving intricate kiʻi and doing general maintenance. Tava was born in the Marquesas. When he was a teenager, he traveled to Tahiti to learn to carve kiʻi from an uncle. Papeete, the capital, was a place where young Tahitians liked to rough up boys from the outlying islands, so Tava learned to box. "When I went boxing, I got proud," he recalls. "I was amateur, six rounds. I won't drink anymore. I exercise, forget kid stuff, no more smoking cigarettes." What Tava doesn't say is that he boxed so well he earned the title of heavy-weight champion of French Polynesia.

After Tava had immigrated to Hawaiʻi, he settled down to become an American. He expected he might lose some connection to his Polynesian roots but when he saw Hōkūleʻa the opposite happened. "It all comes back to me," he remembers, "my ancestors. I feel my ancestors all around me."

THE SPACESHIP
OF THE ANCESTORS

Chapter Seven

A seagoing vessel is an exquisite structure. Her shape is sinuous, composed of compound curves that fold into one another—that never seem to end. She has a beauty that most human beings perceive directly and that appeals to some so completely they are struck silent. There is a dream in those shapes—of voyaging to far-off lands and of confronting something deep within you, the limits of your courage and endurance. An ocean-going vessel is like a poem because it stands for so much more than its mundane purpose of carrying sailors and cargo across the seas. It's a metaphor of freedom, of casting off the lines, of shaking loose from land-bound cares and setting out on a voyage of self-discovery.

These attributes of a sailing vessel are universal—their allure crosses cultures and time. An aficionado of such vessels equally appreciates boats that sailed the Nile five millennia ago, those that carried Lord Nelson into battle at Trafalgar and those that compete today in match races to win the America's Cup. But for Hawaiians who beheld *Hōkūle'a* something stirred in addition to all this—something that was deeply personal. "I feel my ancestors all around me," Tava had said. The canoe carried a song from a time before remembering, a time so far in the past that it had been forgotten, or worse, a time that had been erased from memory so as not to reawaken an ancient hurt. "Better to look forward, not back," as some Hawaiians said. But *Hōkūle'a* overwhelmed such resistance. She sat there. She was real. She was "the spaceship of the ancestors," as Billy Richards had put it. Sam Ka'ai saw the canoe as a flower in the *lei* of memories that extended back to the first people to set sail from an unknown place in Southeast Asia.

When Sam Ka'ai talks, he closes his eyes. He breathes deeply. Then he speaks in a combination of English and Hawaiian without seeming to need additional oxygen. He enters an altered world. His speech becomes poetic and mesmerizing. He blends ancient Hawaiian *'ōlelo* and *mele*—stories and poems.

Hōkūle'a under sail

He strives for the richness of Hawaiian allusion—what's known as *kaona*—multiple meanings. He fashions his *'ōlelo* as he does the *ki'i* or the fishhooks he carves. Metal tools, he says, do not change as you use them. But tools of coral and stone do, so as they shape an object they are also shaped by it. So it may be with Sam and his stories. His *'ōlelo* evoke an ancient reality that moves forward in the telling. He seems to enter a trance. Old-time Hawaiians clearly believed that words have power and so does Sam. Emotion overcomes him. He tears up.

One of Sam's favorite images is of the *mo'o*—a lizard or "dragon" as he sometimes calls it—that represents the Hawaiian family. The lizard's back is the *kūpuna*, the elders, the senior representatives of the living past. They carry the "song of songs"—the everlasting story of their lineage. "They are closest to the source. They are the vertebrae that remember all. They are the back of the dragon," Sam explains. "*Mo'o* also means lineage, *mo'o kū'auhau*, our genealogy," a line of ancestors extending back to the beginning of time, and it also means the story of that lineage. "The word for history is *mo'olelo*. *Mo'o*—the dragon; *'ōlelo*—to speak. The dragon song—*mo'olelo*." The lizard's tail is "the corridor of time" or the "*lei* of bones" that stretches back from the present to the original founders of the lineage. The vertebrae are the generations of the lineage and in their *kaona*, their poetic meaning, they also represent the island stepping stones that led them into the Pacific.

For Sam, *Hōkūle'a* brought a revival of that ancestral story and restored an ancestral blessing that appears as a light moving from the past down the *lei* of bones to the present. Sam calls it "the light that cares," the light that "flickers, moves ever so slightly and sends its token of love down each vertebra, down the corridor of time. Now it is crackling, each bone making its sound, each adding another portion of light, of *aloha*, for you their son, you their daughter. It is coming. And it will change your life. You must enter that light and bring your warmth to the campfire of all those who have gone before you. The light is waiting in the darkness. You must be the light."

"*Hōkūle'a* is the living dream, the dream come true," says Sam. "*Kēia ka maoli.* This is real. Every time *Hōkūle'a* moves she picks up that kind of awe. Before her time we looked for inspiration in occidental and oriental places. Everything was western. But here was something that none of them had their fingerprints on. It

Sam Ka'ai steering *Hōkūle'a*

was affirmation after affirmation, these layers and layers, they came. The *lāhui o ka lani*, the heavenly hosts, spoke—and we began to listen."

❖❖❖❖❖

The canoe stayed in Kailua for a time, and then went to Kawaihae. Shorty Bertelmann lived a few miles away in Puakō, once an ancient fishing village. At the time, he was employed by the Park Service to help rebuild Pu'ukoholā, a famous *heiau*, or temple, erected by Hawai'i's great king, Kamehameha the First. Stone by stone, as he labored on the *heiau*, Shorty was discovering a deep connection to his own ancestry. "When *Hōkūle'a* came along I knew I had to be part of it, to help bring back our traditions and to learn more about my ancestors." The day after *Hōkūle'a's* arrival, Herb Kane showed up at Pu'ukoholā. He took pictures of the workmen as studies for his illustration of ancient Hawaiians building the temple. Herb met Shorty and talked to him about *Hōkūle'a*. "Herb spoke so well," Shorty recalls, "that I decided I wanted to sail with him. Wherever he went, I wanted to follow him." Herb invited Shorty to try out for a crew position, so Shorty sailed aboard *Hōkūle'a* to Maui, then on to Moloka'i and O'ahu.

Along the way, the canoe continued to gather what Hawaiians call *mana*—spiritual power that can be dangerous. In Hilo, she tied up at a pier fronting the Naniloa Hotel and people came out to admire her. John Kruse noticed that tourists readily approached the crew with questions, but older Hawaiians seemed to watch from a distance. "They kind of hid out behind their cars," he remembers. "Some were skeptical. 'What the hell is this? And who are these guys who do this?' They knew that such canoes used to exist but now they actually see one. They are talking full on Hawaiian, but they kept their distance."

John Kruse grew up in Hilo, living with his grandmother. In 1897, she had signed the Kū'ē Petition along with 40,000 other Hawaiians in a doomed attempt to protest the annexation of Hawai'i to the United States. "When I was a kid, Hilo was a small little hick town," John remembers. "My family struggled. My grandmother taught me all the Hawaiian values that she knew. You did everything as a family and you stuck together. No matter how hard it was, you never gave up."

John's grandmother was a *kahuna lapa'au*—a traditional Hawaiian healer. She cultivated Hawaiian herbs in a gulch near her house. "I remember Hawaiian people always coming and getting medicine. They would talk in Hawaiian. They had aches and pains and she would make poultices." Once a month, John's grandmother and her second husband would climb into a Model T Ford with John and his sister bundled up in the rumble seat and drive thirty miles to Kīlauea Volcano. They stopped the car near Halema'uma'u crater 3600 feet up the slope. John's grandmother got out alone with her offerings. John watched as she chanted and threw her gifts into the crater. "She had one foot in the past," John says. "She was going to the Mormon Church but she still had the Hawaiian church that she would go to. That was her Hawaiian religion—up there with Pele, the goddess of fire and volcanoes."

Like so many Hawaiians, John's grandmother was secretive about her religion and her curing arts. In the days before the *haole* arrival, the art of the *kahuna lapa'au* was passed on to apprentices who showed an innate, almost spiritual skill for the laying on of hands and the mixing of remedies. A complex system of diagnosis had evolved that included a model of the human circulatory and digestive systems. Specific symptoms required specific cures. If a remedy failed, there were alternatives. It was a body of knowledge certainly equal to that of Captain Cook's surgeon. Today, some consider Hawaiian remedies superior to modern ones. At the new hospital in Waimea on the Big Island, for example, the Hawaiian arts of massage and herbal medicine are employed alongside those of the most modern western treatments. But this is a recent development. When John's grandmother was growing up, most *haole* considered the *kahuna's* practice a dangerous native superstition, so they passed a law to forbid it. As a result, the *kahuna lapa'au* went underground. Even in her own family, John's grandmother would not reveal her secrets. She had resolved to take them to the grave. "I would ask, 'Grandma, why all these people come?' " John recalls. " 'How come the Hawaiian men always over here asking you questions—all these guys talking Hawaiian?' But she didn't like to tell me that stuff because maybe it wasn't meant for me. 'Maybe you children are not going to be Hawaiian,' she told us. 'Maybe you got to learn the new *haole* way.' "

When Sam Ka'ai speaks of the pain inflicted on Hawaiians by their *haole* overlords he does not mince words nor is he politically correct. "When these islands were seized by the *haole* we all became just niggers," Sam once said, "and they wanted to get rid of nigger jibber so the Hawaiian language was suppressed. I heard the old folks talk about how painful it was. They would say 'Boy, stop talking Hawaiian, or bye and bye you cannot get a job. A German man doesn't speak German, he speaks English, because he wants the *kālā*—the cash. The Japanese doesn't speak Japanese, he speaks English because the boss speaks English. You like to get a job or you just going to stay over here? But at that time there was some *namunamu*—some grumbling. Hawaiians knew something was wrong. They knew the rent was too high. They knew that the schools were getting too old. They knew that Hawaiian kids were okay until the third grade and all of a sudden in the fourth grade when they started to teach them social history they started to collapse and not make it. That is right. Because some guy in a silk stocking and powdered wig is not the father of *our* country. Because Daniel Boone is not *our* hero. We had our heroes, but nobody was singing about Hawaiian heroes. Everybody was singing of some other hero. So you did not belong to that society. And unless you were in that society—in a family that was very European-oriented—you are never going to get anywhere. Never."

As the canoe sailed from island to island, she evoked complex emotions. Older Hawaiians mostly accepted their place in a society dominated by *haole* and, increasingly, by Asiatic migrants who were moving up into the managerial classes. Hawaiians learned to endure what they felt could not be changed. But from across the American Great Plains and through the disturbed cities of the seventies a wind was blowing that carried a message of renewed power among American minorities—blacks and Native Americans—and the wind began to buffet young Hawaiians. One of the places it blew most strongly was on the remote island of Moloka'i which is still regarded, along with Ni'ihau, as the most traditional and least-developed of the Hawaiian Islands.

Moloka'i is redolent of an old way of doing things. There is a single main town and in the town there is a single main street. Many of the stores are false fronted, like frontier settlements in the American West. Even today, the largest grocery store boasts maybe six aisles and there are few buildings over two stories tall. The island's few hotels are still small and cars are drawn up directly in front of the rooms. A single macadam road winds around the southern side of the island and degrades to dirt, then to a footpath as it heads north. The North Coast is accessible only by boat. It's not surprising that a different kind of culture flourished here—one dedicated not just to hanging onto, but to restoring Native Hawaiian values.

From the main pier in the town of Kaunakakai, you can look out to a barren low-slung island called Kaho'olawe. Kaho'olawe has long been an irritant in the otherwise quiet Moloka'i lifestyle. In World War II, the island was taken over as a military bombing range. For a time, people approved of this. But in the midst of the Vietnam War, as many young men in America were called to rethink their patriotism, the constant thumping of bombs stimulated an already swelling antiwar consciousness on Moloka'i. And gradually, antiwar sentiments entwined with rising anger over the past two hundred years of cultural oppression.

Moloka'i, like all Hawaiian islands, is largely owned by absentee landlords descended in many cases from the original *haole* businessmen and missionaries who took the land from Hawaiians in the 1800s. The biggest landowner is the Moloka'i Ranch, 65,000 acres, about forty percent of the entire island. The ranch lands are marked with signs that say *"kapu*—no trespassing." Mel Paoa grew up in Moloka'i and encountered adolescence as America encountered the war in Vietnam—the sixties. For young men like Mel and his friends, the *kapu* signs barred them from prime hunting lands and from the best reefs for fishing. But they recalled a previous right, an ancient Hawaiian one, that gave access to everyone for these purposes and also to visit ancestral shrines and temples, of which there were many on private lands. In 1973, Mel joined a group called Hui Ala Loa, "the society of the long trails" which began public marches to restore access to fishing and hunting places. "A lot of guys my age were getting involved with trying to find out who we were, what rights we had as Hawaiians. What we did on Moloka'i was open up a lot of access areas with quiet protest, marching and petitions. We didn't do anything really radical like burning or things like that. But the protests opened up avenues for us."

George Helm Jr. began a series of "invasions" of Kaho'olawe to stop the bombing of what many Hawaiians considered sacred *'āina* (land). Sometimes acting alone, sometimes with a group of friends, Helm would paddle to the island on a surfboard and attempt to hide. When the Navy learned that people were on the island they were forced to cease bombing and go look for them. Helm's activity garnered a great deal of press. "I used to hang out with George Helm," Mel remembers. "He would talk about *aloha 'āina*, about loving and taking care of our lands, about being proud of who we are and what we represent and how things should not be taken for granted—we should get back what spiritually belongs to us." George and his companions in resistance knew they were practicing a dangerous game. It surprised no one when he was lost at sea on March 7th, 1977, paddling one last time between Kaho'olawe and Maui.

In 1975, *Hōkūle'a* sailed into this growing spirit of Hawaiian activism and revival that was now being called the "Hawaiian Renaissance."

"The canoe—from the moment she was launched, and with momentum increasing as she went to neighboring islands—unexpectedly became a symbol of the renaissance of Hawaiian culture," Dave Lyman recalls. "People would rally around the canoe because she was and is a beautiful thing to look at and because of what she represents. The achievements of our ancestors is so deep in every Hawaiian that the canoe generates this sense of pride. No matter how tough it might be living on a Spam and rice diet and losing the opportunity to subsist by fishing and farming, that canoe instills a sense of innate pride."

"The timing of the canoe was fortunate because of the general feeling of desperation that the culture was slipping away, and if we did not reach out and grab it now it would be gone forever," says Herb. "There was a general revival of interest in the culture. I can't think of any area in which there was not a revival of interest."

Hawaiians had called themselves *kanaka*, which simply means "human," for a long time. But as the renaissance of values continued, a new term emerged—*kanaka maoli. Maoli* means "real" or "true," so a *kanaka maoli* was a "true Hawaiian." For some Hawaiians that meant native to Hawai'i; for others, it required a certain amount of Hawaiian blood—*koko*. But most Hawaiians thought *kanaka maoli* signified a deep feeling in the *na'au*, the gut, of being Hawaiian and a commitment to back it up with action. At least that's the way Sam Ka'ai thought: "You say you are Hawaiian? Can you light the fire for the *imu* (earth oven) without a match? Can you kill a pig without a knife? Can you take his hair off without a razor? Can you cut him open without a knife? Your father's father's father's father could. And so we are not *maoli*. We are just children. We have forgotten our father's footsteps. If we don't care—nobody else cares. A *kanaka* has got to care. So when Herb brought that vessel to us it was time to care. Forget everything. Take your honor and your resources and go."

♦ ♦ ♦ ♦ ♦

Wally Froiseth had been present at *Hōkūle'a's* creation. "When they were building the canoe," he remembers, "I swept out the workshop." In his appearance, there was nothing Hawaiian about Wally. He was blonde, light-skinned, blue-eyed. He was tall, with the lanky physique of a surfer—which he was, and a famous one. Froiseth and a few friends were among the first to ride the huge ocean walls that crash ashore on O'ahu's windward coast. "Wally and a couple of guys went up to Waimea," Nainoa remembers, "and they saw these mountains of water. His heart was pounding. Nobody was around. He couldn't sleep all night because of the surf. He got out of his station wagon when dawn was coming up. What scared him most was no footprints on the sand. You don't go here. It's too dangerous! But off they went. It took them two hours to catch a wave. And they caught one and they went in. What an incredible man."

Wally was more than a surfer—he was a lover of the sea in all its forms. He raced and built outrigger canoes. He swam, bodysurfed, snorkeled, fished and sailed the first catamarans seen in Hawaiian waters since the days of King Kamehameha a century and a half earlier. He sailed them far distances, from California to Hawai'i and on to Tahiti and the Marquesas. Wally was aboard when *Hōkūle'a* went through the 'Alenuihāhā Channel from O'ahu to Maui and he was invited by Herb to sail back from the Big Island to O'ahu. On O'ahu, Wally was known and revered for his skill as a surfer and he had been accepted into that island's Hawaiian community. But when he boarded the canoe on the Big Island, he encountered a new crew and the beginning of a new idea—that the canoe was a Hawaiian canoe and Hawaiians only should man her. Who was this tall *haole* guy and what right did he have to come aboard the spaceship of the ancestors?

"When I got on board all these Hawaiians start rushing me to throw me overboard," Wally remembers, "and Herb had to stop them. I don't think any of us really knew how emotional it was for Hawaiians."

"It must have been confusing," Ben Finney wrote, "for a Hawaiian from one of the outer Islands to behold what he thought was a Hawaiian canoe, only to discover that *haole* as well as Hawaiians ran the project and that a multiracial crew would sail to Tahiti. I saw the confusion on Hawaiian faces when, at outer island anchorages, I stepped aboard the canoe and was introduced as the president and cofounder of the Polynesian Voyaging Society."

"No one could foresee," remembers Dave Lyman, "how pride in the canoe, reviving pride, would turn into possessiveness. 'This is my canoe because I am Hawaiian and this is not your canoe because you are *haole* even though you, Mr. *Haole* Man, are largely responsible for building and creating this. Thank you— but give it to me.' "

Dave knew that the community was diverse and that many did not feel that way. Most just wanted to put their heads down and get on with the task.

"But the voice that was heard," he remembers, "was the voice that said 'This canoe should be given to us.' "

❖ ❖ ❖ ❖ ❖

On her final training voyage, *Hōkūle'a* sailed to the island of Kaua'i. She put in at Hanalei Bay, a crescent of white sand that fronts a deep valley filled with *taro* gardens. It's a place so redolent of paradise that the movie *South Pacific* was filmed there in 1958.

"We came into Hanalei Bay and people just were rising out of the ground," Herb remembers. "Everybody was just looking. They could not take their eyes off the canoe."

Hōkūle'a was greeted by the island's *hālau hula* (Hawaiian dancers). There was plenty of food, beer, dancing and pretty women. A few days after the arrival, Roger Ka'awaloa found himself aboard *Hōkūle'a*, cleaning her decks. He watched an outrigger canoe put off from the beach and paddle alongside. In it was a young Hawaiian girl, a dancer from one of the *hālau* that had entertained them a few nights before. Roger recognized her—but there was something different about her appearance. The girl handed a simple paper bag up to him.

"This is my gift to the canoe," she told him. Then she paddled away.

Among Hawaiians, one of the most personal gifts that can be given are strands of hair. Such a gift implies complete trust because, in ancient times, an evil *kahuna* could use a person's hair to pray their victim to death. When Roger opened the bag he understood why the girl had looked different. It contained long ringlets of her hair.

PILIKIA[‡]

Chapter Eight

"*H*ōkūle'a is sinking off Kaua'i."

The telephone call came as a shock to Ben Finney. In recent weeks things had been going well. What had happened?

The canoe had set off from Hanalei in the early afternoon of October 3rd, 1975. Upon clearing the harbor, she encountered strong east-northeast trade winds. Her destination, Honolulu, lay about a hundred and twenty miles directly into the teeth of the wind, so the voyage would be a good test—in fact the first real test—of the canoe's ability to tack to windward. Herb Kane trimmed her sails in tight. At midnight, *Hōkūle'a* was eleven miles off Kaua'i having made good only eighteen miles toward O'ahu. Herb and Boogie Kalama checked the bilges and found the starboard hull had taken on water. They bailed it out and sponged it dry. Herb tacked the canoe and turned command over to the two most senior sailors aboard, Dave Lyman and Tommy Holmes. He slipped into his *puka*, his berthing place in the canoe's hulls, to sleep.

Discipline had been relaxed during the canoe's stay in Hanalei. Her mission was to train her crew, but days had passed with the canoe serenely at anchor, the crew celebrating on shore. During the midnight to six watch, the compartments were not bailed. The canoe's outboard motor bracket deflected spray into the starboard hull. Imperceptibly, sea water accumulated in the bilge. Sometime during the evening, caulking between *Hōkūle'a's* compartments gave way, allowing water to flow into the full length of the depressed leeward hull. The canoe developed a slight list. No one noticed. The list increased.

"Lyman awakened me at 6:00 a.m.," Herb recalls. "I scanned the canoe and saw the starboard hull low in the water. We pulled back the canvas cover and started bailing, but the hull was boarded by a wave and swamped."

Ben caught the first inter-island flight from O'ahu to Kaua'i. From fifteen thousand feet, he saw the stricken canoe, a tiny spot in the frothing sea below.

[‡] The English translation for *pilikia* is "trouble."

His first thoughts were for the crew shivering in the cold ocean. A few hours later, he watched as the canoe was towed slowly into Nāwiliwili Harbor. "*Hōkūle'a* was a sad sight," he would later write. "The starboard hull was down, except for the tips of the prow and stern pieces, while the port hull was thrust up and canted over to one side. The deckhouse was gone and the crew left on board was clinging to the rail along the port hull. Then, just at the harbor entrance, cross swells caught the canoe and dumped water into the port hull, which then also began to settle. By the time she had been maneuvered alongside the pier, the canoe was totally swamped. Both hulls were completely filled with water and the raised deck was awash... Never before did the voyage to Tahiti seem so remote."

Fingers were pointed following the swamping. It was the captain's fault. Those on watch were to blame. The board of directors should have been more vigilant. The crew had not been trained properly. To channel the anger and redirect efforts toward getting the canoe ready for the voyage, now only six months away, Ben Finney established a Board of Inquiry. Rudy Choy, a well-known boat designer, would be chairman. Wally Froiseth and a Coast Guard officer would help analyze what went wrong. A few weeks later the report came out.

"*Hōkūle'a* swamped due to lack of seamanship, an absence of knowledgeable command at sea and the omission of acceptable standards and procedures for all oceangoing vessels," the report said. "The euphoric aura present during the launching and most so-called training trips whether day sailing or inter-island jaunts, the remarkable success of *Hōkūle'a* despite major warning signs that serious command and organizational deficiencies in fact existed, and the lack of serious problems due to favorable weather conditions and good luck all contributed to laxity and poor seamanship which led inevitably to the swamping."[9]

There was sufficient blame to go around, but Herb Kane, as captain, took the brunt of it. Herb was in many ways the perfect leader during the Voyaging Society's learning phase. He understood what the canoe meant to Hawaiians and to the rebirth of their culture because he was personally stepping back in time to recover his own identity. His passion was contagious. He was confident in his authority. He was tough. Some say he was too tough. "I sailed with Herb a couple of times around the islands," one crew-member recalls. "Herb gave the impression that an *ali'i* was in control of the ship. He could be a hard man to be on the water with."

"The whole project was eating up Herb's life," says Ben Finney. "He left, leaving me at the top just at the time that everyone was attacking the project. The whole thing was about to collapse."

The Coast Guard could have judged the canoe unsafe and forbidden the voyage to Tahiti, but the Board of Inquiry found the canoe to be basically sound. Her crew had failed her. The canoe's watertight integrity, however, was suspect. Her bulkheads did not extend all the way to the top of the hull, so if she shipped sufficient water it could flow into adjacent compartments. A number of simple changes were recommended to fix the problem—the outboard engine mount would be removed, bulkheads would be made watertight and new deck hatches would be fabricated. *Hōkūle'a* was shipped to O'ahu on a barge and put up on 40-gallon oil drums at Snug Harbor.

❖ ❖ ❖ ❖ ❖

Snug Harbor is a gritty place under the flight path of big jets landing at Honolulu International Airport. *Hōkūle'a* sat on a cement apron that kicked back the sunlight. It was hot. Her crew worked out of containers donated by Matson Lines. Some lived in the containers, curled up among marine detritus with their toothbrushes hung on nails. It was primitive, but many of the men who labored over *Hōkūle'a* came from the impoverished town of Wai'anae and they were used to hardship.

John Kruse and Wally Froiseth directed the work. Wally redesigned the gunwales, curving them up toward bow and stern to deflect the spray. Lashings, rigging, masts and boom had to be renewed. The to-do list was long and time was short. It was now January, 1976 and the voyage was scheduled for May. The treasurers' report, read at the January 9th meeting of the Voyaging Society Board, revealed that the cost of barging the canoe and rebuilding her had drained the coffers—the Society was in financial crisis. The need to do so many things at once imposed a harsh division of labor. Herb had seemingly retired, Ben Finney and Tommy Holmes were fully occupied with raising funds, planning a long sea voyage, arranging permits and visas. The only time the crew saw their leaders was when they came down to give orders—but they seldom stayed to help.

"It was a bad thing," remembers Snake Ah Hee. "If you're on the board of directors or are the president you're supposed to come down because all the crew people like to see how things are going. But every time they came down it was always 'Do this or don't do that.' When they do that everybody's morale goes down."

"I was in the service and I thought, 'typical military bullshit. We are the peons,' " says John Kruse. "They gave orders but they would never stay so we drifted apart."

The rift was aggravated by the fact that some of the crew considered themselves kānaka maoli—true Hawaiians—and during this emotional time of cultural renewal they began to consider some of their leaders to be pure haole, particularly Ben Finney who was born and raised in California. Even worse, Ben was a professor who seemed to embody a western scientific view of things—who saw the voyage as an "experiment" of some kind, not the culminating dream of revival that some of the crew considered her to be.

"Some of the guys were getting swept up in the Hawaiian Renaissance," says John Kruse. "They thought the culture side was more important than the scientific side. But on the science side were the people who thought the project up, who raised the money, and who created the organization to make the voyage."

"There was gross miscommunication," Dave Lyman recalls. "And it came about because the leaders of the Voyaging Society did not fully explain that the voyage was a scientific research experiment to show that it was possible for Polynesians to make purposeful two-way voyages between Hawai'i and the islands to the south, the Marquesas and Tahiti and New Zealand."

"You had someone with a Ph.D. from Harvard versus someone who never got out of high school," Ben Young remembers. "How do they communicate? We had a caldron of ethnicities, of cultural backgrounds, of economic backgrounds, of social status. Some people came from very affluent backgrounds and some didn't know where their next paycheck was coming from. And thrown into that was a deadline for getting the canoe ready to go after the capsizing. There were enormous pressures on the group at that time."

Among the crew it became a matter of faith that "someone was making money" while they slaved over the canoe without pay. What happened to all the funds that had been raised? Why was there nothing to help the crew out? Ben Finney was going to write a book—whose pocket would that money go into? The crew didn't know that Ben had donated his ten thousand dollar advance to PVS and pledged all profits from the book to cover the costs of building and sailing *Hōkūle'a*. It was another example of what Dave Lyman calls "gross miscommunication."

"It was chaos," says Nainoa. "If you could have integrated the two sides it would have been powerful, but the two worlds had to talk to each other and they didn't know how."

Wally was one of the few *haole* who could bridge the divide. He was a famous waterman, one of the first big wave riders. He lived on the beach in Mākaha, just a few miles down the road from Wai'anae where most of the crew lived. "He was the guiding force in keeping the crew together," says Ben Young. "No one would dare go up against Wally because he was such an accepted waterman. He was able to put a stop to some of the tension and just put them to work."

❖ ❖ ❖ ❖ ❖

With Herb Kane out of the picture, a new captain was needed. The ideal candidate would have significant sailing experience—especially aboard catamarans—and be able to bridge the growing gap between the factions. Wally Froiseth seemed the natural choice. Wally was an experienced seaman, he had sailed on both monohulls and multihulls. Ben Finney believed he was the only man who could command the respect of the Hawaiian crew and he begged Wally to accept the position. But Wally had been raised among Hawaiians and he knew what the canoe meant to a people who had long been oppressed in their own homeland. *Hōkūle'a's* captain, he felt deep in his heart, must be Hawaiian.

Kawika Kapahulehua soon emerged as the right person to captain *Hōkūle'a*. Kawika first went to sea on a raft he built with sails of bed sheets. He sailed aboard Rudy Choy's catamarans in four TransPac races, two of them in the "first to finish" boat—*Seasmoke.* He had delivered yachts across wide stretches of ocean. Perhaps most important, he had earned a 100-ton Master's license that would be looked upon favorably by the Coast Guard. In addition to all these qualifications, Kawika was a full-blooded Hawaiian. In the 1970s this was a rare quality. Intermarriage had been so common over the centuries that only a thousand or so full-blooded Hawaiians were known to exist. Most of them lived on Ni'ihau—where Kawika grew up—a tiny island off Kaua'i. The Ni'ihau Hawaiians were considered the last guardians of an ancient culture. Kawika had learned to speak Hawaiian at the knees of his grandparents. Surely he would have the *mana* to heal the rift between Hawaiians and *haole*. "Everybody was excited about him," Dave Lyman recalls. "Not only could he speak fluent Hawaiian but he also had experience sailing."

❖ ❖ ❖ ❖ ❖

For a number of weeks, the leaders had not visited the drydock at Snug Harbor. Finney had been incapacitated with bronchial pneumonia partly brought on by stress. Tommy Holmes was out beating the bushes for money. Herb seemed to have retired. One very important task remained, lashing the *'iako*—the crossbeams—that joined the twin hulls. The crew sat and waited for orders. Finally, someone asked Mau if he could lash the canoe.

"They asked me, 'Can you make the canoe?' " Mau recalls, "because the bosses they never come, only Hawaiians like Kimo, Billy, Shorty, Buffalo—they stay waiting for the bosses to come and show them how you lash the canoe. We wait for them about two weeks and then too close to the time for leave so they ask me, 'Can you lash the canoe?' I say, 'No problem. I can.' "

Mau lashed *Hōkūle'a* as his father and grandfather had taught him using a technique of "up and down" lashings. The rope is wound around the two pieces of wood to be joined and made as tight as possible. Later, another rope is wound around the up and down strands, perpendicular to them, and pulled taut. This last strand of rope cinches the lashing and makes it strong. The technique worked for Micronesian navigators during many centuries of voyaging.

"Mau was the guiding light," says John Kruse, " 'You do this,' he told us, and that's how it was going to be. Mau was the calm in the storm." The crew joined Mau with renewed fervor. They were learning an ancient skill at the knees of the master.

Within a few weeks, four miles of rope had been consumed and the lashing was almost finished. Then Herb Kane returned from his self-imposed exile to

Lashing the *'iako*

inspect the canoe. "That's not how you do it," he told them. "This lashing is for a little twenty-six foot Micronesian outrigger canoe and it doesn't belong on an eight-ton vessel."

"None of the real decision-makers had been down to the canoe while we were working away on her," Dave Lyman remembers, "and they came down and said the lashings were no good. They have to be cross lashings like the Hawaiians do. We had a long drawn-out emotional meeting and Tommy and I said that we agreed that Mau was in charge. 'No, no you need cross lashings,' they said. It was one of the most awful situations I had ever been in in my life because after the meeting they said the lashings had to come off and the canoe had to be re-lashed."

When confronted with the decision to remove his lashings, Mau was angry and probably more than a little humiliated. "Now is not *pau* (finished)," Mau told the leaders. "Don't take off. Now is not ready because too many people talk, talk, talk." The lashings were, in fact, loose because Mau had not yet cinched them tight with the final strands of rope.

"Mau's English was rudimentary," Dave recalls, "and he was totally frustrated and he said 'But not finished, not *pau* yet.' 'Sorry,' that's what the leaders said, and off they came and we started redoing them. That really divided the crew from the leaders. *Big time.*"

"They no like," Mau remembers. "They say not Polynesian way because Micronesian way. Then I say, 'Okay, better you guys pay me, I like go back home.' "

For a year or so, a National Geographic film crew had been following the process of building the canoe for a major documentary film. The film's producer, Dale Bell, had focused his camera on Mau as the living embodiment of ancient knowledge. Without him the film would be lost. Fortunately, Bell convinced Mau to stay.

LEAVE YOUR PROBLEMS
ON THE LAND

Chapter Nine

An article announcing the crew for the voyage to Tahiti appeared above the fold in the Honolulu Advertiser on February 7th. The list began with Kawika as captain, Dave Lyman as relief captain, Mau as navigator, David Lewis as scientist and Ben Finney as writer. The crew list followed: Rodo Williams, Kimo Hugho, Richard "Buffalo" Keaulana, Sam Kalalau Jr., Billy Richards, Dukie Kuahulu, John Kruse, Shorty Bertelmann, Clifford Ah Mow and Tommy Holmes. Nainoa and Snake would join eleven others on the return trip from Tahiti. Wally Froiseth was on the crew selection committee, but he had not been consulted on the final choice of crew. Shortly after the article came out, Kawika called Wally to explain that the process was unexpectedly rushed and they had no time to get in touch with him.

"Well, Kawika," said Wally, "you're the captain, so if you're satisfied then it's okay because you're going to have to live with them."

But Wally was worried. He knew that Kawika's strength was in his professionalism—his experience as a captain of catamarans; and he was a pure Hawaiian so that should carry some clout with the crew. But Wally also knew that a few of those chosen were unsuited for the rigors of a long sea voyage and it was obvious that the schism between leaders and crew had opened wide. He worried that no one could take his place as peacemaker.

❖ ❖ ❖ ❖ ❖

On April 22nd, the lashing complete, Hōkūle'a was put back in the water. When the expenses to repair the canoe were tallied, only four thousand dollars were left to pay the crew during the voyage to Tahiti and back. It was not enough. On April 24th, the rift between crew and leaders became an open rebellion. With the National Geographic film team and a local television cameraman on hand, crewmember Kimo Hugho rose to speak. He complained about the pittance that was being paid the crew to tide over their families during the voyage, about the previous swamping and insufficient safety precautions, the inadequate training program. It would require months of work before they were ready to go, he told them.

"I agreed with him," Nainoa recalls. "It was fair to question our preparedness for the voyage. We were not well trained. The canoe was not tested."

"I think I know what the Hawaiian people deserve," Kimo said to the television cameras. "They have been taken for granted. Two hundred years later, gang." It was a stunning rebuke that referred to the past two centuries of cultural oppression. Once again, he implied, the Hawaiian people—the crew—were being taken advantage of by the uncaring *haole*—the leadership.

"Kimo had a meeting," John Kruse remembers. "The media was there and he started chastising the higher-ups. We were supposed to get pay for the families, whatever we make in a month to the family. But since we swamped, all that money was used for the rebuild. We never generated more money. Guys were like—'I can't go.' "

The producer of the National Geographic film saw the dramatic potential of the rift between crew and leaders and, according to some on the crew, encouraged it. "It was probably the worst time in my life," Ben Finney remembers. "Dale Bell is egging it on. He told me he smelled an Emmy. He is actually urging people to revolt. It's on his own sound tracks in the outtakes. It's a circus."

Kawika rose to the challenge. He told the crew that if they did not wish to go they could choose not to. It was up to them, but now was the time to decide. "You can sign on as crew members for the trip," he told them. "For those of you who don't want to go, if you don't want to sign for it there's no problem. But we have a lot of work to do."

On Sunday, April 25th, *Hōkūle'a* left O'ahu and arrived at her departure point, Honolua Bay on Maui the next day.

Kimo Hugho continued to worry that *Hōkūle'a* was not ready. After a long discussion with Captain Kawika Kapahulehua, he decided not to make the voyage.

"Kimo was really worried about being prepared for the voyage," Nainoa says. "He stuck to his guns. It was an agonizing decision for him, but it was *pono* (correct or proper)."

Sam Ka'ai was on hand to help bless the canoe. He was disgusted by the continuing dissension, the *pilikia* as he called it. "At Honolua Bay they were losing track of why they were going," he recalled.

"You listen to me," Sam told them. "If all of you were lepers and they asked me to go, I would go. You're supposed to affirm the song of our ancestors. It's not a matter of are you mad with Ben Finney. That's playing games. You're the crew—the family of the canoe. This is the day when all the training ends and only walking the walk will be proof that we're Hawaiians. Now we're going to look south from where we came and we're going to hear an ancient song not flavored by modern education or European ideas. The song will change us all. What was just a whisper on the wind, a murmur, a growling in the heaven, will become a living song about where we came from."

On the morning of May 1st, just before the canoe shoved off for Tahiti, Mau Piailug stepped forward to address the crew. He spoke in Satawalese. His words were translated by Mike McCoy, who was married to Mau's niece:

"I want to tell all of you how you must act on the ocean to survive. On the ocean you don't eat the same, or sleep the same, or work the same as on land. Everything we do is different. On the ocean all the food, all the water, is under the control of the captain. When he says eat, we eat. When he says drink, we drink. Before we leave, throw away all the things that are worrying you. Leave all your problems on land. On the ocean, you are under the control of the captain and the navigator of the canoe. Everything the captain says we follow. If you have a problem, come to me first and I will talk to the captain. When on the ocean we cannot see any islands. All we have to survive on are the things we bring with us. That is all I have to say. Remember, all of you, these things and we will see that place we are going to."

"I told them that when we go to sea we must *aloha* each other," Mau remembers. "We must be like a family together. Take care of each other. I told them that the canoe is our mother and the navigator is our father."

"Mau was completely calm," John Kruse remembers. "He was already in the zone. The canoe was facing the sea and the wind was coming out of the valley so we opened the sails and let go the hook and we were gone. I saw Nainoa in a powerboat with all the canoe members on the return trip. They were waving goodbye."

HEAVY WEATHER

Chapter Ten

*H*ōkūle'a set out into a chill trade wind. For five days she tacked east to clear the Big Island before turning south toward Tahiti. "We got the shit kicked out of us," John Kruse recalls. "Trade winds, storms, stuff all over the deck. It was mishmash." The deck, fabricated of planks and half-round bamboo, allowed spray to seep through. "Your feet were raw. The deck was all wet. You can't dry off."

The crew slept in a tiny *hale*, a hut of woven *lauhala* leaves. "It was horrible" John says. "You try to sleep but only four spaces—and all big guys. Once you're inside you're stuck, can't get out. You felt trapped. One guy was sneezing and snoring right in your face. We were the guinea pigs."

"The first three days was really something," recalls Dukie Kuahulu. "We were getting wet and cold and it was raining and it was kind of miserable. I think that was the roughest spot when we were leaving the island because we had good winds and we had a lot of spray that was coming from the sides and underneath and we were getting wet."

Meotai, a 65-five foot steel ketch followed in *Hōkūle'a's* wake. The Voyaging Society and National Geographic chartered her to carry film equipment and to rescue the crew should something happen to the canoe.

At the end of the first week, Mau observed the height of the North Star astern and the Southern Cross ahead. "About the same as Saipan," he told David Lewis who recorded Mau's navigational techniques. Lewis logged the position in western terms as 14 degrees 30 minutes north. When checked against the position recorded by *Meotai's* navigator with instruments, the actual figure was 14 degrees 6 minutes, a difference of only twenty-four miles.

David Lewis was a natural choice to document Mau's navigation. In 1972, Lewis had published *We the Navigators—the Ancient Art of Landfinding in the Pacific*, a book detailing his voyages with noninstrument navigators in Polynesia, the Solomon Islands, and Micronesia. Lewis was a polymath who planted his feet in many worlds. He was born in 1917 in Plymouth, one of England's most famous seaports, but he was raised in Auckland, New Zealand and in Titikaveka in the Cook Islands, where he attended school and went on to college. He returned to England to earn degrees as a medical doctor and surgeon, then served as medical officer in a British parachute battalion during the Second World War. After the war, he established a general practice in London's East End. Lewis loved sailing. He competed in the first single-handed transatlantic race in 1960 and placed third. Francis Chichester won the race and went on to fame and a knighthood. In 1963, Lewis led an expedition to Greenland. He competed again in the solo transatlantic race in 1964. In that same year, he abandoned his medical practice, purchased a catamaran—*Rehu Moana*—and set out to circumnavigate the world with his wife and two young daughters. He completed his voyage, with stops in Easter Island, Mangareva, Tonga, Fiji, the New Hebrides, and New Guinea. Along the way, he learned that non-instrument navigators still plied ancient searoutes among the Santa Cruz Outer Reef Islands, the Solomons and the Admiralty Archipelago—all of which he visited in a second expedition in 1968 and 1969, aboard a 39-foot auxiliary gaff ketch, *Isbjorn*. The Caroline Islands were reputed to be home to a pristine navigational tradition, so he sailed there and spent months voyaging with Hipour, a famous navigator from Puluwat, recording his navigational techniques in detail. Now, aboard *Hōkūle'a*, it was Lewis' job to document Mau's navigational lore.

Before the voyage, the crew had been told the trip might take as long as a month but after only six days at sea, one crewman approached Dave Lyman with a disturbing question.

"Hey, we almost there?"

"No, it's going to be another three weeks," Lyman told him.

"I think they thought it was like going to Kaua'i," Dave recalls. "No island could be that far away."

About eight days into the voyage, the canoe seemed to have developed a severe weather helm, a tendency to turn into the wind, and the crew struggled to keep her on course. The balance of any sailing vessel is affected by its trim. If she sits too deeply in the water aft, she will turn off the wind—lee helm. If she sits too deeply forward, she will turn into the wind—weather helm. John Kruse noticed the canoe's bow had settled. Perhaps that's the problem? Without consulting Captain Kapahulehua, he went forward with Billy and Boogie and dropped into the hull. Billy examined the front bulkhead that seals the canoe's bow compartment. He took up a hammer. Tap. Tap. Tap. Thunk. Thunk. "Hey," he told the others, "we got some water in this compartment. That's why she's sitting so low."

John retrieved a chisel from the canoe's tool kit and made a small hole in the bulkhead. Water rushed out. "Problem solved," John recalled. "The canoe was leaking through the cross pieces in the front. The lashings stretch and contract with the canoe's motion and allow water to get in. The captain didn't know about it. We took matters into our own hands. We fixed it."

For the crew, this was another example of the incompetence of the so-called "leaders" who didn't even notice the problem. It's not surprising, given the communication breakdown between the two factions, that Ben Finney recalled the incident differently. He remembers that the leak was discovered and resolved by Dave Lyman.

Nine days out, John Kruse and Buffalo decided to rig a jib—a small modern sail—to allow the canoe to sail faster. "We put it up on my watch," Dave Lyman recalls. "Real simple, I'm a sailor. I allowed it, knowing we weren't supposed to, but it made everyone on our watch smile for a while." When Ben Finney and David Lewis discovered the jib they were furious. The whole point of the voyage was to test the sailing abilities of a traditional Polynesian canoe. Any deviation from *Hōkūle'a's* authentic sails would destroy the experiment.

"Get that down," Finney ordered.

"Ben was right to take the jib down," Dave recalls. "It compromised the purity of the experiment. And that was what the voyage was for. I was wrong. I didn't realize it at the time but it was cause for resentment by some people. I would not have done that if I had known it."

For the crew, it was another arbitrary decision. Did the *haole* think their Hawaiian ancestors were not smart enough, after thousands of years sailing across the Pacific, to invent a simple jib?

DOLDRUMS

Chapter Eleven

During the second week, *Hōkūle'a* made good progress with daily runs on the order of a hundred and twenty-five miles. The mood of all on board improved. The sky remained cloudy so Mau steered by the swells. Dave Lyman recorded course, speed, weather conditions, and the state of the ocean in *Hōkūle'a's* log. He remembers one day trying to detect the most prominent swell, but the sea appeared to be "mishmash" – confused. He decided to consult Mau.

"Mau, what do you call this?" he asked. "I call this a confused northeasterly sea and swell. What is it?"

"It's not confused," Mau said. "Look."

"And he pointed out five different swells to me," Dave recalls, "and once he pointed them out I could see them clearly."

"There is also a swell from the west," Mau said.

"West?"

"Yeah," Mau said. "You watch."

"And every now and then—every five minutes—he showed it to me," Dave recalls. "This long, low westerly swell would come in underlying the northeast swell and that was the one that would slap the underside of the hull and get us all wet. He showed me that and I just thought, 'Man, I thought I knew something about the ocean. Jesus, I know nothing.' "

Without a chart to mark their positions, it was difficult to perceive the canoe's progress. One day seemed to blend into another in a monotonous grind toward a blank horizon. Food soon became the common topic of conversation, as it does on any ship. It's the key to morale. As part of what the crew derisively called "the experiment," they tried to eat the food of their ancestors—*taro*, breadfruit, sweet potatoes, coconut, dried bananas, sugar cane, *poi* and fresh fish—when they could catch it—salted and dried fish when they couldn't. They were supposed to have begun this diet a month before the voyage, but with the rush to get the canoe ready and the constant bickering this crucial preparation had gone by the wayside. Constipation is always a problem during the first few days at sea, but the ancient diet made it even worse. After about two weeks, Captain Kapahulehua ordered the food experiment abandoned. "We couldn't continue," he recalls, "because our bodies weren't conditioned prior to the trip. Eating ancient Hawaiian food wasn't nutritionally adequate. The old-time Polynesians survived because their bodies were conditioned to eating it."

On the evening of May 11th, Mau examined the height of the Big Dipper and reported it to be lower than at Saipan and just a little higher than at Satawal. "The Southern Cross," he said, "is high like at Satawal." Lewis interpreted this as eight and a half degrees north latitude. *Meotai's* navigator calculated the position by instruments as nine degrees—within thirty miles. "It was a real opportunity for David Lewis to continue his research on non-instrument navigators," Dave Lyman recalls, "Mau understood why David was there so he was very open with him, but some people resented it. They would have preferred that David was not aboard so that they could have more one-on-one time with Mau—that time was so special."

"I just watched Mau," Boogie Kalama recalls, "how he set the sail, read the ocean. One time there was one storm. Nobody knew it was coming. He saw it. He jumped up. 'Everybody up.' We changed the sails again. We turned the boat into the wind. We look. We see this big black cloud coming over the ocean. Everybody says 'Wow.' We look at Mau, he's putting his jacket on. Everybody started getting ready for the storm—but he knew already it was coming."

On a Micronesian canoe, the navigator always eats first, so Shorty made it his duty to serve Mau before anyone else. "Shorty has chosen to be Mau's understudy and personal servant," Ben Finney wrote in his book, *Hōkūle'a—the Way to Tahiti*. "He behaves as an island navigator's apprentice should. He keeps quiet, is attentive to Mau's every need and sticks close by him, even to the point of sleeping out on the open deck at his master's feet."

As the voyage settled into the routine of watch standing, a not so subtle segregation took place. Six of the crew—Boogie, Buffalo, Dukie, Billy, John and Clifford—took over the forward *hale* (shelter), claiming it as their turf. The National Geographic film crew, on board to record the voyage for a major documentary, stayed to themselves—tending their gear, holding their own counsel. David

Lewis and Dave Lyman, Ben, Sam Kalalau, Captain Kapahulehua, and Tommy Holmes stayed aft. Shorty tended to Mau who was almost constantly on watch, seated on a platform near the great steering paddle. On occasion, Buffalo joined the aft watch. "A lot of times Buffalo would come up on my watch at night," Dave Lyman recalls. "He would say, 'Oh you guys having good fun—always talking story. In my watch everybody real quiet.' "

Buffalo told Dave about growing up in Wai'anae, a predominantly Hawaiian town on the beach. He talked about Waikīkī where he was one of the most famous of Hawaiian watermen. "He came from a different era," Dave recalls. "He was real smart. He excelled in the water and he had earned such a name for himself—for his accomplishments. One of the neat things about making the trip was getting to know Buff as a friend. His depth goes way beyond just being a really hot surfer. He liked being out on the canoe."

On the sixteenth day at sea, *Hōkūle'a* entered the Doldrums. The passage through this zone of fickle wind, clouds, and squalls lasted a week during which the canoe barely moved, averaging only twenty four miles a day toward Tahiti.

"One night a crew member dropped his food bowl overboard," recalls Capt. Kapahulehua. "Next morning it was still thirty yards from us. In twelve hours the canoe hadn't gone anywhere."

The sea smoothed to a vast skin of heaving mercury under a copper sun. The sails hung slack. The booms swayed from side to side as *Hōkūle'a* wallowed in a deep swell that marched from empty horizon to empty horizon. Some of the crew slept through their watches. Why bother when the canoe was not moving? Without the wind, *Hōkūle'a* rotated slowly, like a needle in a shifting magnetic field. Everyone sought shade. Mariners know that the Doldrums are caused by a belt of rising air at Earth's midriff called the Intertropical Convergence Zone. Here, windless days are punctuated by squalls which bring gusts then die off. The zone moved with the seasons. Sometimes it spread over hundreds of miles, sometimes just a few dozen. Now, unfortunately for the already anxious crew, it was a vast region of calm that grated on nerves already flayed by dissension and bickering. It would take six days for *Hōkūle'a* to drift through this slack ocean and those seemingly endless days sapped the energy of even the most experienced of mariners aboard. For one of the crew, the endless horizon and dead air became overwhelming. He could not sleep. He was tormented by hallucinations. The other watermen watched over him ceaselessly. They tried to calm him—with little effect. Later, when Dr. Ben Young was told of the man's symptoms, he would call it a classic "psychotic break"—a steady loosening of the man's grasp on reality leading, eventually, to a listless despondency that was near-suicidal. It was a time when the breaking point of all on board was very near.

"Then the fun part started," Dave Lyman recalls. "The whole thing boiled down to inner dynamics between people. There were some people on board who may have been shit disturbers. Buffalo was consciously trying to avoid getting sucked into the negative aspects. From what I saw, he was making a wonderful effort to be positive and keep the guys who were down on an up and positive beat, but he may have had some inner turmoil fighting off the negativity, knowing that it would be easy to slip into the role of 'This is no good,' but he fought it."

Toward the end of the third week, the crew decided that the *hale*, shelters on each side of the canoe, were weighing *Hōkūle'a* down and slowing her progress. After a brief confrontation, Ben and Captain Kapahulehua gave permission to remove them. For the crew it was a positive step. Dumping the *hale* lightened the canoe and allowed her to sail faster. Why couldn't the leaders understand that? To the experienced sailors on board, the idea that eliminating a few hundred pounds would affect a fully loaded twelve-ton canoe was ludicrous.

SPACE-TIME COMPRESSION

Chapter Twelve

As the fourth week began, *Hōkūle'a* finally crossed the equator. "All of a sudden," Boogie recalls, "we see the clouds just lift up—right on the horizon. There was a big hole. I swear it was one tunnel in the clouds. We were heading straight for that opening. Through it all, we could see the stars in the back. As we got closer, it got bigger and we went right through the hole. When we came out the other side, the whole sky was up and we were heading straight for the Southern Cross. Buff was saying that was one of the most religious times of his life."

On the twenty-fourth day out, southerly winds forced *Hōkūle'a* off course. In Honolulu, the Voyaging Society monitored the canoe's progress on a large chart. *Hōkūle'a* was now moving west with alarming speed—sixty miles a day. During a meeting on May 26th, Rudy Choy briefed the Society's Board of Directors.

"During the last two days the canoe has veered to a course of two hundred and twenty degrees," he told them. "If they continue on this course, they will pass six hundred miles to the west of Tahiti. The crew may be aware of their course but only time will tell."

If the westward deviation continued, the Board would consider abandoning the navigation experiment. But aboard *Hōkūle'a*, Mau was completely aware of the problem and had a plan to deal with it. He would continue on for four days and if they had not found an island by then, Tahiti would be upwind, so they would tack and search for it to the east.

The crew got word from the escort boat that the Voyaging Society was concerned about Mau's navigation and that the "experiment" might be called off. To them, it was another example of meddling by bosses in a far-off office and it increased the growing disaffection on board. "Mau knew how to get back on course," Dukie recalls. "He knew what he was doing—he was never lost." Prior to departure, it had been agreed that absolutely no navigational information would be transferred from escort to *Hōkūle'a*. Now this. Ben and David Lewis were infuriated by the breakdown in communications discipline. Such information might lead to questioning the purity of Mau's navigation, and it certainly heightened dissension among the crew.

Toward the end of the week, the wind shifted, allowing Mau to hold a course toward Machemeias, the rising Southern Cross—south-south-east. Her projected track would now intersect the Tuamotus. Everyone in Hawai'i was relieved. But aboard *Hōkūle'a*, Mau worried about the mounting tension. He tried to stay awake as much as possible, keeping watch on both his crew and on the natural world around him for clues to direction, speed, and location.

The segregation of the crew was now complete. John, Billy, Buff, Clifford, Boogie and Dukie spent their time together. Sometimes they reported for watch, sometimes they didn't. Among professional sailors, horror stories abound concerning inattentive watch standers and many have paid for it with their lives. On a naval vessel, refusing to stand watch would lead to a court martial and severe punishment. The crew, however, were oblivious to this long-standing maritime tradition. They felt they *were* standing watch. What difference could it make if they were back aft with the rest or up forward talking—or playing cards for that matter? They decided among themselves who was on watch and who was not. If someone needed sleep—let him sleep—others would take his place. But to Ben Finney and David Lewis, it appeared they had a quiet mutiny on their hands.

As a professional mariner, Dave Lyman had sailed aboard sleek racing yachts and lumbering cargo vessels, an experience that had given him perspective on maritime social dynamics. Captains of racing yachts carefully select each crew member, keeping in mind both seafaring skills and intangible human qualities that allow a diverse group to bond as a team. But the captains of merchant vessels do not have the luxury of choice. Sailors are assigned by seniority and their place in line at a union hiring hall. The composition of such crews is the luck of the draw, and it often means that men with nothing in common find themselves living together in tight quarters for months at a time. They are professionals and this helps. Yet even so, fights are common and tensions occasionally rise to the point that homicides are entered into a ship's log. "What I saw on commercial ships," Lyman says, "was that lots of men from diverse backgrounds in a small space after a period of time will tend to get into arguments and fights. On an old rust bucket, it takes about three months for that to happen. On *Hōkūle'a* it happened more quickly. I call it space-time compression. The space was so compressed on the canoe—compared to the quarters you have on a big ship—that time became compressed. But I can't think of anything I saw on the canoe as far as people not getting along that I can't equate to some prior experience on merchant ships, and I have seen worse on merchant ships than I saw on the canoe."

In hindsight, a major problem was the chain of command. Mau had told the crew to obey the captain, but the crew naturally gravitated to him. "We were under Mau's command," Dukie recalled after the trip. "We were not under Kawika because Mau was the one with navigation in his head."

The captain, for his part, viewed his role as a kind of facilitator for Mau. "Mau was actually in command as the sailmaster and navigator," Kawika recalled shortly after the trip. "He was the only one with the experience needed to make the trip to Tahiti without any modern day instruments and using only Polynesian methods of navigation. So actually he was the commander of the trip."

Ben Finney occasionally felt the need to step in and issue orders. The purpose of the voyage was to test *Hōkūle'a's* sea-keeping abilities and he was not about to have the experiment jeopardized. The problem with the jib was a case in point.

There was also the issue of what might be called "leadership style." The watermen were accustomed to an environment that's more Darwinian than most. Leaders were expected to assert their authority with strong words and occasionally with their fists. Captain Kapahulehua led by example and by mediating between factions, trying to find the balance—to make things *pono*—as Hawaiians say. "The captain never showed us any kind of command presence on the boat," Boogie would later—tellingly—recall. "Not once. You figure he would get mad and yell or swear or something, but he never really turned our heads."

The presence of the National Geographic film crew didn't help. One of the filmmakers was diligent and quiet, but the other tended to grate on people's nerves and everyone felt the camera's glass eye constantly upon them. Yet even with all this latent friction, the factions aboard the canoe remained peaceful.

THE GUINEA PIGS

Chapter Thirteen

On May 31st, the thirtieth day of the voyage, Mau predicted landfall the following morning. Sure enough, at 4:00 a.m. on June first, the island of Mataiva appeared off the starboard bow—a low dark smudge on the horizon.

After a day celebrating with the people of Mataiva, *Hōkūle'a* departed for Tahiti, arriving off Tetiaroa Island on the afternoon of June 3rd where they hove to—waiting for dawn to sail on to the port of Papeete. Dale Bell, the National Geographic producer, filmed their arrival from a chartered yacht. In spite of warnings from Herb Kane, he brought with him a dozen bottles of French champagne. After more than a month at sea, the alcohol had a powerful effect on the crew. They reviewed all that had gone wrong on the voyage:

The captain was not a strong leader.
The food experiment was a bad idea.
The crew had to take things in their own hands—like dumping the *hale* to reduce weight.
The crew had done all the work rebuilding the canoe and sailing her between the islands.

"The press were filming and we had this big meeting," John Kruse recalls, "and the discussion got heated. Next thing you know, Buffalo—from where he was sitting in the back by Mau—flew across the side railing and he hit Kawika right square in the jaw, and then glanced off and with another blow dropped Ben Finney, and then David Lewis. David Lewis was sitting on the railing and he fell down into the compartment. Then Mau said, 'Hey, enough already, *pau*.' That's all he said, 'Buffalo—*pau*.' It was over."

"None of us had anything to drink for over a month," Dave Lyman recalls.

"I think that the punch might have been as much a surprise to Buffalo as it was to Ben and the others."

"Then Buffalo went forward all the way on the right side of the canoe and dove off," John Kruse continues. "Buffalo swam under the canoe and there was a tag line—he grabbed the line and jumped back on board. The press boats saw all this shit."

It was out of character for Buffalo to react violently. Dave Lyman recalls that he was the peace-keeper among the crew. Later, Lyman would explain Buffalo's action as the result of severe physical pain. A few days before arrival, while chopping firewood, a steel splinter flew off the hatchet and into Buffalo's foot. "It got infected real badly," Lyman recalls, "and he was really hurting. You can't sleep and the next thing you get grumpy and you want to lash out at someone. Things you might normally just laugh off—because of pain and lack of sleep— that's where Buffalo was."

✧ ✧ ✧ ✧ ✧

At 9:30 a.m. on Friday, June 4th, with tempers still simmering, Hōkūle'a passed through the reef off Papeete and into the harbor's sheltered waters. The Tahitians received the Hawaiians as long-lost brothers. Schools were closed for the occasion; so were many stores and most places of work. The Governor had declared a public holiday. "The Tahitians had started coming down to the waterfront the night before to spread their sleeping mats and to await the arrival of the strange canoe from Hawai'i," Ben Finney later wrote. "Now they were everywhere, standing knee deep in the surf surging around the reef, jammed along the shore, perched atop waterfront buildings and weighing down the limbs of shade trees lining the water's edge."

Among the welcoming crowd was Snake Ah Hee, who had flown to Tahiti to sail Hōkūle'a back to Hawai'i. "In Tahiti it was chicken skin," he recalls. "They had a huge celebration, I think the biggest celebration ever. Thousands and thousands of people were on the beach, in the trees, everywhere, waiting for the canoe. They had Tahitian drums. They were making so much noise. It was unreal."

Finney estimated the crowd to be at least fifteen thousand strong. As the canoe approached the shore, the onlookers fell silent. A church choir began to sing and thousands of voices joined them. "Although the song was a church hymn," Ben recalls, "the spine-tingling effect of the massed chorus was that of an ancient chant."

A song contest had been held to celebrate *Hōkūle'a's* arrival and almost two hundred entries were received. The winning song summed up Tahitian feeling for the canoe:

> Many times, children of Tahiti
> You were lost into the sea.
> Now is the time the Lord has made ready
> For you to come back to Tahiti.
>
> It is the star of the heaven above
> That will guide your trip, *Hōkūle'a*
> It is the light wind of the sea
> That will bring success for your trip, *Hōkūle'a*.
>
> You sailed from Hawai'i
> through the deep blue sea,
> To search for the heartland
> through many long days of journey.
>
> You are searching, *Hōkūle'a*, for your heartland
> In the far distance of the sea,
> It is royal Tahiti, Tahiti has become the heartland
> For you *Hōkūle'a*.

In the end, all that mattered to those greeting *Hōkūle'a* was that the canoe and her crew had reopened an ancient voyaging route. They were heroes who had proven the brilliant achievements of their seafaring ancestors. The difficulties among them were a natural outcome of the stress that such a voyage would produce on anyone—and it measured the extent of their achievement.

"We were happy they made it," Snake Ah Hee recalls. "They were like guinea pigs. They were the first to do it the way Hawaiian sailors did it way back—five hundred years ago—our ancestors. Even if they had problems on the canoe they still made it."

TAUTIRA

Chapter Fourteen

On the evening before he was scheduled to fly to Tahiti to join the crew to bring *Hōkūle'a* home, Nainoa Thompson lay curled on a large *pūne'e* (couch) in his grandmother's house, gazing through a picture window at a bucolic view of horses grazing among scrubby *kiawe* trees. He appeared to be nursing a severe cold. He had no fever yet his muscles ached and his head throbbed. He felt disoriented, dizzy. *Am I sick?* he wondered, *or just terrified?*

Nainoa had a lot to worry about. He had monitored reports from *Hōkūle'a* with intense interest. The first week seemed to go well, but soon there were rumors of dissension. According to newspaper accounts, some of the crew refused to stand watch. The captain had lost control. One crewmember had become despondent in the Doldrums. "I was struck by the enormous dysfunction in our leadership," Nainoa recalls. "Am I going to risk my life with that kind of leadership? I didn't want to go but I didn't have the courage to say it. What excuse could I create not to go? Get sick. And that's what I did. I got sick right before the plane was going to fly down to Tahiti with my crew."

Nainoa's father, Pinky Thompson, had fought in World War II. He volunteered to be an Air Corps pilot but was told that his skin was too dark so he was sent to flight engineer's school. Then the war took a bad turn. Foot soldiers were needed, so his entire company was sent to boot camp. After basic training, he was assigned to the 44th Infantry Division where his skin color once again determined his fate. His assignment officer thought Pinky looked like an Indian so he was made first scout. "And that's an extremely dangerous occupation," Nainoa says. "Scouts lead infantry columns. The life expectancy of a first scout in combat is about five minutes." Pinky landed in Normandy and led his comrades across four hundred miles of hostile France until, outside a small village in the Vosges Mountains, a German sniper saw him on point, moving alone up a hill. The bullet entered just below Pinky's nose and exited his jaw. Pinky's war was over. Now, observing his son's deep anxiety, Pinky recalled something his own father had told him just before he volunteered for military service.

"I was thinking about going to war," Pinky told Nainoa, "and my father said 'You will choose. Whatever you choose, I will support you. If the reasons for going are important enough, then it's okay if you don't come home.' "

"I was trying to decide if the voyage was meaningful enough to risk my life," Nainoa remembers, "and my father understood my choice and he wanted me to be comfortable with it. The next day I was on the plane."

◇ ◇ ◇ ◇ ◇

Early in the morning of June 6th, Snake Ah Hee woke in the Tahitian hostel where he and other members of the new crew were sleeping. He dressed and made his way out onto the quiet street in front of the hotel. A gentle wind stirred palm trees. Snake walked a short distance to the main road leading into Papeete and waited. Soon a truck appeared, carrying produce for the open-air market in the center of town. Snake raised his hand. The truck stopped and he got aboard. Entering the outskirts of town, the truck moved down a broad boulevard and stopped near a beach under sheltering palms. Hōkūle'a lay at anchor offshore. "The canoe was kind of far out," Snake recalls. "I took my clothes off and swam from the beach, at night, out to the canoe. A big Tahitian guy was on watch. I slept aboard because I couldn't sleep in the hotel. I thought I had to be on the canoe so my mind would be at peace. It was my time to take care of her."

After arriving in Tahiti, Mau Piailug had quietly slipped into seclusion. He sent a message to Ben Finney: "Ben," he wrote, "I like go home. I no go back to Hawai'i on canoe."

"Mau explained how he had been thinking of quitting for a long time because of the way the gang had been acting throughout the trip," Ben later wrote in his book. "It was their violence that finally made him decide. Mau came from a small island community where peaceful cooperation is a requirement for survival. Violence disgusted him, particularly the unreasoning violence against authority he had witnessed."

Within days, Mau was on a plane home, leaving behind an angry statement: "When we leave from Maui, I say, don't take your problems with you to the trip. Okay, when we leave from Maui, you don't leave the problem in the land. Everybody take problem to the trip... But second crew I don't know good or no good. But I'm think maybe same as first crew. First crew very, very bad. I very pissed off about first crew. The second crew, I feel sorry about the second crew. Now is last, last I'm see you, you see me. Don't ask me to come to Hawai'i ever again..."

"Mau's departure was devastating," Nainoa remembers. "He was going to be our leader and teacher. Here's a man who deserved our full respect and confidence—someone who can maintain leadership and security. And he says 'First crew no good and you guys probably no good too.' He was shocked by the behavior of the crew. He could not fathom their inability to get along because their behavior had threatened their ability to survive. I was horrified. I was thinking of going back home. The fact that Wally would be aboard gave me some comfort."

"I felt sorry about Nainoa," Mau recalled later, "because I know he like learn about the navigation but I fly from Tahiti because I am a little bit scared about the crew on *Hōkūle'a*, maybe they going to make a little bit wrong on the trip. I say something in Tahiti with the tape recorder because I am mad at the crew. And sad, because not too good because they start make the problems from O'ahu to Maui, from Maui to the ocean, ocean to close to Tahiti. That's why I mad at them because plenty time mistake."

The recent troubles clouded the mood of many on the second crew. Would the return voyage be as difficult as the one coming down? How would they stand up to the rigors at sea? Mau's words hung over them in his absence. "I wanted everybody to be together because we represented Hawai'i," Snake recalls. "We were chosen to take the canoe home. Because they had all these problems I wanted a meeting. So I invited everyone to my hotel room."

"Forget all the problems," Snake told his crewmates. "Our job is to get *Hōkūle'a* ready—to make her safe to sail back home. We have got to be close to each other. We were chosen out of hundreds of people to bring home the canoe, so that's our job. Forget what happened in the past. We're going to take care of the canoe."

"To me it was like *ho'oponopono*—a healing ceremony," Snake recalls. "Everybody said their *mana'o*, what they thought. Everybody cried and hugged and felt happy."

Hōkūle'a had been damaged during the voyage and by the admiring Tahitian throng as they climbed aboard to welcome her, so Wally Froiseth flew down to oversee repairs and serve as first mate on the return trip. He found much to do. A few of the *'iako* that spanned the hulls were delaminating. The bamboo decking had cracked badly. A new deck was needed. The hulls had worked and were slightly canted. They had to be torqued back to their centerlines with cables. For two weeks, Wally and a few crewmembers labored tirelessly over their canoe.

On June sixteenth, Wally judged *Hōkūle'a* ready for sea. There was some urgency about her departure because the Southern Hemisphere winter was fast approaching and with it would come diminishing trade winds. If it had been up to the Tahitians, *Hōkūle'a* would have stayed forever. The crew was in great demand. Everyone was eager to give them feasts and parties. "After we got the canoe going, we visited different groups in Tahiti," Snake Ah Hee recalls. "They had different canoe clubs and we sailed to different places to meet the people."

As part of her grand Tahitian tour, the canoe anchored inside a fringing reef off the town of Tautira. Above the lagoon where *Hōkūle'a* was anchored, tall, deeply eroded mountains rose like knife blades to form the Vaitepiha Valley that sliced inland, channeling a shallow river that snaked between the peaks. The mountain slopes were green with ferns. Mango trees stood above the ferns and lower down were stands of pandanus. Lower still were ironwood and *milo* groves and *'ulu* trees with broad leaves shaped like human hands, yellow in the palm, dark green at the fingertips. Coconut palms fringed the shore. Small fishing skiffs were parked in lawns and outrigger canoes were drawn up by the *bureau du maire* near where village women washed their clothes at a public tap, hanging them to dry in the yard—brightly colored *pareu* of many designs. "It was like going back in time," Snake Ah Hee recalls. "It was so quiet and peaceful and the people were so nice. The canoe builders all lived in Tautira and they were all champion paddlers. They had fishing boats and fishing nets. It felt like the old days."

Hōkūle'a was moored close to shore with an anchor astern and the bow tied to a coconut tree. There was to be a party for the crew, but Nainoa worried about the canoe. "The current was strong," he recalls. "What if the anchor dragged and we damaged the canoe?" Captain Kapahulehua agreed that Nainoa could stay aboard on watch. The sun began to settle over the nearby mountains. The canoe bobbed serenely. Nainoa enjoyed the twilight solitude.

"Finally, the sun went down," Nainoa recalls, "and I saw this little girl, maybe four years old, on the beach. She had a flower in her ear and she was waving to me to come on shore. She just kept waving. So I went on shore and she grabbed me with hands so small that she could just hold two of my fingers."

Nainoa followed his tiny escort down the dirt road toward the village. She walked barefoot, he with flip-flops that made a slapping sound on the road. The distant music of 'ukulele swirled through the sweet aroma of vegetation cut by the sharp tang of frangipani and ginger growing alongside the road. The little girl led him on. Nainoa had to bend slightly to accommodate her stature. Even so, she occasionally lost her grip on his fingers and he bent lower still to find her comforting tiny hand. He was uncertain about leaving the canoe and more so about intruding on the gathering that loomed in the glow of gas lanterns in a house down the road. The din of laughter and music beckoned and taunted him. "I should not be here," he thought. "I don't deserve this. None of us do."

"She led me into a house with a dirt floor," he remembers. "They had the whole crew in there and they were feeding them shrimp and steak and all kinds of food they could not afford to eat themselves."

The Tahitian men wore bathing trunks and tee shirts, a few of them emblazoned with an image of Hōkūle'a under full sail, gifts of the Polynesian Voyaging Society. The women wore flowing mu'umu'u or draped pareu and they moved in and out of the kitchen with plates of rice, taro, kimchi, poisson cru, steaming pork, beef, and baked fish arrayed on breadfruit leaves. On the lawn in front of the house, a group of men sat on homemade wooden chairs and played instruments and sang. For Nainoa, it was like stepping back into a distant dream of Polynesia—the music, the Tahitian language flowing through the trees, the laughter of his fellow crew members, the food, the colorful pareu. Wally Froiseth sat between two powerfully built Tahitian men, their dark faces bent toward him as he told a story using a smattering of French and Tahitian he had learned sailing among the islands. The men made a place for Nainoa on a wooden bench drawn up to picnic tables.

The house belonged to Puaniho Tauotaha and like most of those in Tautira, it was a simple place—cinderblock walls, tin roof and a dirt floor. "Puaniho had powerful eyes," Nainoa remembers. "He was very strong. He couldn't speak

English and I couldn't speak French or Tahitian. We sat there."

Nainoa had been to other, more formal parties sponsored by canoe clubs and government officials. This one was different. It was more intimate, simpler, more direct in some way that he could not clearly define. Perhaps it was the presence of Puaniho—his quietness, his welcoming gaze? "Like we are family," Nainoa recalls. "I was overwhelmed by how much the village people gave when they had so little to give. Somebody would stand behind you and if your beer glass was half empty they would fill it. They didn't have floors in their houses, much less beer and steak to share. I felt awkward, we didn't deserve all this." The party continued deep into the night. Heaping dishes of food replaced depleted ones. Glasses were filled. Only when Captain Kapahulehua gave signs that it was time to leave did the Tahitian hosts rise to say goodbye. Plates of food were placed in hands to be carried back to the canoe.

TAHITIAN STARS

Chapter Fifteen

The following evening, Nainoa stayed up all night examining the stars from a vantage point near Tautira's harbor. He was already quite familiar with the night sky. He had studied the stars in his grandmother's yard and in a soccer field next to the Hui Nalu canoe house a little down the road. And often, he had cranked up a battered fifty-horsepower Evinrude and set to sea in a 16-foot skiff to observe the sky as Mau would, surrounded by ocean. "I slept on my boat all the time getting ready for the trip," he remembers. "I anchored it outside Maunalua Bay and I would sleep in it with my star book and a little penlight. That's how I learned the stars—a book and the night sky. Any amateur who wanted to learn the stars—that's what he would do."

Nainoa's star book was written for children. Its title was simple—*The Stars*—and its author was H.A. Rey, famous in the world of children's books for his *Curious George* series. On the first page of *The Stars*, Rey wrote two sentences that might have been composed especially for Nainoa: "If you know the stars, you are not easily lost. They tell you the time and direction on land, on sea, and in the air, and this can be valuable on many occasions." From Rey, Nainoa learned that the naked eye can see only about two thousand stars—not the "billions and billions" that Carl Sagan promised. Of these, only thirty stars are "particularly bright or interesting" and they can be found in the thirty or so constellations (of eighty-eight total) that Rey says will provide "a good working knowledge of the sky."

The Egyptians were probably the earliest astronomers to systematically observe the stars and the most famous of them was Imhotep, an architect and physician who created both the first pyramid (for a king named Zoser in about 2720 BC) and the first systematic ordering of stars into constellations. The Greeks would later memorialize Imhotep (while transforming him into one of their own culture heroes) in a constellation called Asklepios—a physician they elevated into the heavens as the god of health. Stories like these helped Nainoa personalize the constellations and remember them more easily.

It was winter in the Southern Hemisphere, so the sun began to set a little after 5:00 p.m.. Nainoa saw the dark outline of mountain peaks descending to the sea, punctuated by upthrusting coconut palms at the shore. A stone jetty, protecting the entrance of Tautira's tiny boat harbor, led his eye to the horizon where he observed a sliver of moon, pale against the darkening sky, and a bright spot —Venus. He waited for the stars to appear. *Where is the Big Dog? Where are The Twins?* he wondered. In Hawai'i, just a few days ago, these constellations were high in the sky, but here he finds them low on the horizon. "I got to Tahiti and I said, 'This sky looks different.'" Nainoa remembers. "The relationships that I built in my mind—the pictures in my mind that came from the star book and the boat. Wait a minute! These things are different than in Hawai'i."

Nainoa had brought a spiral notebook and a pencil with him. His scrawled observations of the northern stars contain names familiar to him from his sessions in Hawai'i: Draco, Cepheus, Perseus, Pegasus, Little Dipper. These would also have been familiar to Greeks, Egyptians, Akkadians and Babylonians—the people who first named the stars observable in the northern hemisphere. But in Tahiti it is the southern portion of the sky—what he cannot see from Hawai'i— that interested Nainoa most. He looked up. *Here they are,* he thought. *How clear! There's the Whale. The tail of the Wolf. Ship's Sail.* For the first time he saw the Telescope, Indian and Phoenix. *Look at that. Those are the constellations that the first European explorers would have seen hundreds of years ago!*

The southern constellations are as unfamiliar to Nainoa as they would have been to the earliest recorders of the night sky. In the first century of the Christian era, the Greek astronomer Claudius Ptolemy listed forty-eight constellations. Ptolemy resided at the time in Alexandria, in Egypt, in the Northern Hemisphere—so he could not see many of the southern constellations. For fifteen hundred years, the southern sky was a great Celeste Incognito to Europeans, until 1603 when Johann Bayer, a German astronomer, used the work of navigators exploring the southern ocean to publish *Uranometria*, a star atlas with a dozen new southern constellations. The work of mapping the sky continued for three centuries, leading to a final ordering of them into a total of eighty-eight constellations in 1930 by the International Astronomical Union.

Nainoa was largely oblivious of this history as he jotted down what he observed. He noted that Fomalhaut rose at 10:00 p.m. At midnight he saw what he calls the "mouth of the Whale" and at about twelve-thirty "the tail of the Whale." He jotted down times for other constellations—the "center of the Ship's Sail," "tip of the Ship's Sail," "Belly of Peacock," "nipple of Peacock," "bright star in Indian," "the Fly." By convention, solidified into professional dogma by the International Astronomical Union, each star in each constellation has a name. What Nainoa called "the bright star in Indian," for example, the astronomers call Beta Indus, the "nipple of Peacock" is Kappa Pavo, and "mouth of the whale" is Deneb Kaitos. But Nainoa used H. A. Rey's simple star book as a guide, and not all the stars were named there. So he gave them his own names. It was not arrogance on his part, but rather simple ignorance of refined astronomical conventions. He could have studied books other than Rey's, but he figured it was better to go directly to the source—the night sky. "I wanted to learn the sky first hand," Nainoa remembers. "If you look in books for astronomers they have all this clutter in them. I could not learn the sky that way. Rey broke the sky up into small sections. His book is a children's book, but if you are an adult and you don't know the sky you are like a child."

During his evening with the Tahitian stars, Nainoa was transported beyond his fearfulness of the voyage home. He scribbled his notes under the glittering sky dome, backed by steep mountains and engulfed in strong fragrances. Dogs barked in the night. Time slipped away, marked only by the imperceptible movement of the constellations. There was so much to learn. And now, without Mau, he must learn it alone—by watching and watching some more. Thirty-four degrees of latitude to the south of Hawai'i, this Tahitian sky presented new vistas. Many were puzzling, but none more so than what he saw just after dusk in the newly dark firmament. He searched for the stars Sirius and Mirzam in the Dog, and Castor and Pollux in the Twins. Looking west, he watched Sirius and Pollux arc down to the horizon and set together. He checked his watch, 6:55 p.m. Finding new stars—that he expected. But finding old familiar ones following different timetables to the horizon—that he did not expect. "In Hawai'i Sirius sets first," Nainoa explains, "Maybe two hours later Pollux sets. But here was this strange thing, stars setting at the same time. They didn't do that in Hawai'i. I was puzzled. Why did that happen? I knew the answer could be found in the change in latitude but I didn't understand why. I had no intention of being a navigator, and there was no vision of ever sailing *Hōkūle'a* to Tahiti again, so I studied just to learn. I was not over there thinking, 'Well, now I can tell latitude'—because there was no need to. I learned that the stars are different in Tahiti from Hawai'i—that there's a blueprint for the stars in Tahiti and another one for the stars in Hawai'i. So I thought maybe these were like signatures for the different places."

At dawn, Nainoa made his way through the village. The sun rose, an orange disk behind low scudding clouds. High cirrus clouds were brush strokes of yellow and white. Children scurried home bearing baguettes, trailing the sweet aroma of fresh bread. The lagoon was calm. Palm fronds were motionless. During Nainoa's evening vigil, a few showers had cleaned the sky. Potholes in the dirt road, filled with water, blinked back the sunlight. Tautira seemed a revelation. It was as if he had stepped back to an earlier time—to Hawai'i a hundred years ago.

Nainoa walked along the lagoon. He paused to watch an outrigger canoe slice through the waves. Maire Nui was practicing—Tautira's most famous canoe team, known throughout Tahiti, throughout the Pacific actually, as "the old men." "They were so smooth," Nainoa recalls. "Their movements were fluid, no lost energy, and their canoe seemed to leap forward—faster than anything I had ever seen."

Mate Hoatua was the steersman for Maire Nui and Puaniho Tauotaha was the stroker. Everyone aboard *Hōkūle'a* remembers Puaniho for his immense strength. One day, when three of the canoe's crew were struggling to carry *Hōkūle'a's* outboard motor, Puaniho stopped them. He reached down with one hand and threw the motor over his shoulder. "Where to?" he said, using sign language because he spoke no English. Puaniho stood about five foot ten. Brown eyes were set in a round open face. His shoulders were broad and his forearms thickly muscled. "He was good looking," Snake recalls. "They called him the Marlon Brando of Tahiti. He was a strong, strong person. You look how he was dressed, almost like the old ways. How my dad used to be. No shirt, shorts on, barefooted. Puaniho was like an ambassador to me. No matter who you are, he says 'Come, come, to my house.' "

"You could be in the canoe house," Nainoa remembers, "and there was laughter and singing and people talking, but when Puaniho got up to speak there was complete silence. I didn't know what he was saying but it felt like an oration. And if he wasn't doing that he never said anything. When he coached the canoe paddlers he hardly said a word. He was an extremely quiet man. Very religious, very disciplined. He was the edge of the old times."

PUANIHO'S GIFT

Chapter Sixteen

A few days later, *Hōkūle'a* departed Tautira and continued her triumphal tour along the Tahitian coast, eventually sailing to the island of Raiatea for a ceremony to honor the first canoes to voyage to Hawai'i centuries ago. During this time, Wally—who was chosen to be first mate on the return voyage—often served as the canoe's captain. "Wally was picked for all the right reasons," Nainoa recalls. "He was just so perfect." Wally had helped fashion many parts of the canoe—the *paliwai*, *'iako*, sideboards, masts, booms. He had built racing canoes, had jury-rigged torn sails and broken booms on transpacific voyages. He was seasoned. As far as Nainoa was concerned, Wally was the only experienced sailor among his crew.

At the end of June, *Hōkūle'a* sailed back to Tahiti and anchored in Papeete Harbor where the crew prepared for sea. They loaded food and water aboard. They made small repairs to the rigging—parceling a line here, serving one there. They stowed their personal gear. On July 2nd, Gordon Pi'ianai'a and Kimo Lyman, both seasoned sailors, arrived from Hawai'i to help bring *Hōkūle'a* home. Kimo had studied boat building in Oregon. He had served aboard the pilot boat in Honolulu, had spent a decade delivering yachts throughout the Pacific and he was an experienced instrument navigator. Gordon was a Navy veteran. He had sailed TransPac races. He was a graduate of the California Maritime Academy and a professional merchant mariner.

Shortly before *Hōkūle'a*'s departure, Wally Froiseth developed a virulent leg rash that resisted treatment. He decided he would be a liability on the return trip—better to fly home and greet the canoe in Hawai'i. When Nainoa learned that Wally would not be aboard, he was dumbfounded. "I was shocked. Mau had left, but—I thought—at least Wally would be on the canoe going home. There was a lot of fear associated with that trip. The whole issue of the unknown. And I questioned the leadership that was left." Nainoa did his best to convince

Wally to stay on the canoe.

"I screamed at him—'You got to go,'" Nainoa recalls. "I was almost begging him, 'Please come on the trip back to Hawai'i.' Wally was yelling, almost sobbing, 'No! This trip is for you young guys and you got to just go do it—so just go and do it.'"

"I'm not going," Nainoa told him.

"Wally just turned to me," Nainoa recalls. "His eyes were tearing and he was pissed and he was yelling, 'Boy, it's your time. You have to go.' He was angry—part of the anger was that he so much wanted to go himself and when he heard that I was giving away my chance I think that hurt him. 'Get your head straight,' he said. 'Get on the canoe and take it home. That is your *kuleana*—it's your duty to take the canoe home.'"

At 4:00 a.m. the next morning, in the crew's bunkhouse, Nainoa was wakened by someone pulling on his toes—Puaniho's wife. Wordlessly, she led him outside to a waiting pickup truck. "We drove back to Tautira as the sun came up," Nainoa remembers. "We went to every house—every house—and they filled that truck with food. When we drove back to Papeete I was sitting on a huge mound of banana, *taro*, mango and breadfruit. Puaniho drove right up to the canoe and they loaded all the food aboard."

A wooden cross dangled from a leather lanyard around Nainoa's neck—a gift from his friend Mike Ceasi. "Mike gave it to me as a blessing so that I would come home safely. He knew that I was scared. It was his way of giving me his *aloha*. When Puaniho picked me up and filled his truck up with all that food it reminded me of my family. You go to my grandmother's house—the doors are always open and you are always given something to eat. Puaniho evoked that kind of generosity and the cross was the only thing of significance that I could give. I put it around his neck. Somehow Puaniho knew that I was nervous about the trip. I was even considering not going. By taking care of us he was saying that the voyage was important—he reaffirmed the purpose of the voyage. That was when I knew that I had to go."

❖ ❖ ❖ ❖ ❖

At sunrise on July 4th, the day *Hōkūle'a* was to depart, a squall swept over Papeete. Gusting winds buffeted coconut palms shading the harbor and shook plump fruit off mango trees in gardens a few blocks inland. Dark clouds slid over the canoe, moored to the quay, and higher clouds billowed into the sky, etched by the rising sun. Looking to sea, Nainoa saw a low, thick wall of cloud, somber and formidable in the early morning light. At about noon, *Hōkūle'a* moved slowly beyond Papeete's breakwater where she spread her sails to the wind. On shore, a large crowd from Tautira waved until the canoe was out of sight. Among them were Puaniho, his wife, and his daughter Monique.

There were no fireboats with sprays of water to send the canoe off; only a few yachts and small powerboats accompanied her beyond the harbor. In one of them was Wally Froiseth. The sails were set and *Hōkūle'a* picked up speed. Wally's boat circled the canoe slowly, then turned back to shore. As Nainoa watched the boat grow smaller, he realized that the man he most trusted among the crew was gone.

"The wind was cold, blowing about twenty-five knots," he recalls. "We went around Mahina Point. Night was coming and I watched Tahiti going down below the gray horizon. Everything about that moment was scary. I didn't trust the crew but mostly I didn't trust myself. I was young and inexperienced and afraid—purely afraid."

STEERING BY THE STARS

Chapter Seventeen

*H*ōkūle'a forced her way north, close hauled, into a twenty-knot easterly wind. Her crew watched the mountains of Tahiti sink slowly below the horizon. Clouds were stacked up over the mountains and the light, reflecting from the lagoon, painted their underbellies a faint blue-green.

Leaving Tahiti was more difficult than Nainoa imagined. "The people have so much feeling that it was hard to say goodbye," he wrote in his log. "I'm learning to grow and express my feelings without being embarrassed. They have so much love. I have learned that it's not the head that must be strong to keep you going—it's the heart—from Puaniho." Nainoa cried openly for the first time he could remember. *Why so much emotion?* he wondered. *I just met them. I spent so little time with them. It's the bond between us,* he concluded. *It is ancient. We are family. We're descendants of the same ancestors.* In his notebook he drew a simple diagram:

Tahiti ⟷ Hawai'i.

Now in her element, *Hōkūle'a* rode easily over ponderous swells. When she had set out from Hawai'i, no one really knew if she could withstand the rigors of such a long voyage. That she did so, and admirably, comforts her crew. Still, for all of them, it was a voyage into the unknown.

Eleven men were aboard: Snake Ah Hee, Andy Espirito, Kawika Kapahulehua, Mel Kinney, Kainoa Lee, Kimo Lyman, Gordon Pi'ianai'a, Leonard Puputauiki, Nainoa Thompson, Maka'ala Yates and Dr. Ben Young—and two women, Penny Rawlins and Keani Reiner. Kawika was captain. Gordon replaced Wally as first mate. Kimo and Lele would navigate, this time with compass, map and sextant, Mau having departed. Of the thirteen crew—only five had been to sea before. The others were familiar with the near ocean but they had never spent more than a few days beyond sight of land. And this voyage might last a month or more.

By almost any standards, conditions aboard *Hōkūle'a* were primitive. The crew bathed in saltwater from a bucket. To relieve themselves, they grabbed a rail and hung over the side, always watchful of large swells that might sweep them overboard. They slept in a small *lau hala* (pandanus leaf) hut amidships— eight berths, four over four. Rain and spray seeped between the *lau hala* mats and into sleeping bags. "Water seemed to come in everywhere. We were wet all the time," recalls Dr. Ben Young, the canoe's resident physician. "There was only one entrance to the hut," Nainoa recalls. "It was claustrophobic. I slept with my hand sticking out through the *lau hala* matting so if we capsized I could find my way out." On deck, there was no protection from the elements. Many were seasick. "When we left Tahiti I didn't know how I would be," Snake recalls, "especially on a long voyage. I got sick on the first day. Then right after that I got my sea legs."

Nainoa served as what merchant mariners call an "ordinary seaman," the lowest-ranked sailor in a long hierarchy of ranks. But even that term, given his lack of deep sea voyaging, was optimistic. He needed time to adjust to the open decks, the motion, the spray. Like the rest of his crewmates, his first priority was to endure these rigors. But unlike them he had an additional mission—to learn as much as he could about the ancient way of navigating. He began by making a list of what he wanted to accomplish:

> Write up changes in the stars
> Orient myself with as many guides as possible
> Use swells as guide
> And sounds the canoe makes in that particular direction to the swell
> Set of sails give clues to direction

Nainoa stood his first watch. *Concentrate on steering,* he told himself. *Pay attention to the swells and stars. Get a feel for the wind.* Off watch, he wrote in his log: "Didn't feel too good. Took things slow including eating. Night was pretty cold and a little wet. Stars were good—really dig them." He reminded himself to look for patterns. When do the stars rise and set? How do their paths across the sky change with latitude? How to use all this to navigate? Without Mau, he must teach himself. He had read everything he could find about Mau's star compass. "I knew the compass as a concept," he recalls, "but I didn't know how it worked. It was an intellectual idea. I knew there would be problems trying to apply it on the ocean."

The concept was straightforward—stars rise in the east, arc overhead, and set in the west, defining points on the horizon to steer by, or "houses," as Nainoa called them. He had observed this on land, but could he actually find his way at sea by a heavenly compass? He decided to experiment during this first evening watch. The canoe moved easily into a gentle wind—nicely balanced—just a touch of the steering paddle to keep her on course. Nainoa observed the magnetic compass dial—twenty degrees. Big Dipper was to port, its handle almost vertical to the horizon. He aligned stars in the handle with Hōkūleʻa's shrouds. The Southern Cross was astern, the Scorpion on the starboard quarter. He covered the compass with a tee shirt. *Okay now, Hōkūleʻa, let's see what we can do.*

Clouds sailed across the Big Dipper so he steered by the star Mau called, Mailap, also known as Altair, just forward of the starboard beam. *Hold her there.* When the clouds hid Mailap, he found the Southern Cross astern. *Right where she should be. Hōkūleʻa* moved on, riding gentle crests. Time, measured by the hands of his wristwatch under a flashlight, ticked by. Fifteen minutes. He uncovered the compass. *Twenty degrees, right on course.* A small beginning perhaps, but it proved he could find direction by the stars alone. Still, there were problems.

It was easy to steer by a star low on the eastern horizon, hovering just above the house from which it had risen, but after an hour or so, it was too high to be an accurate guide. Confounding the problem, he knew the stars rose four minutes earlier every day, so a star rising at sunset when the canoe departed would be useful for only a week or so. *If I'm going to use the star compass, I've got to memorize lots of stars,* Nainoa thought. As the canoe sailed north, crossing parallels of latitude, the houses where the stars rose and set shifted on the horizon. "The angle of their arc, the time at night when they rise, their path in the sky, the amount of time they are in the sky all change," he wrote in his log. "So it's very hard to use the stars unless you have a magnetic compass to check them by." Observing the sky and testing his understanding of celestial motion,

Nainoa began translating data into knowledge—a distinction he would use all his life. Data are facts—the stars rise in the east and set in the west. Knowledge is applying those facts to a practical end—finding your way across a vast ocean. "I learned so much on that voyage," Nainoa recalls, "because I was prepared to learn from my collection of academic ideas by putting them into practice—until it became knowledge."

"Nainoa was always looking at the sky," Snake recalls. "He was always holding on to something and looking this, looking that. I never asked him about it because that's the way I do it. If you are learning something you don't tell anyone, you just do it yourself."

Nainoa observed first mate Gordon Pi'ianai'a and navigator Kimo Lyman. They were old salts. *These guys are amazing,* he thought. *They feel everything on the canoe. It takes a lot of experience to be like them.*

As first mate, Gordon carried out the captain's orders and maintained discipline. During the first week at sea, he had carefully observed his crew. "I didn't sleep too much that first week because I didn't know what kind of crew I was sailing with, but at the end of the week I slept when it was time to sleep. I had a lot of confidence in everybody."

"I was concerned at first," Snake recalls, "because of all the trouble the other crew had. But everybody helped on the canoe. Whatever you needed to do, people were there to make it easier."

On July 10th, six days out, the wind piped up. "Made good mileage today," Nainoa wrote. "The canoe is really flying. Passed the halfway point to the equator yesterday." Overhead, the Milky Way was a glowing ribbon matched by phosphorescent fire in *Hōkūle'a's* wake stirred by swarms of darting squid. They sailed on a beam reach, the wind steady from the east-southeast. Nainoa lifted the sweep to bring the canoe into the wind, put it down to steer off. Sometimes he steered by the clouds. While this may seem improbable, the atmosphere in the Pacific is so clear you can see cloudbanks far away and their motion, pushed along by steady trade winds, is so predictable you can adjust for it. *Must know the speed of the clouds and the direction they are moving and estimate how far away they are. Plus they change.*

Nainoa was now at home aboard *Hōkūle'a,* constantly jotting in his notebook. He wrote about ways to improve the rigging. He considered the cut of her sails, how to properly use the sweep, the shape of its blade and how to make it better. He observed the booms bending where the sheets were attached. Can the pulleys, or blocks as mariners call them, be moved to better guide the sheets? *The closer you haul in—the closer the angle to the mast step the sheet line should be. When you let the sail out—the farther the sheet line should be from the mast step.*

"Fish on the line!"

Lures trailed in *Hōkūle'a's* wake, tended by Maka'ala and Ben, who were engaged in a friendly competition to see who could catch the most fish.

"My lure, my lure!" Ben yelled as he rushed aft.

Ben had never been to sea before. He was concerned about boredom and the frustration that it might bring, especially in the Doldrums. He kept busy. He made mental lists of what to do in emergencies. He played chess and studied medical books. During the evening, he played harmonica and guitar in an impromptu *Hōkūle'a* band. "The time," he recalls, "just zipped by."

NATURAL SIGNS

Chapter Eighteen

In proper maritime parlance, *Hōkūle'a* is a double-hulled Polynesian voyaging canoe, but any yachtsmen would immediately recognize her as a catamaran. Catamarans are considered a recent innovation inspired by racing sailors seeking speed. But in Polynesia, such craft were invented thousands of years ago—during a time when ponderous single-hull vessels were evolving in the western world. Limited by stone and shell tools and the lack of iron fastenings, Polynesians could not fashion large European style plank-on-frame ships. Small outrigger canoes would not be seaworthy for long voyages, nor could they carry the cargo and people necessary to settle new islands. Large outrigger canoes would be unwieldy. So someone, thousands of years ago, thought of bridging two canoes with a solid deck. An advanced sailing craft was born out of necessity confronting the limits of a primitive technology.

"I've been on a lot of vessels but *Hōkūle'a* is the most stable and best riding vessel I've ever sailed," Gordon Pi'iana'ia says.

A sailing vessel with a single hull heels away from the wind, so monohull sailors must constantly deal with a tilted world that, over many days at sea, produces fatigue. Because *Hōkūle'a* distributes the wind's torque across two hulls, she does not heel, providing a stable and comfortable living platform in even the most terrific of winds. And her hulls are lean and narrow, so she does not pound into the waves. She slices through them with what can only be described as grace. The contrast in oceangoing comfort between one hull and two is like that on land between a truck and a Cadillac. And as the voyage progresses, *Hōkūle'a* demonstrated more than her inherent seaworthiness—the canoe's twin hulls allowed her crew to deploy subtle human senses to determine direction at sea.

Hōkūle'a invited her crew to dance—and she danced differently in a single set of waves than she did in two—or three. She danced one way if she was running with the wind and another if she was sailing into it. The possible combinations are infinite, so the choreography was complex. *Hōkūle'a* demanded attention from her human partners. If they faltered, she reminded them. She turned up into the wind and slowed and shook her sails. "Listen to me," she said, "Can you hear it?" An alert helmsman knew to push the paddle down to help her fall off the wind. Or she might turn downwind, speed up and pull at her tiller. "Pay attention," she said. All these were clues to maintaining a steady course, an important task for any navigator, but particularly so for one finding his way without instruments. Determining longitude depends on dead reckoning, and dead reckoning, in turn, depends on keeping track of your course.

As Nainoa became more familiar with the canoe and the ocean around him, he recognized three patterns of swells—from the northeast, east and southeast. Standing at the steering sweep, he studied the canoe's motion as she sailed through them. Steering almost due north, he noticed that when he fell off the wind only a few degrees the canoe quieted down. *The eastern swell no longer slaps the side of the windward hull and the southeast swell picks up the canoe's stern and helps her surf through the water,* he thought. Turning further downwind, with the breeze now off the quarter, the canoe assumed a gentle corkscrew motion: *one half of the front hull riding up the face of the wave, one half of the back hull sliding down the face of the wave, with the lee hull digging in.* Turning back into the wind it got noisy, the ride became ragged—the canoe pitched and rolled, she took spray over the windward hull and Nainoa felt her pound in the soles of his feet. Under a totally cloudy sky, when no celestial clues were observable, the canoe provided plenty of information to sail a steady course. Any vessel will do this but none so completely as a catamaran. Twin hulls, each reacting separately to the shape of the ocean, tell sailors much more than a single hull can. The double canoe, shaped by a long evolution, communicates almost perfectly with a sensitive human being.

The days merged in an easy rhythm of rising and sinking suns and of spinning stars. Nainoa was comfortable with all of his crewmates but he felt a special connection with his old friend Snake Ah Hee. Snake was generous to a fault, naturally caring and considerate. He worked hard and said little, except to smile and make light of some difficult moment. And what a smile! Snake's serene face broadcasts good will when he's happy, or telling a joke—which he did often—accompanied by soft laughter. He's comfortable at sea. And there were many aboard who could cook—Keani, Penny, Lele and Maka'ala among them—but if a vote were taken for best cook it would be Snake. "You got to sail with the guy to really appreciate him," Gordon recalls. "He cooked and stood his watches. I told him I would take him off the watch list but he said no."

"I had prepared myself intellectually to be able to ask questions of the ocean and the canoe," Nainoa says. "Snake is much more intuitive. Snake is the epitome of the true ocean man. You can see it in his eyes, you can see it in his hair, in his skin. He is a quiet man, very thoughtful, deep. Most of the crew members would focus their steering on the compass. They would watch that needle. They would not pay that much attention to the rest of the world around them. Just hold that needle in its place. But Snake would watch it the least. He used all his senses to steer the canoe. When he held the paddle it was like he was holding the canoe through the shaft of that paddle. His steering was very soft. He made very small corrections. Some people pulled the paddle up quickly to let the canoe run up into the wind then pushed it down hard to bring it off. Snake's corrections were always very small and they were very soft. When he steered, the canoe was quiet."

Snake also liked to play cards so, from time to time, he and Nainoa broke out a frayed pack and slapped them on the deck. Their talk shifted into the easy patois of schoolyard pidgin.

But often Nainoa found himself alone with his thoughts which now, halfway home, turned back to Tautira. Later, when he described the place to his family it would take on a mythic quality. A village under sharp mountains. Waterfalls. Gentle winds. He took them on the journey from Papeete to Tautira— the bustle of the city dropping away as you traveled, the houses becoming few and tiny and set off from the road. The feeling of the jungle encroaching and of a growing serenity. Then the road degraded. It became dirt. And in Tautira, it ended. The place was, "the edge of the old times," as he once described Puaniho. "The people of Tautira are so powerful," he wrote in his log. "A power I don't understand. They just open their hearts and if you have enough within you— you will receive. Must take time to be more aware of Puaniho's wisdom. Beauty is simple—so make your life beautifully simple."

The voyage helped Nainoa simplify. The sea imposed discipline. It slowed things down. You cannot go faster by applying pressure to a throttle; you must deal with what nature provided. That's why he so constantly thought of efficiency—of trimming the sails, steering accurately. Paying attention was more than just a commitment to doing the job well. It was making the best of nature's gift. And nature, Nainoa began to realize, had a sense of irony.

A stretch of fair wind and clear skies, for example, might seem a gift, but it was the opposite. It lulled the crew—made them complacent. Nature's true gift was a stiff headwind because it forced them to focus. First, there was the noise—the constant wind whistling in their ears; the whooshing of water funneling between the hulls; the thud of waves breaking against the bow. The wind stirred the sea into lather and brought tendrils of spray across the decks. So it was cold and wet. But most insidiously, the wind tried to head the canoe, to steal away her course toward landfall. The sailors must learn to "lean on the wind" to help their canoe to windward. They must pay attention. But occasionally, and to Nainoa's disgust, the crew lost their focus. Whether from fatigue, boredom, carelessness—whatever—the result was a penalty in distance made good, or course made good, or both. Not paying attention was an affront to the high purpose of the voyage. *We are on a mission,* Nainoa often thought—always to himself—*and the mission is to learn.* And there was so little time to do it—so each moment was special, hard won and easily lost.

Sometimes when reading Nainoa's log it's hard to remember how young he is. Sometimes it's hard to ignore it. The man he will be is there. The disciplined observer puzzling out patterns in the sky, watching the swells, always seeking signs. The loner is there too, the man who chooses solitude. Aboard *Hōkūle'a,* Nainoa bent his loneliness to his task. He stared into the sky for hours. Did Sirius set before Pollux? Would a line drawn from Gacrux to Acrux point to the south celestial pole? How does the arc of rising Altair tend? Straight up; to the right; to the left? *Hōkūle'a* sailed in an era before psychologists gave meaning to a term now common—"the zone"—yet Nainoa was clearly in one when he observed the heavens and the ocean, and it colored his observations of his crewmates. *Why don't they pay attention to steering? Can't they see the sails are luffing? Can't they hear* Hōkūle'a *speaking to them?* During one night watch, he went forward and found a hatch had been carelessly left open. Because Nainoa was not blessed with the easy ability to explain himself to others, he did it in his notebook. "I must write these negative feelings so that I may reduce the things I have been holding in and also take time to understand that when I make a mistake to learn from it."

On Wednesday, the 14th of July, *Hōkūle'a* approached what Nainoa considered her first real test. "Doldrums," he wrote, "five to eleven degrees north." On the trip down, the canoe languished in the Doldrums for a week of unpredictable calms under blistering sun followed by howling squalls. From all reports, one of the crew nearly went mad. Nainoa braced himself. "Keep busy," he wrote, "stay out of people's way. Be courteous. What is a sailor?" he wondered. "And how will I measure up?"

On Thursday, during the early morning watch, *Hōkūle'a's* sails fell slack. She encountered pockets of deathly calm. She sailed on slowly, stalled for a time, sailed on. The Doldrums. *If this is the Doldrums it's a screwy place. The wind is changing all over the damn place—northeast, southeast, east.* For a time, fluking winds forced *Hōkūle'a* to sail south—away from Hawai'i. In squalls she picked up speed and the crew enjoyed freshwater showers. Then, once again, the winds died and the sky cleared. The canoe wallowed. *This place is like limbo. During the day—the heat. It's just too hot. I become lazy.* Days merged. The canoe moved listlessly north, surrounded by dark knots of squalls. *The rainsqualls have become like clockwork. For the past three days they have come every morning at dawn and again just as the sun sets. Tonight they came again. At 8:30 last night a dark line stretched all across the horizon to the south. The first part of the night it was clear. Then you see this dark line coming. Get your foul weather gear on. It passes overhead. Dark.* July 17th. July 18th. *Hōkūle'a* sailed on. *The mind reacts to the weather. The body reacts to it. In the Doldrums I don't think. I just sit. I don't want to do anything. It's depressing.* During the afternoon of the 18th, *Hōkūle'a* began to pitch to a different swell. *There's something there alright,* Nainoa thought. *It looks like the northeast swell is coming in.*

An astronomer reads flickering starlight to decipher the history of the universe, the birth and death of heavenly bodies millions of light years away. A navigator reads the ocean in the same way, to tell the genesis of winds by the shape of swells.

"Watch the waves," Tahitian crewmember Lele Puputauiki told Nainoa. "The closer the intervals between the swells—the closer you are to the wind source."

If that's true, Nainoa thought, *we're going to be hitting the northeast trades pretty soon and we'll be blasting home.*

On the 19th, the winds accelerated from the northeast. *We're definitely out of the Doldrums. We're going home. It's a good feeling.* During the first evening of trade winds, the sky was overcast so steering by the stars was impossible. Nainoa studied the situation. The moon was to port, a little aft of the beam, but still visible through the cloud scrim. *It looks like the flattened-out part of the moon is pointing toward the south-southwest,* he thought. On the 16th it pointed south-southwest. On the 17th also. *Today, it still points south-southwest. A sign?* Nainoa had observed what astronomers call the terminator, the dividing line between the moon's light and dark faces. He drew an imaginary line along it and extended the line to the horizon. *If you keep that place on the port beam you're traveling to the west-northwest.* Data became knowledge. He also concentrated on the ocean swells. *If you look off the stern you see the southeast swell is picking up the stern and we are surfing a little.* He steered the canoe by moon and swell, his eye on the compass to check his course.

Gordon Pi'ianai'a had been watching his young crewmate and he was impressed. So was Captain Kapahulehua. On July 16th, twelve days out, they made Nainoa captain of his watch. He was the youngest crewmember. It was an honor. But he worried. Would the crew think he's been pushy? Nainoa's anxiety came from growing up in two worlds—*haole* and Hawaiian. *Haole* favor self-advancement. Get ahead! Think for yourself! But Hawaiians seek consensus. They value consideration of others. Be humble! Don't put yourself up! Humility is worthy, but there's a negative side—a deep fear of failure instilled by two centuries of oppression.

Most mainlanders, when they consider Hawai'i, do not think of a place where racism is a problem. Hawaiians are the brown people everyone loves. Romantic dreams whirl about their exploits as surfers speeding down giant waves, paddlers of outrigger canoes, denizens of sea and sun. It's an image that does not take into account the two centuries since Captain Cook sailed into Kealakekua Bay, bringing a new religion and new diseases. Nor the death of ninety percent of the Hawaiian population that came later. Nor the loss of the Hawaiian kingdom to calculating *haole* planters. But this is the backdrop against which all Hawaiians play out their lives. "We learned to be afraid of success," Nainoa says, "because in the *haole* world we failed so often."

"There's the story of the *'a'ama* crab," Nainoa explains. "We catch them and put them in a bucket. The crabs try to get out but as soon as one of them is about to make it, another reaches up with his claw and pulls him back down. It's like we say in pidgin 'no make shame.' How do you make shame? By failing. And how do you avoid that? By not trying, by staying in the bucket with the rest of the crabs. The bucket is the culture of failure that has grown up from so many years of not being able to make it in a *haole* world. So I was afraid of failing and I was concerned with appearing to put myself ahead of the rest of the crew."

After watch, Nainoa went forward to his favorite place between the canoe's twin *manu*. He arranged himself like a mendicant, legs folded under. *Hōkūle'a is beautiful,* he thought. *She has her own heart and soul. If Mau were here I would feel it more. I miss what he could teach me. I spend a lot of time watching the heavens. I'm so unaware. Trying to be aware.* Nainoa watched the sea shimmering between the *manu.* The moon, waning, cast a silver sheen on the ocean. And there, for the first time, he saw Polaris glimmering on the horizon. *I wish I didn't have to sleep. I could become more aware of the stars. I wish I could stay up all night, every night, to watch them change—rise in the east, set in the west, and Polaris rising...* He considered the night when he first examined the stars in that Oregon hilltop and he recalled his professor drawing the celestial sphere on a blackboard accompanied by the squeak of chalk. The stars are for all intents fixed, the professor taught them, they appear to move because Earth is spinning. Astronomers imagine them attached to a sphere that encloses Earth and spins around it, rotating from west to east, causing the stars to appear to move from east to west. The axis about which the sphere rotates—the celestial axis—is Earth's axis projected out to meet the sphere, so looking north or south we see circumpolar stars circling this axis. All except one—Polaris, the North Star—which appears stationary because the earth's northern axis is aimed almost directly at it. The star's immobility makes it useful for navigators because a sailor, observing Polaris in the night sky, knows exactly where north is.

The star has inspired poets through the ages. William Cullen Bryant, for example, who composed "Hymn to the North Star:"

On thy unaltering blaze
The half wrecked mariner
His compass lost

Fixes his steady gaze
And steers, undoubting, to the friendly coast
And they who stray in perilous wastes by night
Are glad when thou dost shine to guide their footsteps right.

Polaris has not always been the North Star because Earth's axis slowly wobbles through an arc of forty-six degrees. One wobble takes about twenty-six thousand years to complete, so over time the axis has pointed to a very large portion of celestial real estate. About ten thousand years after the demise of Neanderthal man, when Homo Sapiens paused to regard the night sky, they saw a stationary star in the north called Gamma Cephei. About the time that people first began to cultivate plants in the Fertile Crescent, the North Star was Vega. When the great Pyramids were being built in Egypt, Earth's axis was pointed at Thuban in the tail of the Dragon. During the ascent of Greek civilization, it was Kochab in Big Dipper's cup. Arab nomads used Kochab to find their way across vast deserts and they called it Al Kaukab al Shamaliyy, "the star of the north." After Christ was born, Earth's axis began to zero in on Polaris and the North Star became an astronomical celebrity. When the fifth-century chronicler Stobaeus called it "ever visible" Polaris was then about seven degrees from the pole. Tenth-century Anglo-Saxons called it Scip-steorra—"the ship star." Spaniards called it Nortes. The Chinese knew it as Tien Hwang Ta Ti—"the great imperial ruler of heaven" with all the stars circling around it. In Damascus it was Mismar—"the nail;" the Turks called it Yilduz—"the best star;" and astronomer Johann Bayer—one of the first Europeans to map the constellations—called it Angel Stern—"the pivot star," a name that early English navigators adopted.

Though the poets don't mention it, Polaris does more than point the way north. It's a clue to latitude. When a sailor looks out over the sea, his vista is enclosed by an empty flat horizon all around. The Earth is not flat, but his view of it is, because light travels in a straight line. The visible horizon is actually a plane tangent to curving Earth. When a sailor observes the night sky from Earth's equator, the tangent horizon is parallel to Earth's axis—pointing due north and south—so he sees Polaris right on the horizon. When he moves north, the tangent horizon moves with him, forming an angle to Earth's axis that is—by a nicety of spherical geometry—equal to his latitude in degrees. What that means in practical terms is that when a sailor observes Polaris to be five degrees above the horizon he is at five degrees north latitude. So when Nainoa first saw Polaris right on the horizon, he knew the canoe had reached the equator. As the canoe moves on toward Hawai'i, he knows the star will rise higher, but it will be some time before he would learn to accurately measure its height without instruments. And accuracy is important because an error in the sky of just one degree is an error on Earth of sixty nautical miles.

HOMECOMING

Chapter Nineteen

"Fish on the line!"

This time Maka'ala's lure had been hit.

"This is one big fish," Maka yelled as he hauled the line in hand over hand. "What the hell is it?"

Over the side came a *mahimahi* as large as anyone had ever seen, a hundred pounds at least. Gordon reached over the side and gaffed him.

"In all the excitement, and not really knowing what to do with a fish that big, I flipped it on deck," he recalls. The *mahimahi* struggled for life, flopping furiously. In a second it was gone over the side. Maka sadly watched it disappear in *Hōkūle'a's* wake.

"No big thing," he told Gordon. "We'll catch another one. That ain't the only fish in the sea."

"That was the first fish we hit in a long time," Gordon recalls. "We had many dry days. Maka could have been negative about it, but he was positive. He turned it into a good situation."

Everyone appreciated Maka's positive attitude and, as the voyage progressed, it seemed to infuse the entire crew. "They were incredible," Kimo Lyman recalls. "Everybody found their own niche and everyone worked hard, no rattlers, no bad times—just people who had to put up with each other—and they did. It was the most mellow trip I've ever been on."

On July 20th, as *Hōkūle'a* forged northward, Jupiter, Saturn and Mars formed a train of planets settling into the horizon almost due west. At about the same time, scientists at NASA's Langley Research Center were busy communicating with a satellite spinning around the red planet. The satellite's name—Viking I—recalls the first European explorers to set off across the Atlantic to discover North America. On command from Earth, a Martian lander eased away from the orbiting mother ship. For a few hours the two spacecraft sailed around Mars together. Finally, tiny thrusters coaxed the lander out of orbit to descend to the western slope of Chryse Planitia, which resembles—as far as scientists looking through telescopes can tell—a desert pocked with impact craters. They call its landing place the Golden Plain. Shortly thereafter, Viking activated a radioisotope thermoelectric generator, tapping electricity produced by the natural decay of its plutonium fuel to send back the first photographs ever taken from the surface of the red planet.

Aboard *Hōkūle'a* Nainoa and the crew listened to reports of the Mars landing via single sideband radio. "July 20th," Nainoa wrote in his log. "Here we are on *Hōkūle'a* sailing home. And last night they landed on Mars. Really turned on when I heard that on the radio. The report. Just incredible. Small nuclear generators and mechanical hands picking up specimens and black and white television cameras. So unbelievable."

As Viking I settled into its new home, *Hōkūle'a* sailed in heavy seas stirred by a tropical storm called Diana. The canoe climbed steep swells, rolled sharply, then pitched into the trough. Nainoa clutched the steering sweep as the stern rocketed up into the night sky, then plunged back—accompanied by a geyser of spray as the port catwalk met a heavy roller. "That night was probably my best experience on *Hōkūle'a*," he wrote. "Steering her in a thirty-knot-plus squall. Couldn't see anything. Had a big rooster tail in back. Maybe making nine knots plus. Just flying. Just hanging on."

From the top of a ten-foot swell, he looked out over a vast conveyor belt of water rolling toward the southwest. To starboard, he saw white caps, froth, and wind scarring the face of swells as they rushed toward him. Then the canoe dropped into a trough. The world contracted within a fold of ocean and all he saw was the night sky blanketed by wind-whipped clouds. "No stars. I haven't been able to see the stars for the last four or five nights now. Plenty squalls. You can see them coming from a distance." *Hōkūle'a* occasionally took a swell hard and shipped whitewater. Yet she always maintained her composure— slicing through the swells, riding over them, channeling tons of ocean cleanly between her hulls — heading straight to her rendezvous with the Big Island. *The first Hawaiians who came across here, I think about them a lot. They must be, by our standards, superhuman. I was freezing, even with foul weather gear. Without it—I couldn't handle it. They must have had a deep love for the ocean and they must have been a fearless people. Maybe dying to them was worth the risk because they cared enough for what they were doing. I don't know. I don't know. I wasn't there.*

Now in northern latitudes, the wind turned colder. *Hōkūle'a's* crew bundled up as best they could but still, when the call came to change watch, it was an effort to leave the warmth of sleeping bags. As the canoe turned west on its final leg, Nainoa observed the North Star. "It's super high in the sky. It's very big and bright. If you cup your hand it's maybe nineteen degrees at the cup of your hand in front of you." This is Nainoa's first written reference to using his hand as an instrument to measure the altitude of a star, a technique that will eventually become a crucial tool. "I've become a lot more aware than I was before of my universe. I know a lot more about Mau's teaching. I can understand how he can be the person he is. Mau is just a genius. He has to be, to be able to compute all these things in his mind. His cross-references tell him where he is in the ocean— where to point the canoe so the land will come to it. It's been a great experience. It's going too fast. When it's over—it's over. I have to prepare myself for that."

Hōkūle'a moved rapidly now with the wind behind her, racing down long, easy swells. Rainsqualls passed overhead and congealed into gossamer mist. Clouds scudded above the squalls, sometimes obscuring the upright Big Dipper, sometimes revealing it dancing there to starboard. Running in a following sea was tricky. Swells rose up behind the canoe, crested, and raced beneath her, lifting *Hōkūle'a's* stern, causing her to turn upwind—then down. Nainoa struggled to keep on course. "I felt really good when the rains came and I couldn't see," he wrote. "The clouds covered all the stars. The only thing I could use was the swell, the feel of the wind on my face and especially the telltales and the feel of the canoe. But I had the confidence to do it. I used the Big Dipper's tail along the shrouds. We sailed in the squall for maybe ten minutes and I adjusted to the telltales and how the canoe felt. When the squall passed, the tail of the Big Dipper was right there along the shroud. Maybe this is the feeling that Mau has all the time—total confidence in what he's doing."

Nainoa had learned the constellations—their rising and setting points, their paths across the sky—and his confidence in this knowledge had grown. *The heavens have become a good friend to me now. I pass the time. I think about it. I think back on how they could navigate.* But his experience had demonstrated the difference between observing the stars during clear nights on land and during cloudy ones at sea. Seldom could he see the entire sky, for example. Often he located familiar constellations—comprising many stars—by finding just the few that blinked between clouds. He had learned the rising and setting points of dozens of stars. But he had also learned that rarely is the horizon clear enough to actually see them rise and set. To add to the confusion, the sky always changes.

Leaving Tahiti on July 4th, for example, when the sun set at about 5:30 p.m. local time, both Altair and Vega were below the horizon. Waiting patiently, he saw Vega rise at about 6:30 p.m. Altair followed a half hour later. On the equator—ten days into the voyage—the sun set fifteen minutes later, revealing Vega already about fifteen degrees above the horizon and Altair just breaking the ocean's surface. Arriving in Hawai'i's latitude, sunset was about 7:15 p.m. Now Altair had risen about fifteen degrees with Vega sailing well above it. So many things had changed. What to make of it? Nainoa knew that the stars rose four minutes earlier every day, an artifact of Earth's voyage around the sun. So an observer, standing on the same spot as the days tick by, would see the stars higher in the sky with each new sunset. But Nainoa was not standing on Earth. He was moving north along it and that presented other changes. For one thing, he was sailing away from Southern Hemisphere's winter into Northern Hemisphere's summer—moving, in effect, along the inclined plane of Earth's axis, causing the sun to tarry. He also sailed north on a round Earth, his view of the sky tangent to it, so his horizon appeared to tilt down in the north and up in the south. Looking east, the star paths arced left when seen from Tahiti, straight up at the equator, and to the right in Hawaiian waters and this caused the stars to appear to rise in slightly different places. Nainoa knew that all these changes occurred because he was moving through both time and space, along a curved Earth—tilted about twenty-four degrees from upright—that was also moving around the sun. Understanding these changes was the key to finding his way anywhere on the globe. But how exactly? "The more I learn, the more I understand. The more I understand, the more I know how complicated the heavens are," he wrote in his log. "As Mau said, 'You have to begin to study them when you are three years old to really know.'"

Perhaps it was just experience then? Perhaps by sailing seapaths all your life you learned to navigate by the changing shape of the sky? Did such experience create an understanding that allowed a Micronesian navigator to pierce celestial complexities in ways that an observer steeped in western science could not? Nainoa envisioned his world in three dimensions—a complex geometry of tilting planes, tangent arcs and curved surfaces upon which the canoe moved. Is he locked into a western way of seeing that may offer explanations but no understanding? *Maybe it's complicated because of the way I am learning how the heavens operate?* he thought.

Well, that's how it was, he decided. He had been tutored in science and so he would begin with what science could teach. *...it will be good enough. In Hawai'i, when I get home, I can make a time schedule for each latitude—how the stars rise, the path of the stars, which ones follow which, and when they rise. I don't know if it will be practical—but it will be enjoyable.*

July 24th. During the early morning watch, gentle rains extinguished the stars and washed *Hōkūle'a's* decks clean of salt. Ruby and emerald running lights now glowed for the first time in three weeks. The canoe had entered shipping lanes—broad ocean highways followed by massive freighters and tankers bound between Hawai'i and the mainland's West Coast. In a following wind, *Hōkūle'a* raced down long, easy swells. The moon was a tiny sliver gliding through ragged bellies of swirling cumulus cloud. Nainoa steered by aligning Polaris with the starboard shrouds. *I really got a thing going with* Hōkūle'a. *I can really feel her now. How she rides on the swells, up and over, pitch and roll. Pivoting on the top, riding down, pulling to one side—the sound of the steering paddle as it bites into the water.*

A little after 3:00 a.m. during intermittent breaks in the clouds ahead, the crew saw a glow on the horizon—the city of Hilo on the Big Island.

KEALAIKAHIKI
THE WAY TO TAHITI

Chapter Twenty

Patrolman Guy Takeuchi studied the situation through the windshield of his parked patrol car, the engine purring. He had never seen anything like it. Kuli'ou'ou Beach Park occasionally attracted rowdy parties and he had been called there often to break them up. When finding lovers parked late at night, he moved them on with a blast from his siren. But what was this? Takeuchi saw a large circle of glowing lights, about sixty feet in diameter. The lights were green, about the size of small Christmas tree bulbs, and they were attached to steel pins stuck into the grass. The effect was extraterrestrial. In the center of the circle, he saw something that disturbed him even more—a body wrapped tightly in a sleeping bag. Takeuchi approached. He poked the sleeping bag with his flashlight.

"Hunh, what?"

Takeuchi stepped back as the bag moved, revealing a Hawaiian male, maybe a hundred and fifty pounds, in his twenties. He wore a dark tee shirt and appeared to be confused, or drugged, or perhaps just momentarily blinded by the flashlight's beam.

"What are you doing here?" Takeuchi asked.

The young man regarded him for what seemed a long moment.

"I'm looking at the stars."

"You're what?"

"This may take some time to explain," said the young man.

"I told him I was studying the stars," Nainoa recalls, "and that went over real well. It took a few minutes before he relaxed and began to believe what I was saying. Eventually, he turned off his flashlight and sat down. He looked at the stars and said, 'Wow.'"

After returning home from Tahiti, Nainoa tried to resume life where he had left off, but the transition from sea to land proved difficult. He was twenty-three at the time. He had completed two semesters of college. For a while, he was content to be a fisherman—placing his traps, diving to retrieve them and hauling the catch to Honolulu's fish market. But often, coming into port accompanied by the whine of his battered Evinrude and the slap of waves, he could feel *Hōkūle'a* move in the soles of his feet.

I made a good start at understanding the sky, so why stop now? he thought.

Kuli'ou'ou Park was a short walk from the tiny house Nainoa rented and he went there often to observe the sky. Mau had steered *Hōkūle'a* to Tahiti using a star compass and Nainoa had learned the rising and setting points of many stars on the voyage home. He decided to continue this study on land.

"I made a star compass big enough so that I could get inside it," he explains. "I gave it a radius of sixty feet, the length of the canoe. Then I sat in the center with penlights glowing all around me, to observe the sky." Although he knew nothing of the druids and their ancient megalithic observatory—Nainoa had created a kind of Polynesian Stonehenge.

Takeuchi reported to his dispatcher and stayed as long as he could, watching the stars, learning a few constellations. Soon, every patrolman at the Hawai'i Kai stationhouse knew about the strange young man studying the sky.

"So almost every night when their shift got slow," Nainoa recalls, "a couple of cops would pick up doughnuts and coffee and sit with me in the ring of penlights and I taught them the stars."

❖ ❖ ❖ ❖ ❖

Gordon Pi'ianai'a had been Nainoa's shipmate on the voyage home from Tahiti and, like Nainoa, he couldn't get the experience out of his mind. Gordon first went to sea when he was three years old on the steamer *Humu'ula* with his father as captain. In 1958, he graduated from Kamehameha Schools and served in the Navy, three years as a quartermaster, learning to navigate. Then came two years aboard a fifty-two foot staysail schooner out of Lahaina. After that he went to the California Maritime Academy, got his mate's papers and signed aboard various merchant ships. "I went to sea because I was born a Pacific Islander," he says. "The sea is my backyard. Mainlanders hike their forests and climb their mountains. The ocean is my road." Eventually, Gordon moved ashore. He earned a master's degree in Hawaiian culture and history at the University of Hawai'i,

Gordon Pi'ianai'a aboard *Hōkūle'a*

taught at Punahou School from 1969 to 1972 and then moved to Kamehameha Schools. A short time after *Hōkūle'a* returned from Tahiti, Gordon was called into a meeting with the Schools' director of extension education, Fred Cachola, where a discussion ensued regarding *Hōkūle'a's* future.

"I want you to develop an educational program that will take *Hōkūle'a* to visit schools and communities in all the islands," Cachola told Gordon.

Gordon was delighted because the educational voyage would not only provide a new mission for *Hōkūle'a*, it would allow him to test one of his theories about an ancient route to Tahiti that he had discovered in his studies of Hawaiian culture. The Kealaikahiki channel, "the Road to Tahiti," passes between the

Hawaiian islands of Lāna'i and Kaho'olawe. The westernmost point of land on Kaho'olawe is traditionally known as a training place for navigators, a vantage point from which both the northern and southern skies are visible, allowing a clear view of both the North Star and the Southern Cross. Gordon examined "the Road to Tahiti" with a practiced seaman's eye.

On its voyage to Tahiti in 1976, *Hōkūle'a* had set out northeast from Maui and zigzagged across the ocean for five days in order to clear the Big Island before turning south for Tahiti. As a result, the crew endured a battering that left them fatigued and demoralized at the very beginning of the voyage. A canoe following Kealaikahiki, however, is more direct. It passes south of the Big Island, which breaks the force of the northeast trades and provides a few days of easy sailing during which voyagers can accustom themselves to being at sea.

"It didn't make sense to get easting by going around the Big Island to the north," Gordon recalls. "It exposes the crew to the elements unnecessarily. The Kealaikahiki route gives the crew a period of adjustment because it's calmer. It's also a more direct route so I believed it was used for long voyages. It is, after all, 'the Road to Tahiti.' "

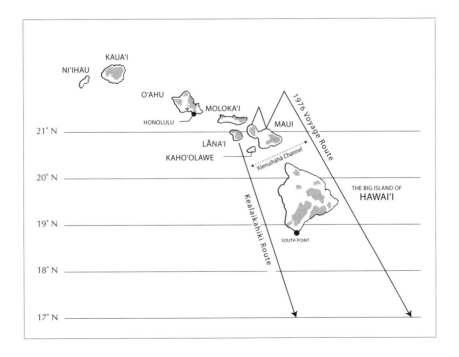

Gordon proposed that *Hōkūle'a* would begin her educational voyage by first following the Kealaikahiki route and proceeding to sea until she cleared the Big Island of Hawai'i and was on her way to intersect the course line taken on the 1976 voyage to Tahiti. Gordon was impressed by Nainoa's attempts to learn the stars, so he also thought the voyage would allow Nainoa to test his emerging skills at sea.

❖ ❖ ❖ ❖ ❖

The promise of the Kealaikahiki voyage stimulated Nainoa to new intensity. Sailing from Lāna'i east-southeast, *Hōkūle'a* would cross four degrees of latitude, from twenty-one to seventeen degrees north, until she eventually crossed her 1976 track. But how to tell when she reached seventeen north? Nainoa knew that the altitude of Polaris, and of any other star when crossing the meridian (the highest point in a star's arc across the sky), is a clue to an observer's latitude— but how to measure it without an instrument? On the trip from Tahiti, he had aligned his hand along the seam between sky and ocean, and observed Polaris rise from one finger, to two, to three. Eventually it rose higher than he could measure with his fingers alone, so he placed his entire palm against the night sky with his thumb on the horizon—a technique he calls "palm out." By rotating his hand until one of his fingers touched Polaris, the thumb directly beneath it, he continued to measure the star's altitude. When the canoe reached Hawai'i, Polaris was perched in the crease between his index and middle fingers. But how high was that in degrees?

A telephone pole stood near the driveway to Nainoa's family home in the Niu Valley. One day Nainoa and a friend who knew how to measure angles with a sextant set out to calibrate the pole. Nainoa climbed a ladder with adhesive tape in hand and marked off twenty-three points that ascended from just above the ground to the cross trees that carried the wires.

"A little higher,"

"A little lower."

"Right there—twenty-three degrees."

When they had finished, the pole was marked in twenty-three equally spaced strips of tape—one for each degree of altitude—and the place from which Nainoa's friend measured the angles was indicated by a stake driven into the

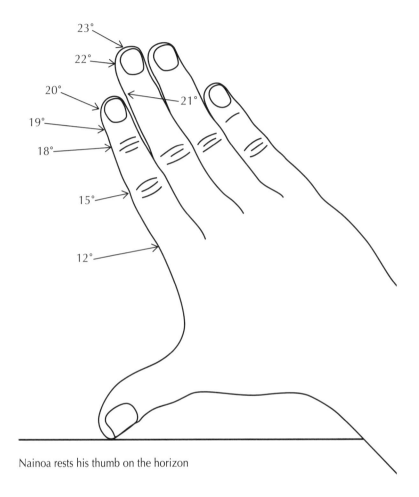

23°
22°
20°
19°
18°
15°
12°
21°

Nainoa rests his thumb on the horizon

ground. During the next few weeks, Nainoa stood at the stake and held his arm out from his body just so—the same way each time—and calibrated his hand.

Holding his hand upright—what he calls the palm-out method— the top of his middle finger measured twenty-three degrees, the middle of the fingernail was twenty-two, the joint between middle and index fingers was twenty-one. He continued to identify landmarks on his hand until he covered the gamut from twelve to twenty-three degrees.

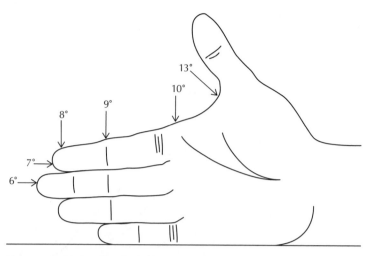

Nainoa rests his hand on the horizon

Laying his hand on the horizon (or the bottom of the pole), he saw the sixth mark, six degrees, near the curve at the tip of his middle finger, seven was just above the space between his middle and index finger, eight near the tip of that finger and so on. He did this over and over until he knew just how to hold his hand so the measurements were identical every time.

Then he set out to measure stars. Looking south, he regarded the upright Southern Cross. Just as the constellation reached its meridian, the top star—Gacrux—was positioned directly over the bottom star—Acrux. From his grandmother's cow pasture, latitude twenty-one degrees north, the distance between Acrux and the horizon was six degrees—just at the curve of his third finger. On the Kealaikahiki voyage, the canoe would move south to about seventeen degrees north latitude. With each degree of southern progress, Acrux would rise a degree higher in the sky.

So, Nainoa thought, *when we reach seventeen north, Acrux will be four degrees higher, or ten degrees total.* Measured by laying his hand on the horizon, the star should dance between the second and third crease of his top finger.

⋄ ⋄ ⋄ ⋄ ⋄

On April 1st, *Hōkūle'a* sailed from Honolulu to Mānele Bay, Lāna'i, to begin the Kealaikahiki voyage. On April 4th, the canoe set out. "We left from Mānele in a nice north wind," recalls Captain Dave Lyman, "with Norman Pi'ianai'a documenting Nainoa's navigation with his sextant and chronometer." Among the crew were Gordon Pi'ianai'a, Sam Ka'ai, Mike Tongg, John Kruse, Kimo Lyman, Sam Kalalau, Maka'ala Yates, Jerry Muller, Bert Barber and Teené Froiseth.

The canoe made good progress, traveling about seventeen miles in three hours to reach the lee side of Kaho'olawe about noon. With the wind out of the northeast, she was then in Maui's wind shadow, almost becalmed. Just before sunset, *Hōkūle'a* encountered the first puffs of wind flowing through the 'Alenuihāhā Channel between Maui and the Big Island, and she picked up speed. Nainoa estimated they were about forty miles west of the Big Island.

Clouds flitted across the horizon and extended into the darkening arc of sky. A star appeared, then another, then a pattern—not yet clear. It was a small constellation, a little to port of *Hōkūle'a's* twin masts and framed by them. Then, for an instant, Nainoa saw four stars—the False Cross—with the red star, Avior, about four fingers high. To the right, the bright star Canopus glistened briefly and was gone behind scudding cloud. For a moment, he saw the Little Dipper in the north—then it was dark there. There was a kind of wonder in this continuing light show, as if some spirit were tantalizing him. "Do you see that star?" the spirit seemed to say. "Do you know which one it is?" And yes, for the most part, he did. Constantly watching the sky, marking each star as it glowed for a time then blinked out, Nainoa constructed the dome of constellations in his mind and he arrayed his star compass—a heads-up display surrounding the canoe. He set a course to avoid the large wind shadow cast by the Big Island.

Nainoa experimented with dead reckoning, an ancient art that requires a navigator to calculate how far he has sailed in a given direction during a known interval of time. The star compass at night and the sun during the day provided direction. To judge speed, he looked over the side of the canoe and counted the seconds required for a bubble in its wake to move from the bow cross beams to those at the stern, a distance of 42 1/2 feet. In one of his notebooks, he had worked out the calculations—ten seconds gave 2.5 knots (2.5 nautical miles each hour), eight gave 3.1 knots, six gave 4.2 and so on. Nainoa strained to keep track of *Hōkūle'a's* changing course and speed and to plot his position mentally at regular intervals—sunrise, mid-day, sunset, midnight. The job was turning out to be far more difficult than he had imagined.

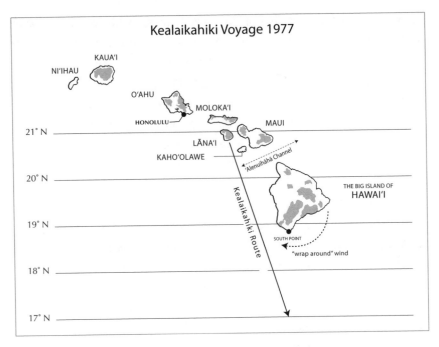

Kealaikahiki Voyage 1977

At about three in the morning the wind became variable—ten to fifteen knots—and shifted to the east. Nainoa had been waiting for this.

The winds are bending around the Big Island, he thought.

This was a rough clue to the canoe's position. When the northeast trade winds encounter the Big Island's high peaks, Mauna Loa and Mauna Kea, they are deflected around the island in a curving path. Nainoa calls these "wrap-around winds."

The evening advanced, marked by the wheeling constellations. About midnight, the Southern Cross sailed past its meridian and descended. The Scorpion rose, dancing on its curved stinger. Nainoa corrected the steersmen when they lost their guide stars in passing clouds. He compensated for their errors in his mind. He calculated the canoe's speed and tried his best to plot her position mentally, using the Big Island as a reference.

At sunrise, he made the transition from steering by stars to using the sun, noting its rising position on his fading star compass. As the sun rose, heavy clouds obscured the Big Island. Soon, Nainoa felt the wind shifting to the northeast, the normal trade wind pattern. *Hōkūle'a* was moving out of the Big Island's wind shadow.

"I think we're south of South Point on the Big Island," Nainoa told Captain Lyman.

Dave consulted Norman Pi'ianai'a.

"Yep, he's right on," Norman told him.

"We didn't tell Nainoa," Dave recalls, "and we kept on going."

Nainoa held the canoe close on the wind. He steered by a large easterly swell that had been driven over long ocean distances by steady trade winds.

At noon, the sun appeared long enough for Norman to take a sight and plot Hōkūle'a's position, but at sunset the sky was again too cloudy to obtain a fix. Finally, a little after midnight, the stars came out. The Southern Cross was upright. Acrux, the bottom star, appeared to rest between the second and third crease of his top finger. Taking this observation into account, along with the wind shift and his dead reckoning—Nainoa figured the canoe had arrived at seventeen degrees north latitude, sixty miles south of the Big Island.

"We're here," he told the captain.

"I remember being so stoked," Dave recalls. "Nainoa said, 'I think we're sixty miles south of South Point' and he says 'Here's the course to Tahiti.' I said 'Okay, that's great, experiment proven.' We were all so impressed with Nainoa because he was able to see such a small change in latitude."

While Nainoa was excited about the trip, his notebook contained reminders of the work ahead:

On trip was not all that confident of my estimations.
Got to cancel out extremes to every side of your course steered.
Heavy memorization of course steered and distance traveled.
Was hard to steer by the swells because seas so confusing.
Wind patterns changed during the day but I did not know until the sun
was low enough to navigate with.

"The trip was a huge learning experience," he recalls. "It taught me how hard it is to navigate under difficult living conditions. There was the issue of staying up all the time. It's one thing to intellectualize the navigation. It's another to do it, to be in command. Kealaikahiki was my first experience with all of that. One thing was certain—I wanted to do it more and more."

THE MIRACLE MACHINE

Chapter Twenty-One

About 7:00 a.m., on an April morning, Will Kyselka, a lecturer at the Bishop Museum Planetarium, was awakened by the telephone in his bedroom.

"I'm sorry to bother you," said the caller, "but I am studying Polynesian navigation and I wonder if you could help me."

"Who is this?" Will asked.

"It's Nainoa Thompson. I'm a member of *Hōkūle'a's* crew."

Will was intrigued.

"Why don't you come over to the planetarium this afternoon, and we'll look into it," he said.

Will is a slender man of average stature with a rather long face and a gentle, somewhat professorial way of contemplating the world. He speaks softly and slowly as if considering each word. He is the author of *North Star and Southern Cross*, a primer on constellations and their meaning to people of many cultures. Will had followed *Hōkūle'a's* 1976 voyage and was vaguely aware that she had sailed on a new mission to trace the "Road to Tahiti." His first impression of Nainoa was that he was "quiet and shy. He was sharp and he knew what he wanted to learn. I like to work with a person like that."

The machine that Will presided over was a Spitz A3-P star projector capable of projecting twenty-three hundred stars onto the planetarium's dome using a 24-inch projector ball. Individual projectors presented the sun, moon, and five planets—Mercury, Venus, Mars, Jupiter, Saturn—and such things as constellation overlays, aurora, supernovae, neutron stars, black holes, and meteors. For Nainoa, it was a "miracle machine." It was capable of moving back to a time when the first Polynesians set out from Fiji to settle the Pacific—just about when Odysseus and his soldiers were busy knocking down the walls of Troy. It was also, at least in some ways, capable of replicating Mau's lifetime of experience by speeding up celestial motion—taking Nainoa on voyages in an

Will Kyselka (center) and Nainoa aboard *Hōkūle'a*

hour that would have required a month in real time. Just as Mau's grandfather had taken him by the hand to face the stars over Satawal, Will took Nainoa to a replicated sky projected on the planetarium's dome.

Nainoa had learned many stars at Willamette College and from vantage points in Hawai'i and Tahiti. He had gone as far as H. A. Rey could take him but that was not a long journey. About four thousand stars are visible to the naked eye, after all, and most of them are not mentioned in a beginner's astronomy book. Nainoa and Will observed artificial stars wheel across the domed planetarium, beginning in the month of March from a vantage point in Hawai'i. They confirmed that they rose and set in the same place, night after night, although the timing of their appearance and disappearance changed. Nainoa called their rising and setting points "houses" on his star compass. "We went down to the equator and looked at the same thing," Will recalls. "Then we went down to Tahiti and watched the same phenomena from latitude eighteen degrees south." Nainoa made a list of stars that rose and set in the same house. Deneb, for example, rises in the northeast as do Almach, Capella, Menkalinan and Delta Cygni, so all of them define the same house on Nainoa's compass. Conveniently, they rise at widely spaced times—Capella about two hours after Almach, Menkalinan a half hour later, Delta Cygni about fourteen hours after that, and finally Deneb an hour after Delta Cygni—so when one star has risen too high to steer by, another can be expected to replace it.

During their training together, Will sometimes turned on the Spitz and set it to go all night. He locked up as if no-one was there, said goodbye to the security guard, and went home. Nainoa lay on the floor and dozed under the rotating stars. He woke up, studied them, dozed off. Eventually, he made a list of one hundred and ten stars to populate his star compass, and committed each to memory.

TO TAHITI AGAIN

Chapter Twenty-Two

Dr. Ben Young, newly elected as president of the Polynesian Voyaging Society, believed that *Hōkūle'a* must continue to link Hawaiians with their past by retracing the paths of their ancestors

"We needed some kind of goal," Ben recalls, "something to push us. *Hōkūle'a* should be sailing on long voyages so I presented the idea of going back to Tahiti."

"We've already done that," some said. "Why do it again?'

"You do it again and again and again," Ben responded, "because you want to learn more."

On January 24th, 1978, after much discussion, the Voyaging Society announced that *Hōkūle'a* would depart for Tahiti on March 16th. Dave Lyman was chosen as captain. Leon Sterling would be first mate. Nainoa would be non-instrument navigator and Norman Pi'ianai'a would navigate with chart and sextant. Norman would plot *Hōkūle'a's* position twice a day, but would not reveal her location unless Nainoa made an error that compromised the crew's safety.

❖ ❖ ❖ ❖ ❖

Crew candidates for the voyage were invited to try out during training sessions aboard the canoe, often under the guidance of first mate Leon Sterling. "He's the best first mate you could ever want," Dave says of him. "He's a real driver, an ocean sailor." Leon was a bear of a man, thick of trunk and bulked up with muscle. His face was broad and often capped by a colorful bandanna that gave him the appearance of a jolly pirate. A cigarette usually dangled from his lips, scattering fine ashes over his beard. Chad Baybayan remembers first meeting Leon aboard a small double canoe, *Mo'olele*, while voyaging between the islands.

Leon Sterling

"We met Leon on the beach," Chad says, "and he came aboard *Moʻolele,* and taught us how to sail. Later, when we had pushed the canoe up on the beach, we began to talk about fishing and in the middle of the conversation Leon reached in his mouth and pulled out a fishhook. We were amazed. He makes fishhooks. He carries a file with him to work the hooks and he keeps one in his mouth so the bone is wet and soft and easy to work. That was my introduction to him. That was in 1975."

Leon had sailed as mate on merchant vessels, visiting ports in the Mediterranean, the Caribbean and the South Pacific. On shore, Leon is reclusive.

He often seems distracted. Aboard the canoe, he focuses. He sees details to be tended to—a frayed rope that needs splicing, a sail that needs mending, an unusual sound deep in one of the canoe's hulls. "He's the kind of person that a voyager long ago looking for land would recruit because Leon brings diverse skills that makes sailing out there safe," says Chad. "He's very sturdy, reliable, and knowledgeable. He's reflective, funny, serious. He has a temperament that is conducive to being in close quarters with a lot of people. He's easy to get along with."

Bruce Blankenfeld tried out for the crew. He had been a waterman all his life, swimming, surfing, paddling canoes and fishing with Nainoa, his brother-in-law (Bruce was married to Lita, Nainoa's sister). Sailing aboard *Hōkūle'a* for the first time, he felt completely at home. *I can do this,* he thought, *and I can do it well.* In the early seventies, Bruce worked for the Hilo Bureau of Land and Natural Resources, forest division—planting trees, putting out forest fires,

Bruce Blankenfeld

building trails. He thought of being a forest ranger. "I loved being outdoors," he recalls, "but mostly I loved being on the water, whether diving or fishing or sailing or paddling." Before *Hōkūleʻa* came along, Bruce, like most Hawaiians, was largely ignorant of his heritage. "When I grew up, I identified with being Hawaiian but I wasn't real certain about it. From kindergarten up through eighth grade there were no Hawaiian studies. Nothing. The extent of what we learned was in a geography class or science class where we had those little booklets from the Bishop Museum about growing plants or building houses. It was a curiosity more than anything else—this was how Hawaiians used to live—that's *pau*, that's all over, in the past. We fished and surfed and paddled canoes. We spoke a little Hawaiian but it was just piecemeal. We ate *poi* and raw fish and *ʻopihi* and crab—but the world we lived in was predominantly an American lifestyle mixed in with an island lifestyle. I think we were confused about being Hawaiian because we didn't do things that the Hawaiians before us did—how they lived, their fishing practices, their beliefs. I felt that you had to know these things or you're not really Hawaiian. Culturally, you're weak. Then I got involved with *Hōkūleʻa*. I started sailing and I never looked back."

Marion Lyman-Mersereau was among the first workers to help build *Hōkūleʻa*, but when the canoe was launched, she discovered that only men would be aboard for the first voyage to Tahiti. She joined the Peace Corps and spent two years in Palau, a Micronesian island surrounded by sparkling ocean. She followed *Hōkūleʻa's* progress by reading clippings her mother sent to her. When she returned to Hawaiʻi she began training for the new voyage.

Also among the crew candidates was one of Hawaiʻi's most famous surfers—Eddie Aikau. During the ten years he had served as head lifeguard at Waimea Bay, one of the most dangerous beaches in all the islands, his supervisors credited him with over a thousand rescues. In 1971, because of his daring and disarmingly humble demeanor, he was voted "Life Guard of the Year" by his peers. Others may have surfed the monster waves at Waimea, but Eddie was the man to perfect the ride. "He'd take off on a big, scary wave and he'd be sliding down it with the biggest smile you ever saw," says Clyde Aikau, his younger brother. "Eddie belonged there. It was home." Aikau lived next door to his parents. He kept his house the same way he did everything else he owned, his surfboards, his car—which is to say immaculate. "You walk into his house

Eddie Aikau

and there are all these surfboards in the rafters—but it was just so neat," Chad Baybayan remembers. "And he used to go to church on Sundays, take his parents to church. Most guys, if the surf was up, they would go surfing, but Eddie had a commitment to his parents. He cared for them that way. He told me that his middle name was *makua hānai*, which means "raised by parents" or "caring for parents." 'It works both ways.' he told me. 'Your parents care for you and you care for your parents.' "

Chad first met Eddie at a meeting of prospective crewmembers in downtown Honolulu. "I went into the room and I saw a lot of big time watermen were there, so I felt kind of intimidated. I was from the neighbor islands and I was real shy. I didn't know anybody. I thought my chances of being chosen for the crew weren't good. And here was Eddie Aikau, a big wave surfer who had just won a surf contest on O'ahu. I didn't want to hang around in *that* crowd, so as soon as the meeting got done I rushed to the elevator. But Eddie got in with me. It was just him and me. I stood in the corner trying to blend into the walls. He looked me in the eyes and in this real Hawaiian way, he said, 'Hey brother, we're going to be trying out for this crew together, more better we start out by being friends.' He stuck his hand out and said, 'Hi, my name is Eddie Aikau.' And that's how I met Eddie. He was this champion big wave surfer, but so what? He was just so humble, just so pleasant to be around, so befriending."

Marion recalls seeing Eddie surf in a professional contest at Waimea Bay. "I saw him make a 30-foot wave and I just assumed that a big wave surfer is a big dude. But when he showed up for training he's about five eight and real wiry and I was shocked. Come on—how can? But I saw how very intense and sincere he was. And he knew how to have fun. We would be out on a sail and he would go up to the bow and sing. He loved to just bellow and it was a shock because he was so quiet and reserved otherwise. It was so joyful. There he was up on the bow—just enjoying being out in the elements."

❖ ❖ ❖ ❖ ❖

The decision to return to Tahiti seemed a natural outgrowth of all that had gone on before. *Hōkūle'a* had proven she could make the trip safely. An experienced crew was available—Dave, John, Leon, Nainoa, and Snake had all made one long voyage—and many competent new crewmembers had shown

Crew training—left to right—Kiki Hugho, Nainoa Thompson, Bruce Blankenfeld, Buddy McGuire, Eddie Aikau—others unknown

up for training. Still, things seemed a little rushed. To avoid the danger of Pacific hurricanes, *Hōkūle'a* would have to depart before the middle of March. That left only about two and a half months to get ready. "We overhauled the canoe, rigged her and went out for day and night sails," Bruce Blankenfeld recalls. "The steering and the mechanics of controlling the canoe were no problem, but God it just seemed like there were so many moving parts. It wasn't easy. I never really learned all the rigging."

Dave Lyman was determined to avoid the crew problems experienced on the 1976 trip. "The crew must be compatible," he told the PVS board. "They must also be financially able to take time off for the voyage, be in good physical shape, have an aptitude for sailing, and fully understand that being selected as crew is a privilege—not a right."

Dave picked Snake Ah Hee to be on the voyage because "he's an absolutely solid guy. Excellent in the water. He enjoyed being at sea for a long time, enjoyed getting wet and has a gentle sweet personality." He chose his sister Marion because she "helped build the canoe in 1975 and I knew how much on a personal level she put into the canoe and how much the trip meant to her." John Kruse, Dave recalls, "was always pitching in to do hard work, to take care of the canoe. He's an incredible seaman. He's physically strong." Tava Taupu impressed Dave with his constant optimism. "Tava is totally enthusiastic—totally egoless. It's something spiritual. No matter how shitty it gets he's always there with a smile on his face." Sam Ka'ai had made the *ki'i* for *Hōkūle'a*. He had greeted the canoe when she first came to Lahaina. He had sailed aboard from Hawai'i to Maui and from there to the Big Island, and he had arranged the ceremonies at Honolua. "If anyone deserved to go, it was Sam," Dave said of him. "He's a man of great depth. Getting wet doesn't bother Sam. And he's funny, funny, funny." Bruce Blankenfeld also made the cut. "He's quiet and intense but he's ready to smile. If I suddenly got a heart attack I would want Bruce there to fish me out of the water. He's a natural on the water."

Everyone in Hawai'i thought that Eddie Aikau was a shoo-in to be chosen for *Hōkūle'a's* crew. He was, after all, Hawai'i's champion surfer and best-known lifeguard. "I hate to admit it," Dave Lyman recalls, "but I didn't really follow surfers. I didn't know what a big name Eddie was until guys started telling me. I tried to spend one-on-one time talking to people, checking them out, getting to know them. I said to Eddie, 'So you're from Maui? You must have graduated from Roosevelt High School?' And he just gave me this silly kind of smile and laughed and he said, 'Well I should have, but I quit high school so I could surf.' I thought, *Whoa, this guy is awesome.* How many guys drop out of school with an excuse like 'I'm going to be a professional surfer?' Most don't make it. But Eddie became one of the most recognized professional surfers in the world. And you could just tell he was totally in love with the canoe."

❖ ❖ ❖ ❖ ❖

To accommodate the crew's work schedule, training was held on weekends. Unfortunately, when canoe and crew were able to join for a sail, they often found themselves on an ocean unsullied by wind. "Almost every time we went out the wind was calm," Dave recalls. "We never had a really brisk sail. Never did. But the departure date was set so we just did all we could to get ready." "The training sails were never a big deal," Marion recalls. "We sailed in five knots of wind. Pretty basic."

In 1976, an escort boat had trailed in *Hōkūleʻa's* wake, serving as a camera platform for the National Geographic and as a lifeboat in case of accident. But on this trip, *Hōkūleʻa* would sail alone. "We couldn't afford a chase boat," Ben Young recalls. "We thought we could do without one because *Hōkūleʻa* had made the voyage down and back without any problems. There was no opposition to it. It was a minor issue."

The new voyage captured the imagination of people throughout the islands. Ron Jacobs, a Honolulu radio personality, presented a special show featuring Eddie Aikau and a song he had written about *Hōkūleʻa*. During the broadcast, Eddie described the immense pressure he felt from all the attention the voyage was getting. "It's unbelievable," he said, "but once we sail out there, we'll be all right. We can settle down and be ourselves." Near the end of Jacob's show, with Kiki Hugho accompanying him on guitar, Eddie sang a song that he had composed a few months earlier.

"I would like to dedicate this song especially to my mom and dad and my family; and secondly to the family of the *Hōkūleʻa* and all of Hawaiʻi," he said, tuning his guitar. The song was called *Hōkūleʻa*.

Hawaiʻi's pride she sails with the wind
And proud are we to see her sail free
Feelings so deep and so strong
For *Hōkū*, *Hōkūleʻa*.
The stars that shine guide her straight path
Across the sea, down to Tahiti
Then back to Hawaiʻi she sails
For *Hōkū*, *Hōkūleʻa*.

Then Jacobs signed off, wishing Aikau and Kiki and their fellow crewmembers good luck on the voyage.

CAPSIZE

Chapter Twenty-Three

On Thursday, March 16th, 1978, the day of *Hōkūle'a's* departure, Eddie went down to Honolulu's gritty port district to help load her. A large crowd milled around. Food and water had already been stowed so Eddie joined a line of people passing aboard the crew's personal gear—duffel bags bulging with clothing, heavy weather gear, snacks, cameras, books to relieve boredom on the long voyage, guitars and *'ukulele*. A holiday mood surrounded the canoe— as if this was to be a joy ride, an overnight sail to the Big Island—rather than an arduous 2500-mile passage across open ocean. Nainoa Thompson worked side by side with Eddie. He would be the canoe's non-instrument navigator, or perhaps better said, the non-instrument navigator "in training." By nature he's a worrier, a person who by foreseeing possible dangers seeks to arm himself against them. He felt personally unprepared. He worried about the readiness of the canoe and her crew. And he worried about the amount of gear that was being loaded aboard. He saw Wally Froiseth and went over to talk with him.

"Wallace, what do you think about this canoe?"

"I think it is way, way overloaded," Wally said.

"That's just what I'm thinking."

Harry Ho was equally alarmed. He watched one crew-member loading two guitars aboard. Someone heaved up a heavy seabag, then another. Harry addressed them.

"Hey, that baby is kinda low in the water, don't you think?"

"What do you mean?"

"The canoe, she's low in the water."

"I looked at the scupper holes," Harry remembers today. "The relationship of the water to the scupper holes—the canoe was way low in the water. She was overloaded. I saw these guys loading all this stuff on."

"Hey, you guys got no weight requirements or what?" Harry asked.

"Weight requirements?"

"Well, you know," Harry said, "each guy should take maybe forty pounds of personal gear besides the food and water."

"Oh, I guess that was all taken into consideration."

Harry said, "Well, okay."

"It was blowing like shit," he remembers today. "Small craft warnings. The whole nine yards. It was raining the whole morning but it cleared up a little in the afternoon. But still, small craft warnings."

Climbing aboard the canoe, Nainoa used his hand to measure the freeboard—the distance between the top of the canoe's hull and the ocean—and guessed it was only about ten inches.

Ben Finney was also among those watching the canoe being prepared for sea. "There was a gale of wind blowing," Ben remembers of that day. "And they were leaving at night which worried me a lot." Like Nainoa, he also worried about the canoe's low freeboard. But what most occupied his mind was that *Hōkūle'a* would sail without an escort boat. On the previous voyage to Tahiti, *Meotai,* a sixty-four foot ketch, had accompanied the canoe. She had carried extra provisions of food and water. Her navigator kept an accurate navigational log of the voyage to compare with the positions plotted by Mau Piailug. But the ketch's most important role was to provide a margin of safety. If anything happened to *Hōkūle'a,* she would be on hand to rescue her crew and call for help with powerful radios. On this voyage *Hōkūle'a* would sail alone.

How serious is this? Nainoa wondered, *and what can I do about it?* Captain Lyman was in charge. The Polynesian Voyaging Society's Board had apparently decided it was okay to go. Who was he to object? He had mentioned his concerns to the captain. What more could he do? Shame was a part of it, he realized later. It was like going to the edge of the cliff at Portlock Point. You had to dive in. There always came a time when you just had to go. But was this really the time?

By six-thirty in the evening, a crowd estimated to be about twenty thousand was on hand to celebrate the canoe's departure. By seven, the ceremonies of leave taking—a ritual drinking of *'awa* to symbolically separate the crew from the land—had been completed. A few minutes later, the canoe set sail into the gusting northerly winds as the well-wishers sang "Hawai'i Aloha."

That evening, Ben hosted a party at his home in the Mānoa hills above the

University of Hawai'i. After his guests had departed and the dishes had been washed, he peered out his dining room window toward the ocean below. He saw an angry sea frothed with white caps. The windows shook. The wind had increased noticeably in the few hours since the canoe left port.

❖ ❖ ❖ ❖ ❖

"The winds were maybe forty to fifty knots and we were smoking," remembers Wedemeyer Au. "The canoe just jumped through the waves. Water was coming in but we bailed it out. She felt real stable, really strong, like she could go anywhere in any kind of weather. That night, when I got off watch, I went to sleep in one of the *puka* and you could hear the water just rushing past the hulls and then there would be a slap, like an explosion, when the water hit one of the *'iako.*"

"The wind had been blowing hard—gale force—and it had been blowing for days so the swells were thirty-foot plus and fully developed and they were breaking." Bruce Blankenfeld recalls, "We had never sailed in anything like that as a crew."

The moon was in its first quarter, but heavy overcast and scudding clouds blocked its light. The wind was out of the north, carrying stinging cold spray across the canoe's decks. At least the wind's direction was favorable because the canoe could point up into it, heading for the Big Island where she would turn east-southeast for Tahiti.

"It was dark," Marion recalls. "We were off Diamond Head and we were flying. We left the flotilla that was well-wishing us in our wake. I remember thinking, 'Whoa, I don't remember the canoe feeling quite like this before.' I was on deck and there were seven other guys around me. I could hear the creaking of the lashing. *Hōkūle'a* was working her way up and over the swells and kind of walking—those two hulls. But I was feeling safe. I knew these hulls were sound. We're fine."

"We were going eight knots in bursts," remembers Sam Ka'ai. "It was like being on a Hobie Cat. We were going like a bat out of hell."

Kiki Hugho recalls that he and Eddie were aft steering the canoe, John Kruse and Sam Ka'ai were forward by the foresail. "The plan was first watch on duty. A lot of people were sick. Two guys on our watch couldn't even stand watch. The canoe was smoking, man, and we were shorthanded right off the bat."

At about midnight, Nainoa sat on the navigator's platform, aft on the port side, clinging to the railing as the canoe plunged into heavy troughs. It was hard to get back into the state of mind he had achieved on the trip from Tahiti. He had not really been to sea since then—and certainly not in this kind of weather. He did not feel seasick, but he did not feel completely well either. Even the most seasoned seafarers complain of the first few days on the ocean. It's a serious jolt to any human body—that change from the stability of dry land to the pitching chaos of being at sea. *The canoe does not feel right,* Nainoa thought, trying to remember what it was like to be aboard in heavy seas two years ago. *Something is wrong.*

Hōkūle'a seemed to be heeling to starboard. That was not particularly alarming. Any vessel will heel away from a stiff wind. Still, it seemed excessive. "We were really heavy on the lee side," Nainoa remembers, "so I went down into the starboard hull and opened up one of the hatches. I will never forget what I saw—that picture of it—just how clear and clean water looks at night with a flashlight in a fully flooded hull. The water was crystal clear. Right up to the top. I put the cover back on."

Bruce was on deck. "Check the windward hull," Nainoa yells to him. "If there's air in it, hold the cover down. Don't let water get in."

Because of the surging crowds, the departure ceremonies and impending darkness, gear was never stowed properly. The canoe departed with duffel bags still on deck along with crates of food, life preservers, coils of rope. Much of it was adrift as Nainoa ran to Captain Lyman.

"The starboard hull is flooded!"

The canoe began to heel alarmingly.

"We've got to get the sail down!"

"I dozed," Marion recalls. "It was a big day. I was on and off and the next thing I heard was my brother yelling 'I don't want this to be like another Kaua'i!' I heard his voice raised and I felt the sensation that we are way over on a serious starboard list. Then I heard 'All hands on deck!' "

Tava Taupu had stood the first watch after leaving Honolulu. When he was relieved at midnight, he went below to sleep. He was not seasick. He knew that it would be a long voyage and was determined to conserve his strength. He remembers someone ripping open the canvas door to his *puka* and yelling at him to get up.

"Oh shit, what happened? What happened?"

On deck, Tava joined Leon Sterling. They both felt the canoe lurch to starboard.

"Tava, get your ax," Leon says, "we got to cut the sail free."

Someone says "Wait, wait, wait!"

"Cut 'em, cut 'em," Leon says.

But the captain is in charge of the canoe, Tava thought, *so I better listen to what the captain say.*

"Cut, Tava, cut!" Leon yells.

Lyman wanted to assay the damage. "Tava, go bail the water," he ordered. But when Tava opened the hatch he found it was too late. "I open and all water inside," he remembers. "All the hull is full."

"We just started bailing," remembers Curt Sumida, "but we couldn't bail fast enough."

"The first thing I saw when I get on deck," says Marion, "is Norman Pi'ianai'a with a five-gallon bucket trying to bail the after compartments on the starboard side, and it was very clear to me that as fast as he was bailing the water was coming in faster and I leaned over the side and puked."

"We tried to turn the canoe downwind," Nainoa remembers. "It was a mistake. The hull was so flooded that when the waves came from astern they came right through the canoe. We rounded back up."

"The sails were strapped in and every wave lifted the windward hull," Bruce remembers, "and the leeward hull, which was already flooded, picked up more water and it was getting heavier and heavier. Eventually the leeward hull was totally flooded and underwater, and then the canoe just stopped because there was so much drag. But the sails were still full and loaded with pressure."

"We tried to cut the shrouds, to get the pressure out of the sail because it was trying to turn us over," Nainoa says, "But it was too late. The canoe was too sluggish to turn into the wind."

"And right after that," says Bruce, "and it didn't take a long time—the wind in the sails just pushed the canoe over."

"Maybe if I listen to Leon the canoe no go down," Tava says, thinking back on the accident. "But the sail catch the water and the canoe turn on her back. That's why she swamp. One hull in the water. If I cut the sail, the bow of the canoe would stay in the wind. But now the boom catches the water, the sail catch the water. The canoe turns around and then swamp."

Nainoa remembers the whole thing in slow motion—the starboard hull slowly sinking and the port hull rising out of the water. The crew scrambled to windward, trying to keep the hull from flipping, but with a slow ungainly motion it kept coming. "By now everybody was on deck. Most of them were perched on the windward port hull. Everyone scrambled to the windward side. When it turned over, we were on the leeward side. We were perched on the keel of the canoe."

"It just happened in seconds," says Snake Ah Hee. "The whole thing just kind of flipped over like a Hobie Cat. A big canoe like that—it just went over. When the canoe was flipping over, I tried to go over to the other side, crawling up the deck. I made it. I grabbed the bottom of the canoe, the keel, and went over on the hull. I was just hanging on."

As the port hull came over, Kiki saw John Kruse cut himself out of his *puka* and free fall into the foaming ocean. "When we went over it was real slow motion. It was like one big swell and one big puff of wind just teamed up together and the next thing we're crawling up the side of that hull as it was coming up. We were just crawling up to get to the top which is now the bottom."

"When the canoe was swamped there weren't a whole lot of decisions being made," Nainoa recalls. "There was no way to communicate. We were sitting on the keel of the canoe. Windy. Rough. You can't really talk to each other. There really wasn't a lot of leadership because there wasn't much to do, just keep calm. But I was pretty young. I was pretty afraid."

Kiki Hugho remembers being in the water with Eddie Aikau on his right and Snake Ah Hee on his left. "We would dive under every wave and when we surfaced we would feel for each other to make sure the guy was next to you again. It was pitch black. We were getting weaker and weaker."

"No matter if you got your foul weather gear your body cannot handle that cold," Snake remembers. "For myself I knew that we had water in the canoe. We had food in the canoe. You don't have to worry about that. The only thing you have to worry about is the ocean because your body can take so much and that's all."

Sam Ka'ai could see that Marion was in trouble. She clung to the side of the canoe, throwing up into the swells. When Sam swam over to her he saw that she was shivering and weak.

"Put this on," he told her, helping her into a life jacket. He knew she could not last much longer in the water, so he helped her climb up on top of the overturned hull.

"I remember looking up at the stars," says Marion, "Do you know the story of the Little Prince? The stars laugh—but it's a joyful laugh. I looked up at the stars and I felt like they were laughing at us—but a mocking laugh."

A slender catwalk extended down the outboard side of each hull. When the canoe was upright, it was used by crew members to tend the shrouds. Now, with the canoe overturned, it was a welcome place for them to stand with the top half of their body out of the water. "So we are standing on the running board and holding on to the top," Snake recalls. "What we did was tie a rope in back of us from one end to the other so that if you fall asleep at least you're secured to the canoe so that you don't go in the water." "We're hanging onto the hull," says Marion. "We're about thigh deep. Standing on that running board. I just started throwing up on this guy and I felt bad. At first I worried that I was going to die, and then I began to worry that I wasn't."

"We were all facing downwind in the shelter of the hull standing on the catwalk," Bruce recalls, "and we were somewhat sheltered from the wind but every hour or so you heard a huge wave breaking. We were drying off and here comes a wave and it buried the whole canoe. Just rolled right over the canoe and us and soaked everybody."

The crew wore foul weather gear but it was not made to keep the water out under these conditions. No matter how they tried, seawater entered through their collars and the openings for their hands. The gear was better than nothing, but not much. It was obvious to everyone clinging to Hōkūle'a's hull that Marion was getting weaker. Someone got the canoe's surfboard and made her lie down on it. She had lost a lot of fluid. She was shivering uncontrollably.

The canoe carried a waterproof emergency radio, known to World War II pilots as a "Gibson Girl" because of its curvaceous shape. The device is powered by hand cranks and is designed to send out an emergency SOS. Norman Pi'ianai'a cranked the thing like hell. It was a simple transmitter, not a receiver, so there was no way to know if the signals were being heard.

At dawn on March 17th, the crew had been in the water for six hours. As the sun rose higher, Nainoa noticed that small baitfish had gathered in the shade of the canoe's upside-down hulls. A few hours later, *mahimahi* began to feed on them. A food chain was being established. "A swamped object is going to float with the current so the bait, which are not fast swimmers, can stay with it. And with all that stuff in the water there were plenty of places for them to hide. The first big fish I noticed was a *mahimahi*. It was like in the Doldrums, if there's no wind we get *mahimahi* in the canoe's shade on the first day of drifting. We get sharks by the second day."

Leon Sterling organized a team to dive beneath the hulls and cut away pieces of canvas to use as padding so his crewmates could climb on top of the hulls to get out of the water. Marion recalls leaning against Tava for support with her legs wrapped around Norman so she wouldn't fall over the side. On the other end of the canoe Dr. Charman Akina was also sick.

"We had been looking forward all night to morning because we thought we would be getting the inter-island flights," Marion recalls, "but we were out of the air traffic pattern. There were no flights." The canoe had overturned in the turbulent Moloka'i Channel about seventeen miles from the nearest land— the small island of Lāna'i. Eddie Aikau suggested he paddle there for help. But the seas were rough, the currents strong and the winds fierce. Captain Lyman refused. "We'll stay together," he said.

"The person I really admire was Sam Ka'ai," Snake recalls. "He was just playing like. He was treading water, going swimming, and going to get this, going to get that. I would think he would be the one guy who would panic, but he was right in there to help."

Sometime that morning, Snake took a surfboard and went off without asking. "I had a feeling that somebody had to get help. So, not telling anybody, I grabbed the surfboard and paddled towards O'ahu. You could barely see it." Shortly after he left, an airplane flew overhead. The pilots did not see the canoe, but Snake heard it and thought maybe they had, so he came back. "That's why I turned around and went back to the canoe. I went pretty far. I could see everybody real small." As it turned out, the plane probably saved Snake's life.

During the night, the crew had seen the lights of passing boats and tried to signal with flares. Some fizzled uselessly. No one had seen the ones that worked properly. During the morning of the first day, the wind continued unabated. Gale Force. The canoe drifted to the southwest, away from land and shipping lanes and the flight paths of airliners.

On the maps of airline pilots are pictured wide blue swaths of airspace called Victors in the parlance of aviators. Though the crew did not know it, the strong winds and currents had already pushed *Hōkūle'a* across two of the most heavily traveled air paths in Hawai'i. Victor two and Victor twenty were flown by almost every airliner traveling from the Big Island to O'ahu, but no one had seen them. Soon, the canoe would be in open ocean with the next landfall thousands of miles away.

"There was a cold north wind," Nainoa remembers. "It was wintertime. People were wet. Hypothermia was an issue. Exhaustion was an issue. Panic was an issue. Sharks were beginning to be an issue. Small sharks are less likely to bite but they are more dangerous because they're more active. But the big shark— those are the man-eaters. But they are slow, they will take their time."

"I looked around and saw that people were getting weaker and weaker," Bruce recalls.

For a while, Eddie Aikau patiently obeyed Captain Lyman's orders to stay with the canoe. But Eddie was a lifeguard. He felt obliged to save his comrades shivering in the cold northerly wind. About mid-day, after a meeting during which the captain relented, Eddie set out for Lāna'i—then a distant mountain peak almost lost in the wind-driven spume. The crew joined hands and said a *pule*—a prayer—for him.

"Eddie convinced David that he could make it," Nainoa remembers. "I was conflicted about it. We're tired, we're somewhat in shock, we're in denial. It was emotionally draining. I swam out with him and he had his life jacket on. We gave him some *poi* and bananas, and I swam with him for a little way, talking to him. I saw that he was scared but that he was committed. I grabbed his hand and held real tight. Then he paddled away. I swam back to the canoe. I remember him taking his life jacket off and throwing it away because he couldn't paddle with it. Eighteen miles to Lāna'i. A long distance in that kind of wind. Small craft warnings."

"Within five minutes of his leaving, the life jacket floats back," Marion recalls. "As he leaves we are all holding hands and saying a *pule* for him."

At about three o'clock Marion is aroused from her stupor by one of the crew yelling.

"A ship! A ship is coming!"

She watched the ship steam directly toward the canoe. Rescue was surely at hand. Eddie had made it! He was bringing help! Dave ordered day flares to be sent up. Some of the crew signaled with mirrors. Everyone was standing, waving, yelling, signaling with whatever came to hand. When the ship was only about a quarter of a mile away, she turned and steamed off. No one was on deck.

On shore, Ben Finney spent most of the day caught up in his normal professorial routine at the University of Hawai'i. Walking from his office to his first morning lecture, he felt the gusting wind tugging at his shirt—a constant reminder of the canoe somewhere at sea. He worried. "So I called up the PVS office to see how they were doing. I called up and they said, 'Oh, we don't know.' "

"Don't you have radio contact with them?"

"No, they're probably observing radio silence because they want to sail naturally."

"It was blowing like hell. I could see huge white caps all over the place. Someone said, 'Ben, relax, someone else is in charge.' That night I went to bed sort of unsettled. And still the same weather."

By sunset on March 17th, the crew realized their situation had become grave. "When the night came on we were all worried," says Bruce, "how is this going to play out? We were slowly drifting south and out of the air and shipping lanes and into the open ocean." The wind had not died at all, maybe even freshened. They dived under the hulls to retrieve food and water. The water, sealed in jugs, was still pure but most of the food was spoiled. They were cold, and hungry, and afraid for their lives. They were also afraid for Eddie. "I remember that I am on top of this hull and the guys are diving down and getting buckets—and cookies, and cigarettes and water—in the watertight buckets," Marion says. "I tried to drink water but I couldn't keep anything down. I lost it. I remember just chanting in my head all day—'Go Eddie go—go Eddie go—go Eddie go'—just trying to send him energy."

Sometime during that night, after many hours in the water, Tava had a vision. "When I'm in the water I see him. He come to me. His face comes to me in my dream. But he look like my mother. I'm thinking to myself—'Why? What's that?' At the time I am thinking too much for Eddie. When he left from the canoe I stay sleepy, but I never sleep. I can hear everything going on around me, but my mind is already asleep. My face is right up against the top of the canoe. I am thinking of Eddie. Everybody thinking of Eddie. In my dream I see a face which looks like my mother. The hair comes down, *hinahina*—white hair. 'Shit,' I think, 'something very strong.' My family had strong power like in the old *kāhuna*. 'Mom,' I say, 'it's my turn. It's mine this one. Mom you leave me alone.' It looks like my mom but it is Eddie. 'Mom you *pau* (finished) already, you *moemoe* (sleeping).' But it was not my mom, it was Eddie. He *pau* already, see? Eddie was not supposed to let go the life vest but he had an idea that he be more free. The wind was maybe fifty miles an hour. High swell. He was a good guy. Me and him. I meet him one week before. The following week we go on the sea to Tahiti."

At nightfall, the crew began to see the blinking lights of inter-island flights passing overhead. With each flight, Dave and Leon fired off parachute flares. They arced high in the sky and descended slowly—lighting up the ocean around the canoe. No one saw them. The flights continued on. "They would go behind us and then go in front of us," Marion remembers, "We would get excited and say 'Here comes another one.' It got to the point that nobody got excited about it when they came over."

RESCUE

Chapter Twenty-Four

At about 8:00 p.m. on the evening of March 17th, Captain Art Dageling, fifty-five years old, a veteran of thirty-two years of flying, commanded Hawaiian Air flight 607 out of Kona. His takeoff had been unexpectedly delayed for two minutes, so his co-pilot, Butch Avalone, had calculated a new flight plan to make up the time—a slightly shorter route at a reduced altitude. In spite of the gusting winds, the flight had been smooth and Dageling was looking forward to ending a long day in the cockpit. Throttling back to begin his descent to Honolulu, he performed a habitual scan of his instruments and then turned his gaze out the window in a perfunctory check of his aircraft. Just as he was about to turn back to the flight deck he caught sight of a flickering light below his port wing. A light where there should be no light. He circled once to confirm the sighting. He got Butch to confirm it too. Then he alerted Honolulu Tower.

"Are you sure you saw something?" the tower radioed back.

"There's something down there," he said, "but I don't know what."

Dageling descended to 7,000 feet and began circling the spot where he had seen the light. He saw a flare rise from the dark ocean, reach its apogee and begin to descend.

Dageling confirmed the sighting of a vessel in distress—and its location—to Honolulu Tower. The tower relayed the report to Coast Guard Rescue Center at Barber's Point.

"They shoot a flare," Marion recalls, "and they shoot again. And they shoot one more time and the plane banks. It circles us once. And it circles us twice."

It's cold down there, Dageling thought. He circled. He wanted to be sure that whoever it was knew they had been sighted. He turned his landing lights on and off—sending a Morse code message that spelled out "okay."

"The plane kept losing altitude and it came straight towards us and it blinked its lights three times," Bruce recalls. "They had seen us."

A commercial aircraft is not equipped for ocean rescue. Captain Dageling had a load of passengers who wanted to get home. He had notified the Coast Guard. There was nothing more to do. "The saddest thing I had to do was say, 'Well, whoever you are, I hope you're thoroughly convinced somebody will be out to help you' and fly away."

Like all aviators, Captain Dageling was a man steeped in engineering, in the practicalities of applied science. He knew all about thrust, power-to-weight ratios, sink rates, wing loading, aerodynamics. In his business of ferrying trusting passengers tens of thousands of miles each year, he was not prone to superstition. He relied instead on Pratt and Whitney, Boeing Aircraft Company, and accepted aviation procedure. Still—there was something inexplicable in his looking out that window at just the right time. Thinking back on it later, he recalled the sky was thirty-five percent overcast. When he passed over the canoe she was in a clear space between layers of cloud. Thinking about that, he remembered the two-minute delay in receiving take-off clearance—a rare event in his experience. If he had taken off two minutes earlier, would the canoe have been visible or would clouds have obscured her? Impossible to tell. Most people on the ground think that an airplane flying overhead must be able to see them. Sometimes land-bound admirers wave. But the waves are almost never seen. A commercial pilot sits before a dizzying array of instruments that occupy his attention. He rarely looks out. If he does, his field of view is severely constricted by a narrow windshield, the placing of the cockpit high on the fuselage, the wings. What if he had not begun his descent—a nose down attitude that provided a better view of things below the aircraft? "When you take all the factors involved," he said later to a Honolulu Star Bulletin reporter, "it would make a heckuva project for some math class. You've got the angularity of our approach, the size of the windshield, the cloud cover, our speed, the duration of the flare, the amount of traffic..."

Late in the evening of Friday, March 17th, or early in the morning of the 18th, someone aboard Hōkūle'a heard the first whirring of helicopter blades. Soon a bright light was switched on, almost blinding the bedraggled survivors clinging to the canoe's upturned hulls. A basket descended from the helicopter's winch. Nainoa swam to the basket and retrieved a radio from it, then swam back and gave it to Captain Lyman.

"Do you read us?" Dave said into the microphone.

No answer. Dave figured the radio was able to transmit only.

"If you read us, blink your lights."

The helicopter's lights blinked.

"Have you seen or heard from Eddie Aikau? If yes, blink once. If no, blink twice."

Two blinks.

"There is a man out there on a surfboard somewhere. He has a strobe light. You need to search for him."

One blink.

"Within minutes we see another helicopter coming from Honolulu on a search pattern," Marion recalls. "I am the first one to swim to the basket—they take five of us up. I got in the helicopter and they wrapped an army blanket around me and I was out. I was out."

"When we were rescued there were already sharks there," Nainoa remembers, "and rightfully so because it was over twenty-seven hours. I saw the sharks at night in the light of the helicopter. I didn't tell anybody; they would freak out. We were up on the hull but to get to the helicopter basket you had to swim."

At about 3:00 a.m., the Coast Guard cutter *Cape Corwin* found the stricken canoe and took her under tow. Three men had stayed behind—Captain David Lyman, first mate Leon Sterling, and navigator Norman Pi'ianai'a. They transferred to the cutter to help with the towing operation. By first light on March 18th everyone had been rescued from the water. Everyone—except Eddie Aikau.

❖ ❖ ❖ ❖ ❖

Wally Froiseth and his wife Moku lived on the flanks of Diamond Head, inland—or *mauka* as Hawaiians say—from the city of Honolulu. The house was a simple bungalow with a tiny yard, but Wally's verandah gave out over a magnificent view of the skyscrapers along Waikīkī and the ocean beyond. Like Finney, he had gone to bed with a scene of frothing ocean in his mind. At 1:00 a.m. his telephone rang. "*Hōkūle'a* has capsized. They're bringing in the crew by helicopter to the old airport." Wally dressed and drove through silent streets. *At least it seems like the crew is okay,* he thought. *Did they all make it? Where's the canoe? Has she been damaged?*

Eddie Aikau's brother Solomon, his sister Myra and his parents—Mom and Pops Aikau—had also driven to the airport in Eddie's green Volkswagen.

"I saw the helicopter come in and drop people off, dressed in their yellow rain gear," Myra recalls. "I saw John Kruse get off the chopper and he was devastated. They couldn't talk to us. There was so much media attention. I remember Michael Tongg coming up to me. He said 'I have something to tell you.' He whispered in my ear, 'Eddie went for help and we haven't found him yet.' I told Mom and Pops that Eddie was missing. My mom was devastated. But what are you going to do—you have to tell them. So I did."

Wally was in the crowd watching the helicopter land. There was nothing he could do for the crew or their families, so he turned his attention to the canoe. He went to the nearest pay phone and called Paul Gay, a friend who owned a sampan called *Hauoli Imua.*

"*Hōkūle'a* is down off Kaho'olawe someplace. We need somebody to tow her back."

"I'll meet you at the dock at Kewalo Basin," Gay said.

"One kid wanted to go with us," Wally recalls. "It was just the three of us. They gave us the position and we got out there at daybreak, and the canoe is upside down, stuff floating around. The Coast Guard was towing her sideways. I dove down and went under with my knife to cut off some of the stuff but the lines were all hanging, and the canoe was moving in the swells and I got worried. I cut off a spar and a mast and they floated free and we put them on the boat."

"It's too dangerous," Gay said. "You'll get caught under there."

Wally decided to take over the tow from the Coast Guard. He released the line from the cutter.

"Thanks for your help, but we've got it now," he told them.

Gay and Wally made a bridle from the bow of the sampan to ease the strain. Slowly, with infinite tenderness, Gay pushed the throttle forward. The towrope went taut. *Hōkūle'a,* encumbered by her dangling mast and rigging, turned to follow them.

❖ ❖ ❖ ❖ ❖

At first light on Saturday, the Coast Guard launched a helicopter and a C130 aircraft to search for Eddie. The Civil Air Patrol sent up two planes. The skies had cleared, but the bright sunlight revealed whitecaps from one horizon to the next.

Eddie's brother Solomon Aikau, David Bettencourt, and Nainoa Thompson flew in a helicopter with pilot Tom Hauptman to search for Eddie. "It was blowing, choppy, whitecaps, the wind was blowing from thirty knots to fifty knots," Solomon recalls. "It was windy. And ugly. Looking at the ocean was just like looking into a washing machine. It was terrible, terrible."

"I was obsessed with trying to find Eddie," Nainoa remembers. "We flew all over the place. We were about twenty miles south of O'ahu when we saw an object in the water. We went down low over the ocean. It was a surfboard tumbling in the white water. We looked carefully. There was no one there. You can't imagine the tension and the pain. The pilot flew up to make radio contact so we could get a position. Then we went back down. We couldn't find the board." They circled to the limit of the chopper's fuel, then returned to the helipad. The surfboard was a bad sign, but not a terminal one. Nainoa did not get enough of a look to say definitely that it had been Eddie's board. *You often find surfboards floating around the islands,* he thought. *People are always losing them.*

❖ ❖ ❖ ❖

Looking out through the sprayshield of his sampan, Paul Gay could now see the familiar rim of Diamond Head and the hotels at Waikīkī. He adjusted his course toward Keʻehi Lagoon, a sheltered yacht basin a few miles west of downtown Honolulu. Wally could not take his eyes off the canoe straining at the towrope behind the lumbering sampan. To anyone else, she would have appeared damaged beyond repair. But Wally was an optimist. He knew better. When the sampan and *Hōkūleʻa* entered Keʻehi's sheltered waters, a crowd had gathered.

"Everybody was crying and mourning," Wally remembers. "Oh god, it was really emotional. 'We lost the *Hōkūleʻa*. She's gone.' We didn't lose *Hōkūleʻa*! I knew we could fix her up."

Wally's first task was to turn the canoe over. Other men might have thought of a crane, but Wally had righted many overturned catamarans in his day. Nothing to it, really. "The water in Keʻehi is shallow, all we had to do was put a line on the canoe, around the hulls, and tow it fast. Everything just drags on the bottom until it fetches up, and if you tow fast enough and don't stop, the canoe will flip over. And that's just what she did."

Soon after the accident it seemed like everyone in Hawaiʻi had an opinion about its causes—most were contradictory.

"The hulls are not watertight."
"You can't make the hulls watertight; they have to flex in the waves and that always pops out the caulking."

"So put flotation bladders in the compartments so she can never sink."
"We can't—we stow all the food in the compartments."

"The crew was not trained for the voyage. The captain made a lot of mistakes."
"The crew and captain were good—things like that just happen when you go to sea."

"She was overloaded."
"She was fine—right on her marks."

"You don't sail in a gale of wind like that."
"She's sailed in worse."

◇ ◇ ◇ ◇ ◇

The search for Eddie continued for five days. Myra Aikau, Eddie's sister, kept vigil with her mother in the Aikau compound on Oʻahu. "John Kruse went looking for him" she recalls. "Our friends, David Bettencourt and Boyce Brown, were looking. We knew so many people and they were all helping us. They went to Lānaʻi. They went to Molokaʻi. And there were people on those islands who were searching with boats and cars. Ricky Grigg was here, an oceanographer, and he spent hours and hours with maps plotting where Eddie might have drifted to."

Psychics joined in the search and many called the Aikau home. Some said that Eddie was still alive—he had made it to shore and was in a cave on one of the islands.

"We made a search that took maybe five days," Solomon recalls. "It took us to Kauaʻi, Hawaiʻi, Molokaʻi, Lānaʻi and we looked in these caves for Eddie. You go into these caves and you call for him. Then you have to come home and Mama is of course waiting to hear if we found him or not. That was the worst part. You got to come home and say, 'No, not today, Ma.' We went to Kauaʻi and one of our friends, Boyce Brown, rapelled down a cliff to explore some caves, and he fell and broke his leg. And so we had to get him back up, through the pastures, to the highway and then get him to the hospital in Kauaʻi. When we came home, Daddy said, 'That's it, that's a sign. Somebody got hurt. Let him go.' That's actually what stopped us from continuing to look for him."

On Wednesday, March 22nd, the Aikau family held a news conference. The search for Eddie would be called off so as not to endanger any more lives. A spokesman said the family hoped that "Eddie's love for *Hōkūleʻa* will not be lost. They hope it will continue to be a symbol of Hawaiian unity and will be used to educate the young."

At that moment, however, *Hōkūleʻa's* fate was very much in doubt. More than fifteen thousand dollars of supplies and equipment had been lost. The canoe was a shambles of broken masts and torn rigging. It would cost a lot to rebuild her. A life had been lost. Was it worth the risk to try again?

"It was a very confusing time," Nainoa remembers. "We had to decide whether it was worth the risk to continue voyaging. We had to figure out exactly what went wrong, and how to avoid it ever happening again. What I most remember about that time was my flight in the helicopter looking for Eddie. I will never forget that sight—a surfboard tumbling in the sea, over and over again."

EDDIE'S DREAM

Chapter Twenty-Five

Ke'ehi Lagoon is a forlorn place, a crease in O'ahu's south coast under the path of jets landing at Honolulu International Airport. The lagoon is bordered by assorted junkyards protected by chain link fences and barking dogs, encircled by a clutter of small businesses catering to the marine trades. Expensive yachts owned by weekend sailors are berthed in a tidy harbor near downtown Honolulu a mile or so to the north. The ones anchored in Ke'ehi are of two distinct types: proud veterans seeking temporary shelter from hard-won miles cruising the Pacific, and their dreary cousins, the abandoned casualties of fantasy slowly settling into green slime at their waterlines. If such boats could speak they would have had a sympathetic word for *Hōkūle'a* as she was towed past them followed by a tangle of ruined rigging.

The mood among onlookers at Ke'ehi was stunned silence. Many stood immobilized by the canoe's wreckage bobbing in the gentle swell. Others helped bring bits and pieces ashore, struggling with the two masts and the spars that had been cut away from the upturned hulls. There were soggy bags of rice, remnants of sail, duffel bags, waterlogged guitars and *'ukulele*. A *pū*, a conch shell trumpet, was handed up to its owner, crewmember Sam Ka'ai. Someone tuned one of the *'ukulele* and began to play a tune—dirge-like and sad. Night fell. The crew and their helpers continued to work on their stricken canoe, emptying her of debris so she could be brought up on dry land. When the canoe was finally unloaded, she was lifted from the water by a shipyard crane and put in a cradle for repairs.

Almost immediately, the Voyaging Society began an internal inquiry into *Hōkūle'a's* sinking. The Coast Guard and the Honolulu Star-Bulletin initiated their own investigations. Quoting several "yachtsmen with years of experience in open-ocean sailing" who spoke on condition of anonymity, the Star-Bulletin raised several issues. Many criticized Lyman's decision to let Eddie Aikau swim for shore. It's a cardinal sin to leave a ship. Others sympathized with Lyman's dilemma. "How do you prevent a lifeguard from trying to save his fellow sailors?" Besides, it looked like the canoe was drifting away from land and sea lanes, and Eddie's dangerous last swim might have been the only chance they had. Some questioned why the canoe had no life rafts. Others pointed out that she had proven herself seaworthy before and that she would float even when capsized. Some pointed to the pressure that Lyman may have felt to depart, given the intense media presence, the departure ceremonies, and the large crowd. Lyman refused comment but he did say that the weather was not a problem. "We've been in worse weather than that. What happened to us was a fluke, a freak thing."

Many yachtsmen were sympathetic. "I've sailed across the Pacific and not seen a whitecap," said one of them, "and then I've sailed to Moloka'i and wondered if I'd ever get in again." "Nobody wants to sit around being armchair quarterbacks," said another, "because everybody makes mistakes out there. It's just that the price isn't often this high." The mood of the informal board of inquiry was summarized, according to the Star-Bulletin, by one of the assembled captains: "The elements are beyond anything that man can achieve as far as a craft or implement to deal with them. When you go out to sea you're counting on luck. What they were doing is a beautiful cause. But the early Hawaiians surely had success in going from A to B because they were in sufficient number that they were bound to succeed. How many do you suppose failed?"

How many indeed? The question begged an answer. Could *Hōkūle'a* continue to journey if there was the continued risk of life? "The Polynesian Voyaging Society was split into two parties," Nainoa recalls. "One party thought the danger outweighed the purpose of voyaging. The other side recognized the dangers but thought if we don't continue our dreams—Eddie's dreams—then the loss of his life will have no meaning."

On the 18th of May, 1978, the Coast Guard issued its report and it came down like a sledgehammer. "Should the Polynesian Voyaging Society continue with their plans to sail to Tahiti," wrote James W. Moreau, commander of the Fourteenth Coast Guard District, "I intend to declare the sail catamaran *Hōkūle'a*, O.N. 571798, manifestly unsafe for this extended ocean voyage." Manifestly unsafe—what could be clearer than that? Permission was given for limited sailing between the Hawaiian Islands, however, providing changes were made to the canoe's design.

The list of changes was not long, but compliance would mean a lot of work. *Hōkūle'a*'s lashings would be replaced. To keep the water out, hatch covers would be raised and reinforced. The canoe's twin hulls would need to be fitted with bulwarks, planks running along the sides that were designed to keep the seas from coming aboard. But should a large wave actually break over the canoe, the bulwarks would prevent the water from getting out, so they were to be pierced liberally with what sailors call scuppers, holes to drain the water overboard. Finally, should all these precautions fail, the report called for bilge pumps so the compartments could be bailed without removing the hatch covers.

Wally Froiseth is a man of few words. His emotions are expressed in simple declarative sentences, but he most clearly expresses himself in work—and here he demonstrated his love for sailing and the sea and for *Hōkūle'a*. It was not surprising that Wally was the leading force behind *Hōkūle'a*'s rebirth—that he showed up to tow the canoe in, to right her, to set her on her cradle and to begin ministering to her. Amidst the debris of *Hōkūle'a*'s defeat, he simply picked up his tools and got to work. He cleared away the rigging and set the masts aside. He began to remove the miles of lashing that held the '*iako* to the hulls. Leon and Jo-Anne Sterling were there, also John Kruse, Keani Reiner, Bruce Blankenfeld, and Chad Baybayan, and soon others began to show up.

Many of the watertight bulkheads had rotted so the crew removed them. They cut off the old decking. The hull had absorbed water, so they flushed it with acetone to draw the water out. They rigged fans to blow away the fumes and help with the drying—but the fans could only do so much. "The hull was full of toxic stuff," John Kruse recalls. Old fiberglass had to be ground off, down to dry wood, before new glass could be laid on. Then new decking was fashioned, also new hatch covers with high combings to deflect water from entering.

❖ ❖ ❖ ❖ ❖

In their final report, the Coast Guard listed the officers in one place and the crew in another. Under ancient maritime tradition, officers are held to blame for an accident and in this case there were three, David Lyman, Captain; Leon

Sterling, Chief Mate, and Norman Pi'ianai'a, Instrument Navigator. Perhaps because they did not know what to make of Nainoa's position the Coast Guard listed him as "non-instrument navigator." It was a category that separated him from the rest of the crew and it tended to elevate him among the officers and imply that he, too, might have suffered some responsibility. For Nainoa, the question of responsibility did not come down to whether someone else considered that he was to blame; he accepted that he was—by default, by not having taken the responsibility of leadership in the first place.

"On the 1978 voyage, I never allowed myself to take a leadership role other than just say 'Okay, I'm going to navigate to learn.' I just would not let myself do it. There were a whole bunch of reasons for that. First, it would separate me from my peers. And second, I was afraid of failing. So my role was to go as a student navigator and they would record with sextants our positions and if I got too far off course they would tell me where I am and we would start over again. So basically I was guiding the canoe and learning but not taking full responsibility. There's a lot that I don't want to remember. I was angry at myself. I knew damn well we should not have gone in that weather. I was young and not in authority, but I knew it. Guilt and shame were attached to that. Nothing that we have done in the last thirty years or the next hundred will justify Eddie's loss."

"I didn't see Nainoa for at least a month after he came back," Will Kyselka recalls, "he was mourning. He was encapsulated in his grief. He felt guilty. I didn't want to bother him."

Nainoa continued to go out in his skiff to watch the night sky, but even the stars seemed to have changed.

"Nothing seemed real anymore. The idea of navigating or voyaging was gone. When we lost Eddie, the feeling of shame was so strong—how could we go on?"

Then Nainoa recalled a conversation with Eddie after one of the crew gatherings in Honolulu. He told Eddie about his dream of learning to navigate and the insights he was gaining by watching the night sky. Eddie listened intently, murmuring approval.

"I've got a dream, too," Eddie said.

"What is it?"

"My dream is about this voyage. I want to see what my ancestors saw. I want to see Tahiti rise from the sea," Eddie said.

"To see Tahiti rise from the sea is a powerful dream," Nainoa remembers. "It means you are approaching an island by sea and, as you get nearer, it appears to rise up from the ocean's surface. That's what our ancestors saw when they voyaged to Hawai'i and back to Tahiti. That's what I think Eddie meant, that he was going to sail in the path of his ancestors and raise Tahiti from the sea. That's a powerful vision. Eddie gave his life for that vision."

❖ ❖ ❖ ❖ ❖

When Nainoa wanted to talk with his parents he would walk up to their modest ranch house in the Niu Valley and sit at their battered Formica kitchen table. While the two men conversed, Laura often shared her views as she labored over a steaming kitchen stove.

"My parents helped me think through my choices," Nainoa remembers. "I could have gone to the other side and said—'Yeah too dangerous, put the canoe in a museum.' They allowed that choice but they made me think it through. My father asked a lot of questions. He asked me what I thought was important. He talked about beliefs. He wanted me to think carefully and he encouraged me to make a decision about my role because the officers on that voyage were devastated, so they backed away and there was nobody emerging as a leader. Eddie's loss was consuming. It resurrected all the anger in me. But what was I going to do with it? That's when I chose to fully commit myself—to take full responsibility. I'm not going to go out there just to learn—I'm going because of Eddie. Eddie made a courageous decision and went for help. He wasn't afraid to fail. So how could I be? That was personal. It became an obligation, deep inside of me."

"We're going to continue sailing," Nainoa told his father, "and we're going to sail to Tahiti."

Shortly afterwards, Pinky called a meeting of the Polynesian Voyaging Society at the University of Hawai'i Medical School.

"If *Hōkūle'a* does not sail," Pinky told the assembled crewmembers and officers of the society, "if the canoe's legacy is tragedy, that will only confirm the expectation that Hawaiians always fail. You must sail to Tahiti. But the only way

Myron 'Pinky' Thompson

you will succeed is if you have a powerful vision. You need to know the path, where you are going and why you are going there. You need to define the values that will guide you on the path, that will navigate you on your journey, not only to Tahiti but throughout your lives. You need to define your community, and community is never about what separates you from each other—your race or your culture—it's about what binds you together. You need to define a plan for success and every single step of that plan. Ninety percent of success is in preparing for it. Come up with a sail plan and I will hold you to it. Don't talk about departure—you will only go when you are ready. And remember always that this voyage is not for you, it is for your culture. You carry the pride and dignity of all native Hawaiians on your canoe. This voyage is for your children and all the children of Hawai'i."

"That was our map for the future," Nainoa recalls, "that single meeting. He pulled it all together."

Pinky was then fifty-four years old and his career was about to arc into the stratosphere of Hawaiian consciousness. In the next quarter century he would lead Hawaiians in a national fight for recognition as a native people and his efforts would be rewarded with many millions of Federal dollars. But even then, in 1978, he had revealed talents that would enable him to lead *Hōkūle'a* and the Voyaging Society out of the deepest depression in its history. Pinky had served in combat and survived a horrendous head wound. He had graduated from a prestigious eastern college—Colby, in Waterville, Maine—and he had labored for ten years as a social worker to help his people overcome the staggering statistics of ill health and abuse that set them on the lowest rung among all of Hawai'i's ethnic groups. He was chosen by Governor John Burns to head up a number of prestigious committees, had helped write the state's first zoning laws, and had been appointed trustee of the Bishop Estate. The Estate was one of Hawai'i's most powerful organizations. Formed in 1884 by Hawaiian princess Bernice Pauahi Bishop, it controlled about 337,000 acres of land—more land than any other private entity in the islands. The Estate used funds raised from leasing these lands to support a school, Kamehameha, for the education of young men and women of Hawaiian ancestry. If there was ever a lever to move things in ways to help Hawaiians, a Bishop Estate trusteeship was it. Through all this, Pinky had learned a number of things, but perhaps the most important was clarity of thought. He understood the need to state lucidly his objectives and then, by analyzing the risks entailed in achieving them, to develop a strategy to succeed. Pinky's objectives were clear. A Hawaiian had perished at sea and his own son had been put in harm's way. That would never happen again. The canoe had accomplished a goal very close to what Pinky had set as his own, reestablishing an eroding pride among Hawaiians. He was now joining his son in a new mission—to be the first Hawaiian to guide a voyaging canoe to Tahiti and back. "If Nainoa was going to commit to guide *Hōkūle'a* to Tahiti," Pinky remembers, "I was going to back him up and be sure that he had the best chance possible of success."

On July 12th, after four months in dry dock, *Hōkūle'a* was launched and taken to Pier Twelve in the Port of Honolulu. Under Wally's supervision, with a Coast Guard inspector on hand, the canoe's seaworthiness was tested. Tons of water were pumped aboard to determine her buoyancy and the integrity of her watertight bulkheads. Heavy weights were used to tip her to port and starboard, testing her stability. She passed the test easily and was declared fit for sea.

Her first voyage was a solemn one. She sailed to the place where she had capsized and hove to as her crew laid flowers on the ocean to honor Eddie Aikau.

Procy
Canis Min
Wezen
Adhara
Canis Major
Sirius
Monoceros
Mirzam
Lepus
Betelgeuse
Alnitak
Alnilam
Rigel
Orion
Bellatrix

THE SHAPE OF THE SKY

Chapter Twenty-Six

Nainoa began to prepare for the voyage by returning to the Bishop Museum Planetarium to huddle with Will Kyselka. They knew that Mau found his place on Earth by "the shape of the sky," but what shapes did he perceive when he looked up from his canoe? And how did he read the clues in them? Mau was lost to the cause, thousands of miles away in Satawal, having vowed to never return to Hawai'i, so they must proceed on their own. But they had some clues—the result of Nainoa's observations in Tahiti and aboard the canoe on the way back to Hawai'i.

On July 13th, aboard *Hōkūle'a*, Nainoa had written in his log: "Beginning to think of the sky as a whole, a painted globe and each star has its own place all moving together as we move north. The globe seems to pivot on an east and west axis. Dipper getting higher and the Cross getting lower." The key to reading the sky's shape was right there, but it had been hidden in a clutter of details. Now, accompanied by the sound of whirring gears as Will maneuvered the planetarium to present differing views of the sky, Nainoa recalled the curious observation he had made that night in Tahiti—of stars setting together on the horizon. "In Hawai'i, I noticed that Sirius always set before Pollux," he recalls, "but when I went to Tahiti, Sirius and Pollux set together and I was puzzled by that. I knew the answer was in latitude but I did not understand it."

"That was a moment of insight," Will recalls, "and once he got that insight his task was to investigate it. He reasoned that 'Okay, so if you go north the horizon is going to tip and one of those stars is bound to set before the other.'"

Nainoa knew that his view of the sky changed with latitude because the visible horizon was tangent to Earth's surface and it tilted north as he moved north. That's why the North Star rose and the Southern Cross sank behind him as he sailed from Tahiti to Hawai'i. But the planetarium allowed him to actually see that effect and to test his theory that stars setting together might

Planetarium view of the sky

be a clue to latitude. And so one evening Will and Nainoa settled into a long night of observations.

"Okay, Will, let's check the sky in Tahiti."

The Spitz Ball moved to a precise position that would replicate the view from Papeete—eighteen degrees south latitude. Will programmed it for late June, 1976, the time when Nainoa first made his observations of Tahitian skies. The two men focused on the wall behind them where a large W was projected to indicate the western horizon. The ball began to spin slowly, projecting the setting stars on the curved ceiling. At twilight, Orion had already set—or almost. Saiph, in the constellation's left leg, was still visible. To the left, the Big Dog and its bright eye, Sirius, dominated the horizon. To the right were The Twins with Pollux trailing behind Castor. The gears whirred. The constellations descended. At 6:40 p.m. local Tahitian time, Sirius and Pollux arrived at the horizon together.

"That's it,' said Nainoa.

"Yes it is," Will said.

When Sirius and Pollux set simultaneously, the observer is at 18 degrees South latitude

To study the difference that thirty-nine degrees of latitude will make, Will programmed the Spitz for Honolulu—twenty-one degrees north. Keeping the time set at 6:40 p.m., they observed that the sun had not quite set in Honolulu but there was Sirius right on the horizon. Pollux, however, was still high in the sky. A little more than two hours of simulated time was required before Pollux approached the horizon. "It was a really exciting observation," Nainoa recalls. "The difference was so great. Here was something that clearly might work to tell latitude."

During the next few weeks, Nainoa and Will carefully worked on the theory they now called "simultaneous setting." They traveled in accelerated time from Tahiti to Hawai'i and back again. At fifteen degrees north latitude, they saw Mirzam and Betelgeuse set together. They moved south, one degree at a time. At six degrees north they observed Alhena and Adhara set together; at three and a half north it was Alhena and Sirius; at six south, Alhena set with Mirzam. Laboriously, over a period of many nights, they made a list of eleven pairs of simultaneously setting stars—celestial steppingstones on the way to Tahiti.

But even as he gained knowledge from the Planetarium's artificial stars, from books, and from naked eye observation late at night, Nainoa knew that something was missing from his training. His ancestors had spent their lives at sea so they had an instinctual relationship to the ocean. Only one man could teach him that—Mau Piailug. "When Mau went back to Micronesia I lost my teacher," Nainoa says. "There were no others like him—his skill and knowledge were unique. He knew the sea in the old instinctual way. It was essential that he join us."

MAU

Chapter Twenty-Seven

In June, Nainoa learned that Mau was visiting relatives in Saipan. He decided to fly there to ask him to be his teacher. For centuries, Saipan had been a refuge for people from the Caroline Islands. The Carolines are mostly low coral atolls and they lie in Typhoon Alley, a highway of storms that often attain one hundred and fifty miles an hour of wind. When a typhoon strikes a low atoll, it sweeps the island clear of houses and canoes. The survivors take refuge in breadfruit trees; when they descend they find their gardens and everything in them wilted and dying. This is one reason for the perseverance of navigators and sailing canoes. They are lifeboats. They ferry some of the stricken islanders to temporary refuge on other atolls and bring back saplings and seeds to replant their gardens. After a particularly vicious storm in 1815, many Carolinians picked up and moved permanently to the high island of Saipan and even more moved there, including some from Satawal, after a series of storms in the early 1900s.

Nainoa's trip to Saipan was a measure of his commitment to Eddie and to his crewmates. It was proper protocol for a Micronesian student to ask a master navigator for instruction, but it was altogether another matter for Nainoa to ask Mau to come to Hawai'i to spend months as his teacher. What would Mau think of such a request? "Who was I to be asking him to give us his time and his knowledge?" Nainoa recalls. "When he left Tahiti he had written a letter to us—'Don't look for me, you will never find me.' But I knew that to succeed we needed Mau's help. I needed to make the request."

From the Saipan airport, Nainoa took a taxi out to the Carolinian settlement, an unprepossessing village of cinder block walls and tin roofs. "Mau and I walked on the beach by ourselves and sat down on a log to talk," Nainoa recalls. "He knew about the swamping and Eddie's death."

Nainoa told Mau about his recent efforts to study the stars. He told him that the Voyaging Society would make another trip to Tahiti in 1980 and that he planned to navigate "in the old way." They spoke in broken English, communicating as best they could with gestures and the few words they shared, yet somehow Mau was able to convey his thoughts. He let Nainoa know that he regretted his decision to not sail to Hawai'i with the new crew. They were young; perhaps they would have been better than the first crew. Still, at the time, he considered the risk was too high. As the conversation was nearing its end, Nainoa gathered his courage to speak plainly to Mau.

"I told him that the voyage was very important, but I didn't tell him why—that was very personal—a strong obligation to Eddie and his family. Without Mau I knew that we could not meet our commitment to navigate as our ancestors did. And the only way we would earn the right to make the voyage, was by sailing in the old way."

"We need you—not to find Tahiti for us—but to help us find it for ourselves," Nainoa told Mau.

"We'll see," was all that Mau said.

Nainoa returned to Hawai'i on the afternoon flight the next day. He remembers thinking that Mau was "finished with Hawai'i—that he had decided he was not going to voyage with us any more."

◇ ◇ ◇ ◇ ◇

When Mau had returned to Satawal after the voyage to Tahiti, he was greeted coldly by the chiefs and other navigators. He had expected this. When he accepted the challenge of guiding *Hōkūle'a* through foreign waters and shared his navigational knowledge with Hawaiians, he had broken an ancient cultural prohibition against giving *kkapesen neimatau*—the Talk of the Sea—to outsiders.

In all human cultures, knowledge that has deep survival value attains an aura of sacredness. It is secret knowledge and it is nurtured, protected and sanctioned by spiritual force. And Mau was not just a *palu*—a term that designates a navigator knowledgeable enough to voyage alone—he was a *pwo*—a master of all the arts of navigation. He was, in fact, the last navigator to be initiated as *pwo* on Satawal.

In 1951, when he received *pwo*, Mau was secluded in the canoe house for a week. He entered a spiritual state, guided by the island's master navigators, in which he reflected on his grandfather's teaching which combined technical matters, such as sailing directions, with spiritual ones, such as chants to calm the winds or to strengthen the resolve of his crew. He was in a liminal existence, as anthropologists call it—a fragile place between things—not yet a navigator and yet no longer a normal human being. Tiny communities such as the one on Satawal are places that breed strong human feelings, and those of respect and love jostle with those of jealousy and hate. Magic could be practiced to heal as well as to harm. During his seclusion, as Mau voyaged toward *seram*—the light—he was particularly vulnerable, so he was protected by the magic of the older *pwo* navigators all around him. His knowledge and his worthiness were tested. He was surrounded by symbols of his new status. He was served special foods. During this time of seclusion, an invisible force emanated from the canoe house that the villagers honored by making detours from their normal paths, expressing their respect by keeping their distance. Those were the old ways.

But the old ways were dying on Satawal. Missionaries began arriving in Micronesia in the late 1800s and by the 1940s they were spreading out from the main islands, Chuuk, Palau and Yap—to the outer islands—of which Satawal was among the outermost. The missionaries meant well, and they provided schools and a modicum of healthcare as they endeavored to nurture the minds and bodies of the people they served. But, ultimately, they were the servants of their God and their goal was conversion to the "one true faith." In this effort there was no room for superstition.

"The old ceremonies were stopped when the church came," Mau once said. "That's why I don't like the church, because when the church come, when Christians come, everything is gone. Missing. The people follow the Christians. That's no good. Why are we going to follow customs from outside? Why we throw away our own customs? They throw away medicine, they throw away magic and now it's too late to try pick them up again. Everybody who knew the old customs has passed away."

Only a few young men came to Mau to learn navigation and those who did show up were not totally committed. School education began to replace the traditional way of learning—master to apprentice—and Mau felt the *kkapesen neimatau* fading away.

Mau understood only too well the pull of the outside world on his people. It was because, he often said, it made everything easier. Maps precluded the need to memorize the directions to islands, compasses made the hard task of learning star paths seem useless and old fashioned, and Loran allowed a navigator to guide his vessel by consulting a glowing screen rather than the stars themselves. Houses could be constructed more easily of cinder block and wood that came to Satawal in the cargo hold of a government ship. As he observed these things being carried across the reef and into the canoe-houses on Satawal, he knew that he was watching not only the demise of the art of navigation, but the death of his way of life.

During his stay in Hawai'i, Mau saw first hand what his people's future looked like. He was astonished to see the skyscrapers, the roads clogged with cars and the opulence of the Hawaiian life-style, but what affected him most was the advanced state of decline of Hawaiian culture. Only a rapidly dwindling few knew how to tend a garden or fish for their livelihood. Almost no-one spoke the language, ate the traditional foods, danced the ancient style of *hula*. The irony of it was that in Hawai'i, in this place of cultural loss, he found students eager to learn his knowledge of the stars, waves and currents. By serendipitous accident, he had discovered an opportunity to pass on his art and by so doing to not only revive Hawaiian culture—but to save his own. *If my people regard the outside world with awe*, he thought, *what would happen if they saw that outsiders valued my knowledge of navigation even more?*

✧ ✧ ✧ ✧ ✧

Early in the fall of 1978, Nainoa received a phone call from Ben Fitial, a member of congress in Saipan.

"Mau went back to Satawal after he saw you," Ben told Nainoa, "and then he came back to Saipan. He's flying up to Hawai'i in the next few days."

Nainoa picked up Mau at the airport and drove him to his small rented house in Kuli'ou'ou. "I will train you to find Tahiti because I don't want you to die," Mau told him. "Then I will go home. I came to teach you because I'm afraid for you. But I'm not going to go with you on the voyage." While Mau unpacked, Nainoa cooked dinner. They chatted for a while, then Mau went to bed. "We start class tomorrow," Mau said.

In the morning, Mau gathered stones and palm fronds to make a star compass. Nainoa helped and when the compass was finished he sat down beside

Mau, waiting for the lesson to begin. Nainoa knew that Micronesian apprentice navigators do not take notes—they learn by repetition—and he expected to learn that way as well.

"Go back and get your notebook and write everything down," Mau ordered. "I will tell you a little bit, but write down whatever I tell you so you don't forget."

"When I learn from my grandfather," Mau recalls, "it was hard because at night he told me about the stars—that's all. Just once. The next day I walk around and play but inside me I never forget because he say 'Next night you come back and I see if you know or not.' In Satawal, students have to remember, but here they write it down because they have paper, they have pencil."

Mau chanted the names of the stars and listened as Nainoa chanted them back. Nainoa knew the western names for all the important steering stars, but the Micronesian names were new to him.

"*Tana Mailap*," Nainoa repeated, "*Tana Paiiur, Tan Uliul, Tana Sarapul, Tana Tumur, Tana Mesaru, Talup, Machemeias, Wuliwulilup*," repeating the names of the stars from east to south.

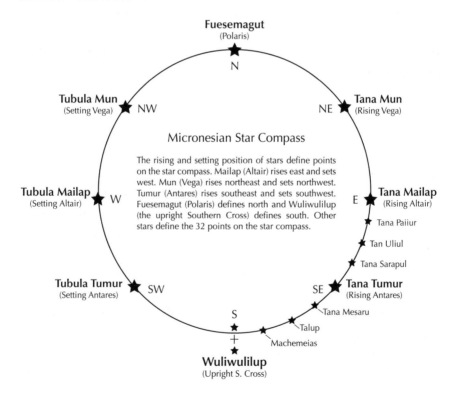

Mau had returned to Hawai'i with serious misgivings. What would the new crew be like? Would they get along at sea? And although he liked Nainoa and trusted his dedication, he was uncertain that he could train him to navigate in such a short time. Harry Ho had befriended Mau in 1976 when, for a time, he had been involved with the *Hōkūle'a* project. But Harry stepped away when he saw the dissention developing between leaders and crew. He had always believed in Nainoa's quest to learn to navigate and now he committed himself to support his young friend. "Mau didn't really know Nainoa that well," Harry recalls, "so I went to speak with him. I told him, 'This guy is serious. Like you, he's putting his life into navigation. This whole thing we are doing now is going to get bigger. You, more than anybody else, can help us.' "

"Harry, I'm worried about my family back home," Mau told him. "How can they get along without me? I think they need some money."

Pinky arranged a stipend for Mau's wife from the Voyaging Society while Harry tended to his other concerns. Mau could not see well with his old glasses, so Harry purchased new ones from a friend in Chinatown. He also gave Mau a new Citizen's watch and when he learned that Mau could write, he bought him a notebook and pen.

"That was typical of Harry," Nainoa recalls. "He took care of everybody."

One night, during the time he was studying in the planetarium, Nainoa had invited Harry over for dinner, forgetting that he had no food in the icebox. "Harry arrived all dressed up and all I had in there was water. He left. The next day the freezer was full of food—Chinese food—frozen wantons, egg rolls, juice. I was out of control with my dreams and Harry was there all the way. Harry donated thousands of man-hours. He represented the new commitment to voyaging that began after the canoe swamped. When we began to train aboard *Hōkūle'a*, Mau discovered there was a whole new chemistry among us. We had a new set of values. Mau could see there were no longer any racial issues among the crew, no fighting for leadership even though I didn't have confidence that I really knew what I was doing. But we all had confidence in Mau. With his training, we knew that we could get to Tahiti and back."

'OHANA[‡]

Chapter Twenty-Eight

"**M**an the tricing lines."

Three crewmembers scurried across *Hōkūle'a's* decks to the foremast, three more to the mizzen. Captain Gordon Pi'ianai'a gave orders just loud enough to be heard above the rush of the canoe moving through Pacific swells.

"Take in the sails."

The men hauled on tricing lines to raise *Hōkūle'a's* boom and gaff and close the sail. Then they used brailing ropes to snug the flapping sail in a neat bundle.

"Stand by to let out the sails."

Taking in and letting out sails are critical because the Pacific Ocean, while not as wild as the Atlantic in winter, is subject to sudden squalls. This is especially true in the Intertropical Convergence Zone, a region of storms in *Hōkūle'a's* path to Tahiti. In a squall, getting the sails in quickly is a key to safety.

For three months now, with November approaching, *Hōkūle'a's* crew had taken in and let out the sails hundreds of times. They had learned to trim them for maximum efficiency—to "lean on the wind." They knew the points of sailing—close-hauled, a close reach, a broad reach and running with the wind. They had mastered the reef knot, sheet bend, bowline, half hitch, rolling hitch, square knot—and they could splice a rope in their sleep. And at night, in heavy seas, they had practiced and re-practiced the man-overboard drill. They knew how to bring the canoe into the wind, to post a lookout to track the man in the water, to deploy the man-overboard-pole, to pay out the rope attached to it, to come about and search downwind for the swimmer.

What spells success in any great enterprise is the ability of many different people to mesh in ways that employ their individual skills in harmony. It's what makes a team. And team-building was what was going on during this period of *Hōkūle'a's* greatest apparent defeat. Those who joined *Hōkūle'a's* crew would

---

[‡] The English translation for *'ohana* is "family."

Crew training aboard *Hōkūle'a*

simply not accept defeat. Harry was one of these people, and so was Wally—but others showed up also.

Snake Ah Hee came from his home in Maui. He had accompanied Nainoa on the 1976 voyage from Tahiti and was aboard when the canoe swamped in 1978, so his return said much about his commitment to voyaging. "Snake is a very quiet guy," Nainoa says of him. "He's uncomfortable talking about what he feels, but he's a very powerful personality. He's a top sailor. He clearly recognizes that when he goes to sea he has made a conscious choice, and that if he doesn't come home it will have been worth the risk. He's fully committed." Among all the crew, Snake was revered for his skill at the steering paddle. In tight situations he was always at the helm. "When he steers," says Sam Ka'ai, "Snake Ah Hee is the backbone and the feet and the nose and the spirit of the canoe."

Tava Taupu, another veteran of the capsizing, came to train from the Big Island. Tava's face is broad and he wears a perpetual look of amused beatitude. Outdoors, he dons gold-rimmed aviator's glasses. Inside, he tips the glasses back on top of his head where they rest uneasily. He has large hands and powerful fingers, yet is delicate of touch. When working, Tava often chuckles quietly to himself. When he listens, he crosses his arms and leans back. He appears pensive and he is quiet. His eyes are full of mischief and humor and they often radiate affection, but you do not want to consider a physical altercation with him. "First impressions of Tava can be off-putting," said one of the crew. "He is clearly a strong man. If you saw him in a dark alley, you would definitely turn around and walk the other way."

Chad Baybayan is about five-feet ten but he seems taller. He has a swimmer's body, suggesting a capacity for powerful strokes and a strong kick. He is dark by genetic makeup—he is half Hawaiian, a quarter Filipino and a quarter Portuguese—and because he spends so much time outdoors swimming and surfing. "I had a great curiosity about voyaging from growing up in Hawai'i," Chad says, "but there was really no way to pursue my curiosity because all the voyaging artifacts of our history and the canoes were all gone by then."

From a newspaper article, Chad learned that Levan Sequeria had formed a group on the Big Island to build a 42-foot coastal sailing canoe called *Mo'olele*. They were looking for volunteers. "I was really a shy kind of kid but I went down because I wanted to get involved so badly. I walked into the garage where they were building the canoe and I said, 'Hey, I want to help. What do you want me to do?' And they threw me into the kind of jobs that nobody wanted, climbing down into the bottom of the hull to sand, fiber-glassing, lashing down the floor boards, but I was just so excited to be part of it that I couldn't sleep at night. I couldn't wait to get up in the morning and work all day long. So I started to learn how to sail on that canoe and I got involved in the launching ceremony, the *'awa* ceremony, and a lot of cultural protocol that I had never been involved in before. I really started to feel my roots being Hawaiian—and it just grew."

Steve Somsen was somewhat of an anomaly among the crew. He was a *haole*, born in New Ulm, Minnesota. He was an ex-Marine. He was fastidious. He was also a sailor. He kept a small sloop in Kāne'ohe Bay and it was aboard this vessel, on a sail from Kāne'ohe to Honolulu, that Nainoa got to know him well. "It was just the two of us on the ocean together. Coming down by Makapu'u we were just smoking. Being out there on this small sailboat—night time, two guys—even though it was a very short experience it was a very intense one." Steve showed up regularly for training sessions. "He was constantly enthusiastic, constantly positive," Nainoa recalls. "I recognized that this guy was here to support us all. I knew that he was not only a good friend to me, he was a good friend to the canoe. There are always times when you're challenged. Someone has a different opinion; someone doesn't believe you can get it done; someone doesn't follow through. There were challenges along the way that raised the question of whether I could do this. But Steve was always just so very positive and supportive."

Another regular on board *Hōkūle'a* was Bruce Blankenfeld. Bruce stands over six feet and he weighs under one hundred and eighty pounds. He is well built but not showy. Thick black hair caps a long handsome face. His eyes are set deep under full lids. His shoulders are large, his waist is slim and his forearms are those of a canoe paddler. After *Hōkūle'a* returned from Tahiti in 1976, Bruce and Nainoa worked together as commercial fishermen. "Bruce is the most natural ocean person I think I have ever met," says Nainoa. "When he leaves the land and goes to sea there is no adjustment time. No nothing. Bruce changes from the land to the ocean by becoming completely relaxed. He calms people down because he's so calm and relaxed himself. If you took the ocean away from Bruce, you would take away half his life. He is just so innately inclined to the ocean."

Shorty Bertelmann had sailed aboard *Hōkūle'a* on the 1976 voyage to

Tahiti. He put his head down, did his job, and stayed out of the fracas. Among Hawaiians, Bertelmann is a famous name. During what is known as "The Overthrow," when *haole* planters deposed Hawaiian Queen Lili'uokalani and established a provisional republic, Henry Bertelmann was prominent in a short-lived rebellion to restore the queen. Bertelmanns are also prominent on the Big Island as *paniolo*—cowboys—herding cattle on the slopes of Mauna Kea. Shorty was singled out by Mau as a man he could entrust with his knowledge. "Shorty is spiritually intense," says Nainoa. "When he goes to sea he is so geared—his whole mind and body are connected—and he is very intense, yet very quiet. He does whatever it takes to succeed and he fights for all of that."

Pat Aiu would sail as ship's doctor. He was thirty-nine years old at the time. Pat spent three years on active duty in the army, serving in Germany from 1966 until 1969. He toured Europe extensively with his family, camping out mostly.

Doctor Pat Aiu.

He completed his residency in 1971 on Oʻahu and then returned to his home island, Kauaʻi. Pat was born the youngest of eight children. He grew up in humble circumstances, living in the Wailua Houselots on Kauaʻi's East Shore. He became the island's first specialist in obstetrics and gynecology and he often traveled to attend patients on tiny Niʻihau island, a unique settlement of pure-blooded Hawaiians. He had a canoe paddler's physique—broad shoulders, well-developed pectorals and large forearms. He carved his own paddles. His full name, Patrick Koon Hung Piʻimauna Charles Aiu, reflected his colorful ethnic background.

Mel Paoa, age twenty-five, came from Molokaʻi—one of the most rural of all the Hawaiian Islands. "Our nearest neighbors were three miles away," Mel remembers. "I grew up as a kid alone on the beach with fish, cattle, horses, dogs, and cats as my playmates. Maybe that's why I'm quiet with people. I'm more easy with kids and animals. The first time I heard about *Hōkūleʻa* was in 1975 when they were doing the island training runs. In that year, they brought *Moʻolele* from Maui and Chad was on board—just a kid out of high school. So we all went sailing together. That was my first time on a sailing canoe. That was the spark that started it."

The same people appeared at the dock every Saturday morning for training cruises aboard *Hōkūleʻa*. It was a process of self-selection. Joining up. Forming a community. The crew found themselves using a Hawaiian word –'ohana—to express it. "An *ʻohana* is an extended family," says Bruce Blankenfeld. "You have that in other cultures, but among Hawaiians it's real strong. I think it comes from our culture of voyaging. For the crew to survive on long voyages they had to take care of each other. And that's what we were learning when we sailed together." Every one of the crew had played team sports but the bond that grew among them was different from what they had experienced on athletic teams. The sea imposed a kind of discipline and a mutual respect that was unique. "Everybody respected everybody's space," Harry remembers. "There was never this competition you have on football or baseball teams. Because of our closeness aboard *Hōkūleʻa* nobody offended anybody."

"When you come on the canoe you separate from your land family and connect with your canoe family," says Mel Paoa. "Every time I sailed I had more people I trusted my life with—Nainoa, Chad, Bruce, Tava. I felt real comfortable with them. The more I sailed with them, the more I got to know their personalities. Their stress level. Sometimes you don't need any verbal communication, it's something special, a sixth sense between each person."

"We were all young and about the same age," says Chad. "We were growing up together. We were not just learning about navigation, but also about life, about leadership, about sailing, and about working with people."

On the first voyage to Tahiti, some crewmembers felt that only 'authentic Hawaiians'—as they defined it—should be allowed aboard the canoe. But now, only three years later, sailing aboard *Hōkūle'a* were men and women of many extractions—Chinese, Filipino, Japanese, Hawaiian, Portuguese, German, English, American. After months of training, they had shared hundreds of hours together during which potential differences between them had become meaningless. "I remember looking around at the crew one day," says Chad, "and it was not just native Hawaiians. We had the entire Hawaiian community on board."

❖ ❖ ❖ ❖ ❖

Pinky Thompson monitored the final selection of crew with the eye of a combat veteran and he liked what he saw. He was particularly pleased with the rainbow hue of the crew's complexions. Pinky knew that to defeat the discrimination that held Hawaiians back for so many centuries, he also had to overcome the anger and frustration that such oppression engendered in his people. It was only natural that Hawaiians resented the presence of *haole* on their canoe—at first—but this would no longer be tolerated.

For Pinky the voyage was about more than proving the scientific truth of his ancestor's seafaring skills; it was about rediscovering their ancient values. In 1974, when he became a Bishop Estate Trustee, he examined the Estate's educational programs which were focused on a single high school on the island of O'ahu—Kamehameha. "Although the Hawaiian children in Kamehameha were doing well," he recalls, "the vast majority of Native Hawaiian children were in public schools and they were not doing well." Carefully studying the will of the estate's founder, Hawaiian Princess Bernice Pauahi Bishop, he found that her intent was to benefit all the children of Hawaiian ancestry, including those in public schools, so he began extending the Estate's programs throughout the six other Hawaiian islands. This effort to reach out was part of an ancient value— *lokomaika'i*, or sharing—that Pinky thought the world needed more of. From the beginning of his professional life, Pinky had looked for continuities between past and present. In his previous job, as Director of the Queen Lili'uokalani Trust, he helped create a book entitled *Nānā I Ke Kumu: Look to the Source* which showed how traditional Hawaiian cultural practices, such as *ho'oponopono*—a way of resolving conflict—continued to be useful ways of achieving a healthy life. What worked for his people in the past, he thought, could work today and into the future. Gradually, he created a holistic vision for what *Hōkūle'a's* voyages might accomplish, all grounded on Hawaiian values. "Before our ancestors set out to find a new island," he said, "they had to have a vision of that island over the horizon. They made a plan for achieving that vision. They prepared themselves physically and mentally, and were willing to experiment, to try new things. They took risks. And on the voyage they bound each other with *aloha* so they could together overcome the risks and achieve their vision. You find these same values throughout the world—seeking, planning, experimenting, taking risks and the importance caring for each other. The values that guided us in the past, are the ones that we should use today and that we will use into the future." They were values, he thought, that would bind together the crew of *Hōkūle'a* and guide them safely to Tahiti. The voyage was not just a way to right past wrongs—it was a journey from anger and fear toward love and courage. Not just for his people—but for all people.

LESSONS FROM THE MASTER

Chapter Twenty-Nine

Under a brightening sky and the glow of arc lamps, boats on trailers converged almost every day at the public boat ramp a few miles from Nainoa's rented house in Kuli'ou'ou. During many such dawns, Nainoa could be found in the cab of his battered pickup truck, with Mau in silent company, maneuvering his 22-foot boat, a Radon especially designed for rough Hawaiian waters, down the ramp and into the ocean. These early morning ventures had been routine for the last four years of fishing trips but now it was part of what Nainoa called his "total ocean immersion program" with Mau. "In the ocean immersion period, I paddled, worked as a commercial fisherman and studied navigation—that was it," Nainoa says. "Mau taught me the conceptual framework of navigation through the star compass. But the next challenge was to apply the concepts to the real ocean and make that work. I had the opportunity to learn that in my fishing boat with him. I watched what he watched, listened to what he listened to, felt what he felt. The hardest for me was to read the ocean swells the way he could. Mau is able to tell so much from the swells—the direction we are traveling, if the wind will change, the approach of an island, but this knowledge is hard to transmit. No two people sense things in exactly the same way. To help me become sensitive to the movements of the ocean, Mau would steer different courses into the waves, and I would try to feel it and remember the feel."

Nainoa could easily distinguish the large northeast swells generated by steady trade winds blowing over a long stretch of ocean. Other swells, set in motion by distant storms, were also evident. But when he tried to distinguish the smaller waves stirred by local conditions, he became easily disoriented. They seemed to come from different directions. "We would go out in my boat every day, out in the Moloka'i channel. I would stop the boat. I would sit on the engine box and look at the swells and waves. I could see the swells but the waves seemed to come from all directions. I couldn't distinguish an individual wave from another individual wave. It was confusing because the wind might be blowing from the east and you would think you should see a wave from the east. And, yes, if you look east you will see a wave. But if you look northeast you also see a wave and if you look southeast you see another wave."

Mau had taught Nainoa on shore by arranging white pieces of coral to represent the thirty-two cardinal points of his star compass. Then he fashioned a model canoe from a pandanus leaf and placed it in the middle of the compass. Using palm fronds to represent waves, he showed Nainoa how they arrived from different points of the compass and caused the canoe to roll in different ways, a teaching technique called *pukulaw*—or "wave tying"—and he used this method to teach Nainoa to name the pandanus leaf swells by their direction. On Satawal, with students fluent in his native tongue, Mau conveyed the secrets of *pukulaw* in great depth, but here, in halting English, a critical element was lost. Looking back on it, Nainoa thinks it may have been the distinction between waves—which are generated by winds birthing in a local area; and swells—which are generated by steady winds over time. "I sat in the boat with Mau and looked at the ocean but I just could not see many of the waves that Mau pointed out. I was becoming a little panicked because on cloudy days this was all I would have to steer the canoe. If I couldn't learn to see what Mau saw, how was I going to get to Tahiti?"

Dixon Stroup, a respected oceanographer at the University of Hawai'i, helped clarify Mau's teaching with a dose of western science. Stroup alerted Nainoa to the fact that local winds create waves that spiral outward; creating not a single easily identified wave train, but a series of waves that flow downwind in a ninety-degree field of view. "Dixon got me to understand that you cannot tell direction from a single individual wave. He knows from a scientific point of view that there is a certain amount of chaos associated with wind being generated locally. The wind that you are experiencing is making waves but the waves don't come straight downwind: they will come from different directions because of the way that wave patterns are formed."

Nainoa began to scan the ocean by looking for an overall pattern—a series of waves—one coming from the direction of the apparent wind, another from forty-five degrees to the right and another coming from forty-five degrees to the left. "If you have wind coming out of the east at twenty knots and it has been blowing that way for a week you will see a big wave train coming from the east. But if you watch the first wavelets when a wind begins to blow over the ocean they are scattered all over the place. These winds are in big gyres so that you get this confused state of waves that will come not straight downwind but also from the sides up to forty-five degrees away. I learned to ignore the individual waves and to look at the whole picture. What are the characteristics of the general wave trend in the big picture? I began to see the wave coming out of the east because I could see the edges of where those waves were coming from."

On Satawal, Mau taught his students in a holistic process that took place in every arena of life, in activities that westerners divide into economics, politics and socializing. His students joined Mau's canoe house. They worked there, ate there, gathered there with others to drink palm wine, and they were taught *kkapesen neimatau*, "the talk of the sea," during formal nighttime sessions under a murmuring kerosene lantern or on the beach under the enveloping stars. The teaching also took place informally. Students helped Mau work on his canoe or tend his gardens and during a break they might ask questions about navigation or be quizzed. There were no grades and very little praise and so a student might be easily confused about his progress. But, over a period of years, he would notice that Mau had loosed the reins a bit—had allowed him to steer the canoe for longer periods of time without correction—and by this he knew he was doing well. This kind of teaching relied on an ancient communal way of life. It was extensive as opposed to intensive. Up to this point, Nainoa's learning had occurred in classrooms where feedback was instant, in the form of grades, and where knowledge was conveyed by lectures accompanied by questions and answers.

At first, Mau's way of teaching confused Nainoa. Many times, aboard the small Radon, they would sit quietly observing the ocean. Often Mau would say nothing. Sometimes, he would ask Nainoa to point out the direction of swells and when Nainoa had done this, Mau would just nod and indicate that it was time to return to shore. Gradually, Nainoa learned to look for Mau's approval in actions rather than in words. "I don't remember the exact moment, but I remember sailing with him on training sails and I could tell when he was confident I was learning. He was heavily scrutinizing my ability to navigate. I looked to see if he was relaxed or not relaxed. I looked for those signs all the time because I was trying to build my own confidence." During weekends, on board the canoe off Waikīkī, Mau assigned a star course and Nainoa would try to hold it, giving orders to his steersman as he would on the trip to Tahiti: "steer up, good, steer down." One clear evening in 1979, after a few hours of steering drill with the lights of Diamond Head a dim twinkle on the horizon, Mau announced that he was tired.

"Now I go to sleep," he told Nainoa. "You follow the star path—*tana wulego* (the rising Big Dipper)."

Then he descended from his perch on the port navigator's platform and disappeared into his *puka*. "It was a huge compliment to me," Nainoa recalls. "I wanted to do well, but I was an overanxious student. I wanted to try some different courses to feel what the wave patterns were like. How the canoe would move in the swells. I thought that he wouldn't notice because he was sleeping inside the hulls."

Shortly after sunrise, Mau emerged from his *puka*.

"Nainoa, what star house did you sail last night?"

"He knew that I had changed course," Nainoa recalls, "and his voice sounded a little angry. And when I told him, he challenged me to make sure that I knew where we went."

"When I wake up I ask him, 'What you do last night?' " Mau recalls. "Then he tell me: 'This course, this one, this one.' Then I look, some good, some no good. Some right, some not right. Then I told him 'Almost exactly but some not too good.' "

"He actually knew each course I steered," Nainoa recalls, "even though he was lying in the hulls. Somehow he can do that."

"You know the sound?" Mau explains. "The swells' sound? The swells hit the canoe, the sound is not same. When I was down below I am hearing that. The sound of the wave is changing when the canoe goes different directions and I know because the canoe is moving not the same."

"It was a lesson from the master," Nainoa says, "he was telling me there's a deeper side to navigation than what I know—a learned mastery that I might never know."

As the months until departure dwindled, Nainoa continued to study the swells and the stars, both on his small boat and on the canoe. He also continued to study the demeanor of his master, seeking subtle clues of affirmation. Gradually, in the ancient way of Satawal's *palu*, Mau began to spend more time in his *puka*.

"The second time Nainoa steer almost all okay," Mau recalls. "Then third time is good."

CAN YOU SEE THE ISLAND?

Chapter Thirty

During Mau's apprenticeship, his grandfather had taken him to Satawal's shoreline where he taught him to predict the weather, to see subtle shades of color in the clouds—red for rain, pink for fair weather and dark blue for squalls. When he observed a "wind house," a massive cumulus cloud at dawn or dusk, Mau's grandfather told him to expect wind from the cloud's address on the horizon. Now it was Mau's turn to pass on this knowledge. Hundreds of times as the rising sun painted the horizon, Mau and Nainoa stood at the Koko Head lookout and gazed into the sunrise. At sunset, they traveled to O'ahu's western shore and continued their observations. "We looked at the colors of the sky, the color of the sun when it was very low to the horizon, to find clues to predict the weather. Mau told me exactly what to look for—what the different signs meant. We came hundreds of times because to learn to predict the weather you must see many sunrises and sunsets."

Mau taught Nainoa to look for "smoke"—a kind of haze low on the horizon. The heavier the smoke, the stronger the winds. If the smoke was orange at sunrise, there would be plenty of wind but no rain. If it was red the rain would come. The darker the red—the more rain. Scientifically, smoke is caused by wind stirring salt and moisture into the sky or by particles of rain that filter out blue short-wave light and allow only red long-wave light to pass through. Early Hawaiians paid a great deal of attention to a red sky at sunrise and sunset. They had specific terms for clouds that exhibited red streaks, or resembled a red eyeball or contained the colors of the rainbow. If they saw red patches in eastern clouds at sunrise they called it *kāhea*, "a call, an alarm," and predicted rain. If they observed a red color at sunset they called it *aka 'ula*, "red shadow or glow," and they predicted clearing skies.

The Hawaiian summer is dominated by smooth, steady northeast trade winds and clear skies so almost anyone can predict the weather. During the winter months, however, the wind turns variable and clear weather vies with rain and squalls. Still, Mau's weather predictions were astonishingly accurate. Nainoa filled notebooks with descriptions that he tried to tally, without much success, with Mau's predictions. A few months would pass before he realized that he was studying snapshots, while Mau was observing pictures that moved. "When I had spent enough time with him, I realized that he was not looking at a still picture of the sky. If you took a snapshot of the clouds and asked him, 'Mau, tell me what the weather is going to be,' he could not give you an answer. But if you gave him a sequence of pictures on different days—he would tell you."

"To find if weather will change look high," Mau told Nainoa, pointing to high-level clouds that Nainoa knew as cirrus. "If clouds move in same direction as surface winds, then nothing will change," he continued, "but if clouds move in different direction, than surface winds might change to direction clouds are moving."

"That was only the first indication," Nainoa recalls, "but Mau taught me that you don't really know yet. If the clouds form lower down and they're still going in the same direction as the high clouds then there's a better chance the winds will change in that direction. When the clouds get low enough, then the winds will definitely change. Satellite technology was in its infancy then so Mau's predictions would often be right and the National Weather Service would be wrong. He practices a kind of science that's a blend of observation and instinct as compared to the laboratory scientist measuring outcomes. Mau observes the world twenty-four hours a day. It's constant. That's his relationship to nature. As I grew up, I learned to see the world through science and math. But he saw the world in a much more internal way—through trained instinct."

Will Kyselka often accompanied Mau and Nainoa on these daily weather briefings. He stood behind them and wrote notes in a big hand because, in the early morning darkness, he couldn't see his notebook. Later, he would transcribe his scribbles and produce a book called *An Ocean in Mind*, a record of Mau's teachings. "Mau was impressed with what Nainoa knew," Will recalls. "Nainoa knew more about the stars than Mau but what he got from Mau was a sense of the sea, of weather and ocean swells. The art is how you integrate those, how you deal from the inside with them like a dance. You can know the steps but knowing the steps is not the dance. That's where Mau came in—to give him the knowledge he needed to dance."

After a year of observing the stars and swells from land and from Nainoa's fishing boat, Mau and Nainoa traveled to Koko Head Lookout to observe the weather signs one more time. They confronted a placid sea. Swells breaking on offshore reefs were dotted with surfers. The sun rose. The beat of surf mixed with the murmur of their conversation as they interpreted signs in the dawning sky. There was a pause in the conversation. Then a question from Mau.

"Can you name the stars in the star compass?" Mau asked.

Nainoa nods—"Yes."

"Can you point to the direction to Tahiti?" asked Mau.

Nainoa pointed to the star direction—south-southeast.

"Can you see the island?"

The question puzzled Nainoa. "I could not literally see the island," he recalls. "It was twenty-four hundred miles away. But it was a serious question. I had to consider it carefully. Finally, I said, "I cannot see the island but I can see an image of the island in my mind."

"Good," said Mau. "Don't ever lose that image or you will be lost."

"I ask him, to see is he like me," Mau recalls. "When I am on the land I know where islands are. When I ask him where is Tahiti, he knows where it is inside of him. A navigator knows where the land is inside of him, even when he can't see it."

"Then Mau turned to me," Nainoa recalls, "and said, 'Let's get in the truck and go home.' And we drove home."

During the weeks that followed, Mau busied himself with various chores. He carved a model of his canoe. He studied his notebooks of English words and expressions. He seemed involved in personal matters. Gradually, Nainoa began to understand that the final exam had been given. "That was the last lesson," Nainoa recalls. "Mau was telling me that I had to trust myself. I had to have a vision of where Tahiti was and that if I held on to it, I would get there. When he said, 'If you lose the image in your mind you are lost,' he was saying I had to see through my own eyes, feel my own feelings and understand the ocean my own way. In his wisdom, Mau recognized that he had to let me go. I was very anxious. I was trying to cling to my teacher. I wanted him to say 'You have graduated. You have arrived. You have the knowledge and skill and you're going to find Tahiti.' When he divorced himself from me I didn't know what to make of it. I was scared."

❖ ❖ ❖ ❖ ❖

While preparing for the voyage, Nainoa lived in a tiny rented cottage in Kuli'ou'ou. The house was shaded by a *kiawe* tree so it was dark. Illumination was by a single overhead 70-watt bulb and a gooseneck desk lamp. The desk was piled high with books on sailing and navigation and the inevitable spiral-bound notebooks. There was a small bed. Two jalousie windows gave out on the front yard and the pool of shade under the *kiawe* tree. "I lived in that little cave of a room for a year," Nainoa remembers.

Nainoa's notebooks began to mount up. They spilled off his desk. They were based on precious planetarium time with Will that could not be easily replicated. As the data mounted up Nainoa began to fret. *Which of these clues are the most important? How will I ever memorize all this?* Going over his planetarium notes for the zillionth time, Nainoa looked for patterns in the sky that might hold clues to direction and place. He was plotting new territory. If anyone had covered this terrain before, Nainoa did not know of it. Concentrating on the search for patterns, he entered a place where time streamed by. He might enter his zone of concentration after lunch with the *kiawe* tree painting its dark portrait on the lawn and come out of it realizing that the moon was up. He did not remember turning on the desk lamp, but there it was, casting a pool of light on his notes. For a moment, in a state of suspension, he enjoyed the apparent momentum of progress. The sky was becoming very familiar. He wandered out to the lawn and picked out the constellations hovering over the peaked mountains. He padded quietly through the darkened house to the kitchen to pour a glass of milk. A moment of peace, sipping the milk at his kitchen table, looking out through the window at the lawn glistening in moonlight and the stars above. But these moments were often followed by ones of crushing depression. *Who am I to be doing this?* he thought. *Where do I get off? How in hell am I ever going to learn this stuff?* Seeing star patterns in lined note pages or in the sky from a tended lawn were one thing. Finding them at sea would be something else again.

"My emotions," Nainoa remembers, "went from sheer excitement and thrill in the adventure, sheer inspiration to be on this incredible challenge, to being just compressed by the weight of Eddie's death—trying to bring out of the rubble of that tragedy some sense of dignity about what the canoe represents as well as carrying around all that guilt in being part of that death. I knew that I needed to deal with those issues. It was just too damn painful not to. I grew up in a time when Hawaiians were not expected to succeed. They were expected to fail. And that expectation became part of who I was. And the consequences of failing were now exponentially more risky because not only was it measurable—it was public. Being afraid of that kind of social expectation translates to being afraid to learn. You have death. You have fear. You have shame."

Fear and shame expressed themselves in Nainoa's dreams. Drifting off to sleep, he occasionally saw himself in a tiny cave. "That little cave of a cottage," he remembers. "I lived in that small world. If I look at myself back then there's a picture in my mind of this little man living in this cave by himself. That's the only place he feels secure because that's where he can protect himself from the things that either he's afraid of or he's ashamed of." At other times he saw a door with a sepulchral light behind it. It was a familiar door, the one to Yoshi Kawano's house in Niu where he was often taken care of while his parents were out for the evening. "I was very young and I was afraid they might not come back," he remembers. "Yoshi made a bed for me in their living room but I never went to sleep. I waited. And I watched that door. I was afraid they would not come for me. Now, in my dreams, I saw the same door—and behind it was everything I was afraid of."

STAR PAIRS

Chapter Thirty-One

L ate one night, after a long session in the planetarium with Will Kyselka, Nainoa returned to his little house in Kuli'ou'ou which he now shared with a roommate, his old friend Mike Ciacci. Mike was a superb athlete and had been invited to try out for the Kansas City Chiefs football team. He needed to train but he was prone to party if given the chance. Nainoa's monastic existence provided a kind of insurance against these proclivities, so Mike moved in and slept on the floor. Returning from a session with Will, Nainoa stepped over Mike's slumbering form and went to bed, his mind filled with visions of wheeling stars. "I was sleeping," he remembers, "and I saw the Southern Cross moving across the horizon and there was a pattern there I had not seen before—top star to bottom star, bottom star to the horizon—it was absolutely clear." It was so clear that he leapt out of bed, dressed in his underwear, jumped over Ciacci and sprinted down the road toward Kuli'ou'ou Beach Park where he expected to see the real Southern Cross. "I ran past all the streetlights to Kuli'ou'ou Park. There it was. Not only was the pattern in my mind but it was physically there in the sky." Nainoa returned to the house, retrieved a ruler and some paint and ran back to the park—still in his BVDs. "Mike chased me. Now there were two guys running down the street in their underwear. Mike had no idea why I was running."

"What the hell are you doing?" Mike yelled.

In the park, at the edge of the beach, a sign was affixed to a tall pole— "Danger, no swimming." Nainoa sighted along the pole at the upright Southern Cross and painted three lines on the pole—one at the horizon, one to mark the bottom star in the Cross and another to mark the top star. "Then I took the ruler and measured the distance between them. It was exact, exact. That was it! I called Will early in the morning. He said, 'Come on back to the planetarium'—and there it was."

The top star in the Southern Cross, Gacrux, is separated from the bottom star, Acrux, by six degrees of altitude. At the equator, the cross upright, Acrux will be twenty-seven degrees above the horizon. But from Honolulu, twenty-one degrees to the north, Acrux will have descended to only six degrees, so the distance between Gacrux and Acrux is exactly the same as the distance between Acrux and the horizon. When a navigator sees this, he knows he has reached twenty-one degrees north latitude—the celestial address of Honolulu. "The answer was always there," says Nainoa. "The Southern Cross was constantly going by but I never thought of it until I saw it in my unconscious mind—in a dream."

Southern Cross

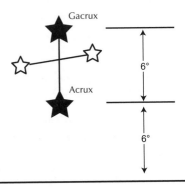

When the distance between Gacrux and Acrux is equal to the distance between Acrux and the horizon - the observer is at 21 degrees North latitude

Will and Nainoa decided to call this kind of observation "equal distance," which, in addition to "simultaneous setting," provided another instrument in the sky. It was an exciting discovery because it could have been made by anyone observing the heavens with the naked eye. It required no understanding of the concept of latitude so it was a way of finding land that would have been available to ancient Polynesian navigators. They would not have thought, as Nainoa did, that they had reached the latitude of the Hawaiian Islands. But they might easily have conceived of the observation— "distance from top star to bottom star, equal to distance from bottom star to horizon"—as indicating something like the "place of Hawai'i." Every pair of stars that cross the meridian simultaneously can be used for "equal distance" observations. Nainoa made a list of them in his notebook: Miaplacidus and Iota Carinae, Hadar and Menkent, Ed Asich and Pherkad—and more—a dozen additional stepping stones on the voyage to Tahiti.

It's hard to explain how important this discovery was to someone who has not tried to navigate without instruments. Simultaneously setting stars, for example, was a big advance—in theory—but in practice, due to atmospheric conditions, a navigator cannot actually see the stars arriving at the horizon. So Nainoa would place a finger on the horizon and observe the stars setting a few degrees above it. But here was an observation that was beautifully direct. That literally required no manipulation. "It was a picture that I could clearly hold in my mind. I could see where I was on the planet in a kind of mental snapshot." It was a first step into a new world—a place of images and intuition rather than logic and calculation. A place where he might actually find his way by the "shape of the sky."

◈ ◈ ◈ ◈ ◈

Nainoa had now solved the problem of finding his latitude by the stars. To find his longitude he would use the ancient system of dead reckoning, of estimating his course and speed over the water, twice a day for a month. He would plot these positions against a series of course lines drawn first on a map and then memorized.

The voyage to Tahiti would take Nainoa twenty-four hundred miles through four varying belts of wind and current. From Hilo to about nine degrees north latitude, the northeast trades blow steadily, accompanied by westward flowing currents. He would then encounter the Intertropical Convergence Zone—commonly called the Doldrums—a belt of storms, unpredictable currents, varying winds and long periods of calm from nine to five north. From about five north to the equator, the westerly currents return but the winds continue to be variable. Finally, just below the equator, the southeast trade winds reassert themselves and the currents grow stronger. He must account for these changing conditions by plotting four separate legs of the voyage.

Plotting the course of a sailing vessel on the planet's surface is like a game of

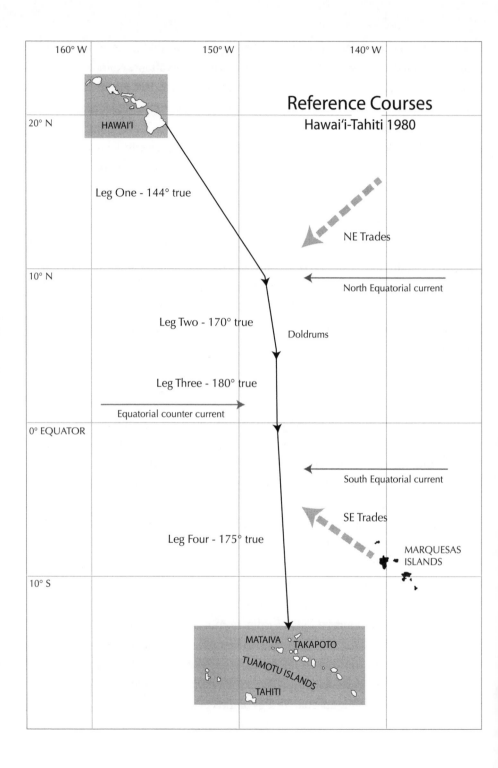

Reference Courses
Hawai'i-Tahiti 1980

160° W

150° W

140° W

20° N

HAWAI'I

Leg One - 144° true

NE Trades

10° N

North Equatorial current

Leg Two - 170° true

Doldrums

Leg Three - 180° true

Equatorial counter current

0° EQUATOR

South Equatorial current

SE Trades

Leg Four - 175° true

MARQUESAS
ISLANDS

10° S

MATAIVA   TAKAPOTO

TUAMOTU ISLANDS

TAHITI

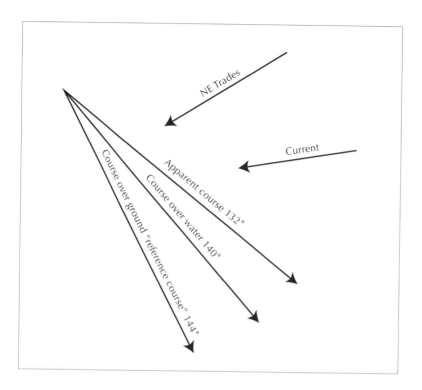

three-dimensional chess because the navigator must account for a complex variety of forces acting on the canoe. A sailing vessel is moved forward by the wind but also pushed away from it, or downwind, an effect called leeway. So the course being steered is only the "apparent course," the course actually sailed "over the water" is the apparent course plus the leeway. In addition to this, the water is moving too, in vast belts of current, so only when the current effect is added in does a mariner know his actual "course over the ground."

To figure his path over the ground, Nainoa first had to estimate the average apparent course he would be able to hold in the four areas of changing wind, then factor in the leeway and the current set. On the first leg, for example, the strong prevailing northeast trades should allow the canoe to sail an average of a hundred and thirty-five miles a day on an apparent course of 132 degrees true. On this leg, the canoe would be set downwind—the lee set—by 8 degrees, so her path through the water would be 140 degrees true. Nainoa estimated that the current would flow from east to west an average of about 13 miles a day. He also estimated that the first leg would take 6 days to complete, during which time the canoe would move west with the current an additional 78 miles, giving him (after a little calculation) a course over the ground of 144 degrees true.

In a similar fashion, he calculated the course over the ground for the remaining three legs. On the second leg the canoe would sail a more southerly course over the ground of 170 degrees true. On the third leg, the course would be 180 degrees true and on the fourth it would be 175 degrees true.

Each of these courses or legs are what Nainoa calls his "reference courses" and they represent the actual path he would try to follow over the curving planet. Without any means of determining his longitude, he would figure the direction and distance he sailed—given the vagaries of the shifting winds—and determine if he was to the east or to the west of his reference course. He thinks of distance in terms of an average sailing day in the trade winds, 100 miles, a number he has chosen for convenience in making mental calculations. He thinks of direction in terms of star houses, one house being equivalent to 11 1/4 degrees on the compass. As an example, suppose he sails from dawn to dusk one house to the west of his reference course for an average sailing day—a distance of 100 miles. He will report his position as one house west of the reference course. To regain his position on the reference course he must sail 100 miles on a course one house to the east of it. This is the simplest of cases. In actual fact, he would often sail multiple courses in one twelve-hour period and the calculations would become exceedingly difficult.

To complicate matters even more, each of these reference courses contains many assumptions about average ocean and wind conditions, and nature is often capricious. On the first leg, he assumed that it would require six days to reach nine degrees north—based on other assumptions—that the wind would hold steady, allowing him to sail an average of one hundred and thirty-five miles a day. Suppose the wind did not hold and it required seven days? In that case, the current would have an additional day to work on the canoe, forcing her an additional thirteen miles to the west of her reference course. It was a problem he would have to deal with on the voyage.

❖ ❖ ❖ ❖ ❖

In November of 1979, Ben Fitial again called Nainoa from Saipan. He would be visiting Honolulu—could he stay at Nainoa's house? After a few days, when

Ben was preparing to depart, he told Nainoa that Mau would be going with him. "I was shocked," Nainoa remembers. "I knew that Mau wasn't going on the voyage but I was surprised that he never said a word to me about leaving. He was in his room packing. He didn't say anything."

Nainoa drove Ben and Mau to Honolulu International Airport and helped them lug their baggage to the Continental Airlines counter where they purchased their tickets. They checked in early, so they went to the airport bar for beers. "I felt real sad," Nainoa recalls. "I was confused, and not prepared for Mau to leave." The conversation was desultory. For the first time, Mau appeared restless—indecisive. After the second beer, he looked up at Ben.

"I'm not going home," he said. "I'm staying here."

"Now I'm even more confused," Nainoa recalls. "So we had some more beers and Mau seemed happy. He had made his decision not to go back to Satawal. We shipped Ben off and we went back home. Later on, as we were preparing for the voyage, Mau came to me and said, 'Can I go on the trip?' "

"After I teach him then I like go with him on the canoe in case he miss the navigation," Mau recalls. "I like go because I'm thinking in case they get lost then I going to make sure."

"Those were the most joyous words that I ever heard. That was a turning point for the Voyaging Society. That was a testament that we were on the right track."

SANDY FOOTPRINTS

Chapter Thirty-Two

The planetarium was a god-send but it had its limitations. It was an artificial sky. It did away with the inconvenience of clouds, for example, and it was a teaching device and prone to errors, so while it was extremely useful for developing hypotheses, every one of them had to be tested against the real world. Nainoa observed the stars in his back yard and from his boat off O'ahu, but he knew that to really understand the sky he should observe it from many vantage points in Hawai'i. So he traveled to Kaua'i—the northernmost of the main Hawaiian Islands—and to the Big Island, the southernmost. To make the Big Island trip easier, Harry Ho shipped his specially prepared surfing van from O'ahu to Hilo. Employing an architect's sense of space, he had designed roof racks to hold surfboards and cabinets to contain maps, clothing, swim fins, masks and water bottles. "I had my side of the van and he had his side," Nainoa recalls. "We were Felix Unger and Oscar Madison—'the odd couple.' There was a demarcation line down the middle of the van. My side was a wreck. His side was completely neat. He even had a little Plexiglas thing that held his toothbrush." Harry and Nainoa drove around the Big Island—to Kohala in the north, Keāhole in the west and to Kumukahi in the east. Kumukahi means "first beginnings" in Hawaiian, the place where the rising sun is first seen in all the islands.

Nainoa and Harry spent a week observing the stars. On their last night, Harry drove the van down Ali'i Drive in Kona to Kahalu'u Park. As the stars rose, Nainoa scribbled copious notes. He paid particular attention to Aldebaran and Rigel—simultaneously setting stars that he was studying as a clue to latitude. "On the Kona coast," he wrote in his notebook, "Aldebaran sets kind of before Rigel even though Aldebaran sets after Rigel on O'ahu. Not too much difference but you can tell." He underlined can tell. The observation suggests Nainoa's ability to perceive tiny clues because the latitude difference between Honolulu and Kona is less than two degrees, which amounts to a small time difference between the setting of the two stars.

That night, Nainoa and Harry slept in the van. In the morning, Nainoa noticed the surf was up. "I grabbed my surfboard and I was gone. The waves were really, really nice. I'm thinking, 'God, Harry you're missing this beautiful day.' When I finally came in, Harry had just finished getting everything organized. On my side everything was folded and rolled up. He had even got my toothbrush in its place. All the anxiety, the pressures and the immaturity, looking back—I needed people who I trusted and had *aloha* with. Harry understood that."

In December, Harry and Nainoa flew to Tahiti for two weeks to observe the stars. After landing in Papeete, they rented a car and drove out the coast highway to Puaniho's house in Tautira. The village was in those days composed of simple houses and dirt roads, hardly more than paths, that spread like veins among the houses. The land was intensely farmed. There was the constant aroma of vegetation and salt. For Nainoa it was a magic place. He could feel the *mana*— the spiritual power—of his ancestors.

In the river that spiraled down from the mountain peaks, the villagers maintained a stone shrine—what Hawaiians call a *kū'ula*—dedicated to a spirit that protects fishermen. An elder who lived in a house by the river had the power to call fish to the *kū'ula,* and one day he called a school of *aku* and fishermen surrounded them with a net. "I remember the kids chasing the fish with sticks," Nainoa recalls, "herding them into the net. The school was so thick you could almost walk on them. Then they would scoop the fish out, taking just what they needed and leaving the rest in the net to keep them fresh, coming down each day to take more out. They would only hold the fish until they got weak and then let them go."

For the first week it rained. When the sky finally cleared, Nainoa, Harry, and Puaniho took a boat around a jut of land to Fare a Cheri, a secluded house where Nainoa could devote himself to study. "We were trying to tell latitude by the stars. We had the system worked out in the planetarium—the scientific basis— but we needed to observe the actual stars." After a few nights of observing from Fare a Cheri, Harry rented a car and they traveled to Point Venus on Tahiti's north shore and to Maeva on the western shore where he could observe the setting stars. "Harry would sleep in the car while I sat and observed the sky," Nainoa recalls.

A little after midnight, on January 24th, Nainoa began observations at Maeva, a long strand of white sand beach near Papeete. He saw lights twinkling on the distant island of Moorea. He oriented himself to familiar shapes in the sky. Orion rode high in front of him with the Taurus, the Bull, lower down. He recorded his observations into a tape recorder. At about 1:30 a.m., he paid particular attention to Capella and a star that he called "the nose of Taurus," also known to astronomers as Gamma Tauri. Slowly, the two stars descended to the horizon. From their planetarium observations, Nainoa and Will predicted they would set simultaneously in the Tahitian sky. "Pretty close," he said to the tape recorder as the stars arrived together at the horizon, "This is a good observation." Now he shifted his attention to Sirius and Pollux. On the voyage to Tahiti, Nainoa would not have a watch. Instead, he had memorized signposts in the sky to tell him when various significant celestial events were about to happen. Looking south he found the Southern Cross in the meridian. Looking north, he found the familiar pointers Alioth and Cor Caroli very close to their meridian. "Very good lineup," he said to the tape recorder. "Won't be long now." At about 4:30 a.m., Sirius and Pollux began to sink below the horizon. "Sirius sets a little after Pollux," Nainoa recorded. This is true, but the difference is only about three minutes, so for his purposes the synchronized setting of the two stars was an accurate skymark for Tahiti.

When Nainoa had first made these observations in the night sky over Tautira almost three years earlier, he was a neophyte. Since then, he'd spent hundreds of hours examining the sky holistically, without instruments, as his ancestors must have done. By discarding the preconceptions of western navigators, he had discovered shapes and relationships in the sky that had not been seen for centuries. He was, as some might say, "thinking out of the box," but more accurately, he had thrown the box away. Looking up from beaches in Hawai'i and from this one in Tahiti, he was asking questions that his ancestors might have asked. He was treading in their sandy footprints.

SPIRIT GUARDIANS

Chapter Thirty-Three

A few months before the canoe was to depart for Tahiti, Sam Kaʻai set out, just before sunrise, to visit Puʻukoholā, a large temple on the northwestern coast of Hawaiʻi. Sam approached the temple from the sea. To his right, the land sloped up across a plateau of lava cloaked in scrubby *kiawe* trees and rose to the peak of Mauna Kea 13,796 feet above sea level—the highest point of land in the Hawaiian Islands. There was snow on the top of the mountain and below the snow the slopes were pockmarked with *puʻu*—cinder cones. Lower still, the skirt of the mountain formed a green prairie where Parker Ranch cattle grazed. The air was still except for a rustling wind that made its way through the saddle between Mauna Kea to Sam's right and the Kohala mountains to his left.

Reaching the temple's western wall, Sam turned to follow a trail that led to the entrance on the northwestern corner. He paused before a worn set of stone steps and listened. He waited for the slightest sign that might indicate whether he should enter or turn away. The wind seemed to die. He heard the beat of surf. There was no bird song. He removed his shoes and began climbing the steps. At the top, he encountered a walled platform and he made his way to a place where the wall was pierced by an entrance into a large inner room. Here Sam knelt and seated himself with his bare feet tucked under his legs. He waited some more. Then he began to chant, his deep voice echoing against the stone wall before him.

Nā ʻAumākua mai ka lā hiki ā ka lā kau!
Ancestors from the rising to the setting sun

Mai ka hoʻokuʻi ā ka hālāwai
From the zenith to the horizon

Nā ʻAumākua ia Kahinakua, ia Kahinaʻalo
Ancestors who stand at our back and front

La ka'a 'ākau i ka lani
You who stand at our right hand

O kīhā i ka lani
A breathing in the heavens

'Owē i ka lani
An utterance in the heavens

Nunulu i ka lani
A clear, ringing voice in the heavens

Kahōlo i ka lani
A voice reverberating in the heavens

Eia nā pulapula a 'oukou 'o ka po'e Hawai'i
Here are your descendants, the Hawaiians

E mālama 'oukou iā mākou
Safeguard us

E ulu i ka lani
That we may flourish in the heavens

E ulu i ka honua
That we may flourish on earth

E ulu i ka pae 'āina o Hawai'i
That we may flourish in the Hawaiian Islands

E hō mai i ka 'ike
Grant us knowledge

E hō mai i ka ikaika
Grant us strength

E hō mai i ke akamai
Grant us intelligence

E hō mai i ka maopopo pono
Grant us understanding

E hō mai i ka 'ike pāpālua
Grant us insight

E hō mai i ka mana
Grant us power

'Āmama ua noa
The prayer is lifted, it is free."

The prayer was dedicated to the *'aumākua*—the spirits of Sam's ancestors. Sam wanted to know if they approved of the upcoming voyage. "My prayer asked the *'aumākua* to please notice us," Sam explains. "We are going to go down the *ala nui o ka moana* to Kahiki nui, down the ancient sea path to Kahiki of the rising sun, so help us go down the correct path as our ancestors once did. Please notice us. Please see us. Please guide us."

Many of Sam's fellow crewmembers were experiencing similar connections to their *'aumākua*. When he was floating in the water beside the capsized canoe, Tava had seen a vision of his mother's face. Others saw similar apparitions in peaceful moments at sea, the faces of their parents guiding them as if in a dream. "We feel our *'aumākua* all round us," explains Bruce Blankenfeld. "*Au makua* means 'my *akua*,' my god. It's your caretaker, your parent in a general way."

Hawaiians believe that the *'aumakua* can take the physical shape of a living thing. For some it is a shark, a turtle, a particular kind of lizard and for many, like Bruce Blankenfeld, it is an owl. "One day my *'aumakua* saved my life," Bruce recalls. "When I was nineteen years old, I was working in Hilo on the Big Island. I finished work and I am driving to Kona, about an hour and a half away, trying to get there before dark. I am flying, making good time. I'm on the mountain road between Waimea and Hualālai. I'm coming to a corner near Pu'uanahulu, when I see a *pueo*—an owl. He's on a fence post, flapping its wings. The *pueo* is my *'aumakua*. He's telling me something. Slow down! And sure enough, after two more turns there's a big accident in the middle of the road, and if I had not slowed down I would have been a part of it."

Pinky Thompson's Hawaiian spirituality had been renewed many years earlier on a troop transport off the beach at Normandy, France. "When I was twenty, we were ready to jump off for the invasion and needless to say I was scared as hell. The night before, we went to services conducted by a Catholic priest and he asked us to call on the supreme powers of our families and of our own personal beliefs to join us that night. He wasn't pushing God, he wasn't pushing Christ, he wasn't pushing anything. He asked us to call the supreme powers of our own spiritual beliefs to be there. I felt a tremendous relief that I could call the 'aumākua that our family had talked about for years in muffled tones and I could have them with me that night and for the rest of the time I was in combat. That was a hell of a relief. That was the first time I felt an intense connection to my family's spiritual beliefs."

Nainoa found his 'aumākua in the stars. When his childhood guardian, Yoshio Kawano, passed away, Nainoa went into the pasture behind his grandmother's home in Niu and he looked up to see Spica rising, so Spica became Yoshi's star. He named Capella for his grandmother Gardie. Alpha Lupus became the Willy star, for Will Kyselka. Eddie Aikau is embodied in the constellation Scorpio, known in Hawaiian as "mānai-a-ka-lani" — "made fast to the heavens" — the fish hook of the great Maui who pulled the Hawaiian islands from the sea.

Maui was half divine and half human, born of the union of the goddess Hina and a mortal Hawaiian man. One day, while fishing with his brothers, Maui threw his hook deep into the ocean. Soon he felt a fierce tug on the line and a battle ensued. The seas all around rose up in great waves. The line was drawn tight. Maui and his brothers fought the fish for two days until, finally, it tired and they pulled together to bring it to the surface. They pulled and pulled and, eventually, they pulled up all the islands of Hawai'i. This creation story is common throughout Polynesia, though the fisherman often has a different name. Many think the legend's kaona—its hidden meaning—is the celebration of great sailors and navigators who, on their long voyages of discovery, literally fished islands from the sea. "A fishhook is Neolithic engineering," Sam Ka'ai explains. "You whirl the hook over your head and you let it down, down beyond your sight, down beyond your breathing capacity, down into a dimension deeper than you can see and you pull up the nourishment of life—i'a—fish. Navigators reach down, down, down with the mānai-a-ka-lani to pull up islands. Hawaiki rising. The signs for finding islands are stars. The islands are hidden. They are the treasures underneath the stars. Hawaiki rising is feeling again the wind. Noticing again the stars. The heavens have not shifted. Hawaiki rising is grasping again that star, knowing where it is, and therefore knowing where you are. All of that is bound up in one ball of string, the spiritual cord and the spiritual hook, the physical cord and the physical hook—all of these things lead together. Herb Kawainui Kane's dream on paper gave fruit as a canoe. We will whirl our hook above us. We will throw it into the depth of another dimension, led by a star, and we will pull out an island. Hawaiki rising."

❖ ❖ ❖ ❖ ❖

With the voyage only two months away, *Hōkūle'a* entered dry-dock at Sand Island near downtown Honolulu. Her crew swarmed over her, inspired by Mau's calm guidance. They replaced her decking. Deep in her hulls, they sanded away many skins of old fiberglass and replaced them with new. They rove new standing and running rigging. They caulked the canoe's watertight bulkheads and the topsides of her hulls. They checked her pumps. They renewed frayed wiring for her running lights and emergency radios. They installed an Argos transmitter that would broadcast to a hovering satellite the canoe's position two or three times a day. It was a safety precaution and an important part of the navigation experiment because it would provide accurate positions that would later be compared with those Nainoa conjured along the way. "Finally, they painted her. Work ran ahead of schedule because there were so many people turning up," Jo-Anne Sterling wrote in her log. "Mau was convinced that the project and attitudes were altogether different from the 1976 trip. After the final coats of paint on her hulls and *manu* she glowed. It will be good."

❖ ❖ ❖ ❖ ❖

On the Big Island, two large volcanic peaks, Mauna Kea and Mauna Loa, rise above skirts of eroded lava punctured by vents and cinder cones. Of the two, Mauna Kea is the highest by a small margin and occasionally its peak glistens with winter snow. On its flanks, is an ancient stone quarry where Hawaiians made adzes to fashion canoes. A month before the canoe was to depart for Tahiti, Nainoa flew to the Big Island, borrowed a jeep and drove up the Saddle Road to a cluster of simple cabins the National Park Service rented to hardy folks who hiked the mountain's slopes. He came here because of an earlier conversation with Sam Ka'ai.

"Sam told me a story about the *kū'ula*. It's a stone shrine for fishermen and it's a family guardian. It has power. It brings good luck."

Inside the lagoon at Tautira, in Tahiti, the *kū'ula* was a small stone shrine, but as Sam envisioned it, Nainoa's *kū'ula* was the entire island of Hawai'i.

"Sam told me that a navigator is not of the land—he is of the sea—so his *kū'ula* is the whole island. When I pictured our return from Tahiti to Hawai'i I saw Mauna Kea—the highest mountain, the mountain closest to the middle of the latitudes of all the islands. Spiritually, Mauna Kea is a very powerful place. The ashes of my grandfather, Eben Low, are scattered high on its slopes. So as I prepared to bring the islands to me I decided I had to stay on the slopes of Mauna Kea."

With the date of departure for Tahiti fast approaching, Nainoa came to Mauna Kea in a state of high anxiety. A few thousand feet above the camps, he found a *pu'u*, a volcanic cone in the district called Pōhakuloa. He hiked up to the cone as the sun was setting. He wrapped himself in a sleeping bag.

"Sleeping on Mauna Kea's slopes was a way to get close to the mountain in both my mind and in my *na'au*, my gut. I had done all my academic study. I had gone to Tahiti. I was physically strong—at my best. I had worked with the best teachers—Mau, Dixon, Will, my father—and I had the support of so many people. But something was missing, my own spiritual preparedness. My own personal journey. I was trying to find my home—inside of me—and Mauna Kea defines home to me. It's the highest mountain. Sam said that the Big Island was my *kū'ula*—my guardian. When we came back from Tahiti we would be approaching from the east so we would see Mauna Kea first. It was my spiritual beacon—a place that I would be coming home to."

HĀMĀKUA STORM

Chapter Thirty-Four

*H*ōkūleʻa departed Oʻahu in twenty-five knots of wind en-route to Hilo, her final stop before departing to Tahiti. On board were Gordon Piʻianaiʻa, Chad Baybayan, Leon and Jo-Anne Sterling, Tava Taupu, Chuck Larsen, and Mau Piailug. *Ishka, Hōkūleʻaʻs* escort, sailed in her wake. *Ishkaʻs* captain, Alex Jakubenko, was a seasoned sailor. Born in 1924, he grew up in Mariupol, a seaport in the Ukraine on the Sea of Azov. He lived a few hundred yards from the ocean. When he was nine, Alex stowed away on a fishing boat. "I always liked the sea. I thought that one day I would build a small yacht and go around the world."

In World War II, Alex served in the Army and was taken prisoner by the Germans when they invaded the Ukraine. He eventually escaped and served in the French underground. After the war, he ran a night club for the American armed forces and traveled throughout Germany to buy liquor. "That's how I met my wife Elsa. Her father used to sell cognac. They were very well off. I remember this beautiful woman came in one day and there you are. After the war we got married—in 1947, I think." Elsa and Alex emigrated to Australia where Alex nurtured his dream of building a boat and sailing around the world. He went to a shipyard near Melbourne and asked for a job. He was thrown out but he returned, manned a broom and began sweeping the floor. "The owner came out and said, 'What the hell are you doing here? Get out.' He picked up the broom and threw me out. I went back in, picked up the broom and started sweeping again. I did that quite a few times. He was really mad, but after a while he thought I must be a little crazy and he just let me do it. I learned to build ships by watching how they did it in that shipyard." At night, Alex took navigation courses. He eventually set up a small yard of his own and began building his first boat, *Hella*, a forty-five foot steel sloop. Alex and Elsa lived in Australia for seventeen years. He became well known for constructing sleek vessels by using large steel plates, an innovation that saved time and labor. He prospered but he still dreamed of sailing the world. So, in 1967, he sold his business and he and Elsa boarded *Hella* and set out. They visited Hawai'i and sailed on to Sausalito where he established another successful shipyard. In 1972, they moved to Taiwan where Alex built a sixty-five foot ketch, *Meotai*. *Meotai* was launched in 1974 and purchased a short time later by Honolulu businessman Bob Burke who used her as *Hōkūle'a's* escort vessel on the first historic voyage to Tahiti in 1976.

When *Hōkūle'a* arrived in Tahiti in 1976, Alex and Elsa were there aboard another Jakubenko-built sloop, the one he now sailed aboard—*Ishka*. "I saw the tremendous reception that the Tahitians gave the canoe," Alex remembers, "you would have to be there to believe it. Within twenty-four hours there were at least twenty new songs about the canoe. The voyage gave the people so much pride and excitement that both Elsa and I wanted to do something to help. But at the time, we had no idea what." Later that year, the couple returned to Hawai'i where Alex worked at Ke'ehi Dry dock where *Hōkūle'a* was brought for overhaul after the 1976 voyage and for repair after she capsized in 1978. In 1980, he volunteered to escort *Hōkūle'a* to Tahiti aboard *Ishka*.

❖ ❖ ❖ ❖ ❖

The canoe and *Ishka* sailed easily over choppy seas stirred by steady trade winds. "God what a relief to get away from land," Jo-Anne wrote in her journal. "At last—it's our first leg of the journey." With only seven people on board, the watch system was flexible, some slept while others kept a lookout in the busy sea lanes off O'ahu. Night fell and a full moon rose. By early the next morning, *Hōkūle'a* had sailed down the length of Moloka'i. The winds diminished, then died. The canoe and her escort lay becalmed. "Moon was yellow," Jo-Anne wrote. "Just drifting around. Looked alongside—*Ishka* drifting—no wind— very still. Eerie. Beautiful and glad to be just where I am." The Hālawa Valley glistened in the moonlight, a green sward expanding to sharp mountains. Archeologists working in the valley had recently found evidence of a settlement dating to about 1300 AD. The earliest households were excavated a few hundred feet from the beach and they revealed the bones of chickens, dogs and pigs. The first Polynesians to land at Hālawa had not come on an exploring mission—they had brought their animals with them so they had come to settle permanently.

The wind died so Alex maneuvered *Ishka* alongside *Hōkūle'a*, passed a line and began to tow the canoe. He slowly throttled up to about five knots with the canoe following astern. The lights of Kahului town glistened in the saddle between the West Maui mountains and the peak of Haleakalā. The coast slipped by, dappled with surf. By mid day, *Hōkūle'a* was off Hāna on Maui's eastern tip. "What a sight from the canoe along the Hāna area," Jo-Anne wrote. "Passed not far from Hāna Bay."

Early that same morning, Nainoa set out in his twenty-two foot Radon powerboat with three University of Hawai'i scientists on a mission to photograph whales. The sea was flat and they were able to make twenty knots, but Nainoa was uneasy because such calms often signaled a change in weather. Arriving off Penguin Banks, a shoal area about twenty-five miles south of O'ahu, the team glassed the ocean with powerful binoculars. A pod of whales swam slowly a few miles away, accompanied by two calves. Nainoa moved in front of the pod and donned scuba gear to photograph them from the water while the scientists took pictures from the boat. It was a good day, perfect conditions for the work, and there were plenty of whales. Nainoa exhausted one tank of air and went down with a second, accompanied by two of the scientists. When he came back on deck, he noticed a thick line of clouds to the northwest off O'ahu. The line was dark and fast moving, and he watched it engulf the island. "The frontal edge was so distinct," he recalls, "a series of black lines. It just covered O'ahu. We couldn't see it. Then I got worried."

"Get the guys out of the water," he ordered. "We've got to get out of here."

The scientists were reluctant to leave. By the time they had stowed their gear, the cloud was upon them, traveling at about twenty-five knots. "Finally that first whisper of wind started to come. That frontal edge cracked the mirror-smooth ocean. In a matter of minutes it was roaring." Behind the front came rain in horizontal sheets. The waves were short and steep and the small Radon bucked as Nainoa throttled up. Steering toward O'ahu, the boat lurched and thudded. A particularly steep wave threw one of the scientists against the forward bulkhead, cutting his lip. Nainoa strapped on a mask and snorkel so he could see to steer in the stinging rain. Everyone hung on. The trip seemed to take an eternity. "I never did see O'ahu," Nainoa recalls. "All of a sudden we started to get in the lee of something—it became really dark and the rain seemed to stop. I found myself off

Koko Head between Portlock and Hanauma Bay and the rain was so horizontal that when we got underneath the cliffs it just stopped. We were on the Hanauma Bay side of the cliff so I drove towards Portlock in the lee."

Nainoa had fished Maunalua Bay so he knew the waters intimately. Three boats bobbed outside the narrow channel marked by towering surf breaking on reefs on either side. Nainoa passed them. They followed him in. Although the wind and rain had abated in Portlock's lee, the clouds were so thick that he was a hundred yards from shore before he could see land. As soon as he docked, he raced to radio Will Kyselka aboard *Ishka.* "I told them to watch out for the storm. You can easily be fooled because the day had been so nice."

Aboard *Ishka,* Alex and Will tuned to a local weather report. The storm was predicted to reach the Big Island in about twenty-four hours—plenty of time to reach shelter in Hilo Harbor, they figured. "Nainoa radioed the escort boat telling them this thing was coming," Chad remembers. "He told us how bad it was going to be. I was really young so I didn't pay much attention to it. What was bad weather? Rain?" "Will radioed back that everything was fine," Nainoa recalls. "Back then I didn't understand how weather systems worked. I was thinking maybe it's okay. I didn't really know the seriousness of the storm. Maybe it was isolated to O'ahu."

By four o'clock, *Hōkūle'a* had passed beyond the 'Alenuihāhā Channel and was off the Big Island's Hāmākua Coast with *Ishka* keeping a steady strain on the towline. Hilo was about forty-five miles away, another nine hours or so at five knots. The sea was calm. Jo-Anne lit the propane stove and began cooking dinner. The canoe's crew of seven was about half its normal complement so there was plenty to eat. Chad Baybayan recalls stuffing himself with Portuguese bean soup.

Suddenly the storm was on them. Everyone remembers its approach.

"I looked up and I could see this big black wall coming towards us," Chad remembers.

"I am looking outside Maui and it is black—all black," Tava recalls.

"Oh, yeah, I remember the storm," says Mau. "We pass Maui, whoooo, the storm come blowing hard. That's why I scared because I thinking the wind is going to push the canoe to the island."

Alex and Gordon Pi'ianai'a conferred by VHF radio. Both had voyaged tens of thousands of sea miles and knew conditions would deteriorate fast.

"Take down *Ishka's* sails," Alex ordered.

Mau ordered the crew to take *Hōkūle'a's* spars and booms down on deck.

"Don foul weather gear and life preservers," Gordon told his crew.

The storm struck the canoe broadside and it came so suddenly that, for a few moments, the ocean was a confused roiling froth on one side and a millpond on the other.

"I am looking at one side—big waves. I am looking other side—clear and calm," Tava recalls.

The wind accelerated to gale force.

"It was like somebody hit the light switch—it just went black. The seas went raging—crazy deep seas," Chad remembers.

Ishka's mainsail writhed in the wind. Furling it was out of the question so Alex tied it to the boom and hoped for the best. He had built *Ishka* with his own hands and he had built her sturdy. Off Sydney, Australia, she had survived near hurricane winds. In that same storm, a large freighter had gone down with all hands. Alex knew his boat could withstand almost anything nature could throw at her. She was equipped with an engine that could move her at eight knots or so, but the best speed she could make towing *Hōkūle'a* was about five knots—and that was in calm weather. Alex turned into the wind and eased the throttle forward. *Ishka* pitched in the wild seas. Her propeller cavitated, losing traction, and the engine raced. Alex jockeyed the throttles to prevent overheating. He had given *Ishka* an oversized prop—eighteen inches in diameter rather than twelve. Now he wished he had provided an even larger one.

Hōkūle'a's crew saw their escort appear high atop a swell and then disappear into a trough. Tava stood at the bow, watching the towrope for signs of wear. "I look at the swells and when a big swell comes then we no see the sailboat—we only see the rope."

"If that rope breaks we're going to be freaking *'opihi* (a snail that lives on rocks)," Chad told him.

Hōkūle'a and *Ishka* were now in a classic sailor's predicament. Caught in a fierce storm off a lee shore, *Ishka's* power and Alex's skill were all that stood between the canoe and the frothing reefs a few miles astern.

Looking toward the Hāmākua coast, Chad recalls rocks surrounded by churning surf and spume—"like teeth ready to eat the canoe."

He watched the distance dwindle. "We were being pushed backwards. The escort boat was pulling us but we were drifting back slowly, slowly, slowly—oh man, it was nasty."

"I am looking and I no can see the canoe moving," says Tava.

"I was holding her—but just barely," Alex recalls.

The strain on the towrope eased as *Ishka* dived into a trough, then took up when she reappeared. "I look at the tow line," says Tava, "It is big then it come small. I say to myself, 'No way—it is going to break.'" Manning *Ishka's* throttles, Alex waited for his boat to settle between waves, giving the propeller some grip. Then he gunned her to gain speed. It was a reasonable plan but he knew it was risky because of the different hydrodynamic properties of the two vessels. *Ishka* is a heavy monohull designed to sit low in the water. *Hōkūle'a*, a lightly constructed catamaran, sits high. Speeding ahead, Ishka would suddenly take a strain on the towrope. *Hōkūle'a* would respond by shooting forward and veering to one side, almost overtaking her escort. "That was big trouble," Alex recalls. "Whenever we tried to speed up, *Hōkūle'a* would overrun us and sometimes she was actually beside us. That was very, very dangerous."

To compensate, Tava and his crewmates struggled to steer the canoe back behind *Ishka*. "The canoe is going by herself. No way you can steer in the swell. *Ishka* just tow us. I look at the rope—it is going back and forth—wzzzzz—freaky. Go back—wzzzz—go back—wzzzz. No way we can steer." Darkness fell. "We no can see *Ishka's* mast—only can see the light on the mast."

Will tuned *Ishka's* radio to the Coast Guard Communication Station at Honolulu and called for assistance. It was not the only distress call that night. A number of vessels were in trouble; two were sinking. If *Hōkūle'a's* towline should break, it was doubtful that a cutter could arrive in time. Will kept this information to himself. He radioed the crew huddling aboard *Hōkūle'a*. "Don't worry," he told them.

"Will's voice over the storm was just real calm," Chad recalls. "He kept encouraging us and that kept me from going totally bonkers."

A few hours into the storm, Elsa popped her head above *Ishka's* companionway. "You had better come down and eat something or I am going to throw it overboard."

"That's Elsa," Alex says. "Nothing rattles her—nothing."

Jo-Anne had confidence in the canoe and her crew, but she was preparing for the worst. "I was thinking that if the canoe started to break up what could I hook up to? I felt that if we all hooked up together by our safety harnesses we at least would drown together."

As the night wore on, the swells built to twenty feet and began to break. "Two big ones rocked the whole canoe," Chad recalls. "They went over us and I heard Gordon yelling 'Is everybody okay?' Then another wave hit us and I remember one guy grabbed me by the shoulders and looked at me with big eyes and a pale face—'This is it,' he yells. 'This is it.' " "One of the guys panicked," Jo-Anne recalls. "He wanted to know if the canoe was going to break up." "I don't know if it was the wave or that guy who scared me more," Chad remembers. "He was yelling at me—'This is it, this is it!' "

Jo-Anne huddled by the galley repeating Hail Marys. "I looked back to Mau," she recalls. "He was standing near the navigator's platform on the port side looking at the ocean. His face was very stern and suddenly he made the sign of the cross." "Big wind," Mau recalls. "I think more than sixty knots. Wind and rain. Me, I scared because the canoe is close to the Big Island. Big waves. If we had been on my canoe, no more canoe."

After about four hours, the winds seemed to decrease slightly. Still, *Hōkūle'a* and *Ishka* continued to slowly slip back toward the rocky coastline. "We were losing ground," Alex recalls. "I thought we might have to swim." Alex conferred with Gordon by VHF radio. If *Ishka* could not keep *Hōkūle'a* off the coast, Gordon would release the towline. *Ishka's* crew would tie a life preserver to it and Alex would circle *Hōkūle'a* to bring the line close to the canoe. Then Gordon and his crew would abandon ship, swim to the rope and be hauled aboard *Ishka.* "I was worried but you couldn't show other people that you were worried," Alex recalls. "I thought that if the engine went out we would be finished. We would have lost our boat and *Hōkūle'a*."

About six hours after the storm hit, Jo-Anne recalls seeing a blue flashing light. The Coast Guard cutter *Cape Newagen* had arrived. "When they came, they told me it would not be safe to come near *Hōkūle'a* or *Ishka*," Alex recalls. "They told us to follow them back to Kawaihae."

Slowly, in abating winds, Alex worked up sufficient speed to begin towing

Hōkūle'a around 'Upolu Point on the northern tip of the Big Island and into the lee on the western side. *Cape Newagen* stood by until they were safely on their way to the nearby commercial port of Kawaihae.

Once *Ishka* was moored in Kawaihae, Alex went below to check his engines. Two engine mounts had worked loose and would have to be replaced. It had been a close call.

"That storm made me come to grips with the danger of voyaging. If you want to be out there, bad weather is part of the bargain," Chad recalls. "Anyone can sail in good weather. I had an opportunity to back out of the trip to Tahiti. I remember thinking 'Do I really want to do this again? Do I want to go through that?' "

"It was something you don't want to go through every day," Gordon recalls. "The ocean has no conscience. We were our own 'Magnificent Seven' on that trip. Everybody just worked as a team."

"To this day," says Chad, "on a good day out there in the 'Alenuihāhā channel, I get really scared that something is going to come down hard and just slam the door. It was terrifying. That's the best way to describe it."

"When we came in from the storm," Tava recalls, "it was like we came in from a long voyage from far, far away. The body relaxing, tired. I said, 'Mau, now I need something warm.' You know Mau, he likes something warm too. 'Whisky,' I say, 'for wake up.' "

THE DREAM

Chapter Thirty-Five

A few days after the storm, *Hōkūle'a* was towed past Hilo's sheltering breakwater and moored in front of the Naniloa Hotel. Sam Ka'ai and Snake Ah Hee flew in to join her from Maui. Pat Aiu came from Kaua'i and Harry Ho, Buddy McGuire, and Marion Lyman-Mersereau arrived from O'ahu. Shorty Bertelmann drove from Waimea. Their families came with them.

Hōkūle'a moored at Naniloa Hotel

During the following week, the weather was grim. Two stationary fronts diverted the normal trade wind flow from northeast to east and then to the southeast. The wind gusted to forty knots and it brought rain. It was a large system and it was stalled. Ocean swells reached twenty feet and crashed against Hilo's breakwater. Nainoa and his crew settled in, waiting for the wind to shift back to the northeast.

Sam Ka'ai brought his *pū* with him, a conch shell trumpet that he used to announce the beginning and end of a sacred event. He had blown the *pū* when *Hōkūle'a* was launched and when she arrived on her first voyage to Maui. He had blown the *pū* to greet *Hōkūle'a* when she made landfall in Raiatea during her cruise around the Society islands in 1976. And when Sam stepped aboard *Hōkūle'a* in 1978, he carried his *pū* under his arm. After the canoe capsized, Sam feared the *pū* had been lost but it was found dangling from a net by a Coast Guard diver working to attach the tow line. "That *pū* was brought back to call again," Sam says, "That was one of the tangible things that I got ready for the voyage besides the toothbrush and the extra this and that."

On Sunday, March 9ᵗʰ, Sam dressed in a short cloak of *ti* leaves, donned a head *lei* of *palapalai* and blew his *pū* at Coconut Island in Hilo Bay to begin an *'awa* ceremony to bless the upcoming voyage. He laid down mats of woven *lau hala* and arranged the crew in a circle. He placed two feather *lei* on the ground before Gordon, Mau and Nainoa. "The rain had been hard," Sam recalls, "and then there was a clear period and we decided to do the ceremony."

The *'awa* ceremony marked the separation of the crew from the land. It signified they were about to travel "in the hollow of the hand of god, in the lap of the mother" as Sam puts it. With the ceremony, the crew became *kapu* — sacred — separate from the routine affairs of men and women. They were about to venture upon an altar, the canoe, and would soon follow the "*lei* of bones," the ancestral route to the homeland. "You will go on the lap of the mother," Sam told them. "You will be in the hand of *akua*, of god, and his breath will fill your sails."

Sam mixed the *'awa*, a mild intoxicant from the root of the *'awa* plant, in a large beautifully carved wooden bowl. "*Hō mai ka wai ola o Kāne*," Sam prayed softly, "bring on the waters of life. *Hō mai ke Kāne* — the water is brought in the body of *Kāne; mai ke Kāne 'awa—ke kīnolau o Kāne*, the body of god." Then he stood to chant:

'O Lono ma mua
Lono in front of me

'O Lono ma hope
Lono behind me

'O Lono ma luna
Lono above me

'O Lono ma lalo
Lono below me

Lono 'ākāu
Lono to the right of me

Lono hema
Lono to the left of me

Lono i loko
Lono within me

"It is the god above me, below me, around me, in front of me," Sam explained to the crew. *"Ko uka o Lono*—it is a condition, a state of mind, the things of heaven surround all of you." As he chanted, Sam faced west and entered a world of spiritual dimensions. "When you face west that means you are not afraid of going forth into death. West is the ending. West is where all the souls go to. Your left hand is facing south. In the south are all the places we came from: Samoa, Tonga, Tahiti ku—the place from which all our ancestral lines come to us. Your right hand is facing north. North is the unknown, the cold, the high portion, the clear white. East is where we sailed to find islands when we came out of the west."

Sam dipped a cup into the large bowl and poured *'awa* into a carved coconut shell that he offered to each crew member. After each man finished drinking, the entire crew clapped three times. "When you clap the first time, it means 'You said it,'" Sam explains. "The second clap means 'I heard it.' The third means 'I hold you to it.' *Pa'i ka lima,* or heaven holds you to it. You make a pledge with the body of god within you and surrounding you: 'I will follow the command. I will be on this voyage. I will be one with the crew.' And those all around you, when they clap, are saying 'We heard you and heaven will hold you to it.' The crew pledges their loyalty and their hand to the *kāpena,* the captain, and the *ho'okele*, the navigator. Everyone speaks the truth, because they drank the body of *akua*. That is what the *'awa* ceremony is. You offer yourself up—to be one with heaven—and to do heaven's work. It is beyond being a man. It is being in the eternal spirit, being the god within you."

Shortly after the ceremony, Nainoa rose to speak. He faced Mau Piailug. "It was you who inspired us and gave us strength," he said. "You live by the sea. We do not. We are your children. Now is our time to learn. We must sail or forever be silent."

Then the crew rose and went aboard *Hōkūle'a*. They tied the *lei huluhulu* to each of her masts and they lashed the *ki'i* to the *manu*. To end the ceremony, Sam blew his *pū* once again. The rain had held off for the last hour or so. Now it began to pour. "When I blew the *pū* the sky cracked and the rain came down," Sam recalls. "The mats were wet, everything was wet. It was like a blessing. The *akua* waited for us to complete the ceremony. Now we must wait until the *ho'okele*, the navigator, the one who knows the mystery of the Earth and all the stars, would decide if the wind was right, if the redness of the dawn was right. There is the time when spiritually the voyage begins, and there is a time when the *ho'okele* says 'Now.' "

The next day, a little after 3:00 a.m., Nainoa rose and dressed in his hotel room. He looked out the window. Hilo sat in a bowl of mountains, protected from the southeast wind, but he saw surf crashing over the outer breakwater and clouds scudding across the bay. It was raining. In hotel rooms all around him, his crew slumbered. "There was all this pressure. All these people were waiting to go. They had jobs they had given up. There were guys flying back and forth between work because they had taken the whole month off for the voyage." Some among the crew were professionals and a month off from busy schedules was particularly difficult to arrange, now it looked like they would need an extra week or two. "Nobody wanted to wait the extra days, nobody. And in Hilo—in that pocket—there was no wind. They didn't see me get up at three o'clock to go to look at the weather."

Nainoa went out to the parking lot, got into his rented car, and began the long drive out to Kumukahi point, the easternmost tip of the Big Island. He drove up the flanks of Mauna Loa and through the tiny village of Pāhoa, wending through dark lava fields and out to the peninsula. In the waning night, a Coast Guard lighthouse blinked at Kumukahi. The cape presented a jagged scene of lava from a 1960 eruption—smooth *pāhoehoe* lava like congealed stone puddles and sharp spikes of hardened *'a'ā* lava. Kumukahi is a sacred place because the rays of the sun first strike the Hawaiian Islands here every morning. Many legends associate Pele with this place and some say that Tahitian sailors first arrived at Kumukahi many centuries ago.

Nainoa stood by the lighthouse. Buffeted by gusting southeast winds, he observed the dawn as Mau had taught him. He watched for a break in the clouds but the sky dome was gray all around the horizon. Ragged banks of low clouds scudded before the wind. "I was making my decision the old way, not by weather reports but by watching the sunrise. I was looking for the wind to die down. I was looking for it to drop into a safe range and come from north of east so we could hold a southeast course. I wanted something that was not due east. I was looking for the rain to back away. It was exhausting—waiting."

Sam Ka'ai saw the delay in his own way. "We had the *'awa* ceremony and it rained and it rained and it rained, and everybody said 'We got to go.' People had to work, the professional people can't wait that long. And it just rained solid. The idea was to be patient, to be obedient, to wait. Don't be uppity. Don't make schedules. It's not up to you. It's up to heaven. If you want to learn the old way, learn patience. And it was a very, very hard lesson to learn. There was a lot of complaining—'God, I got a schedule,' 'I just took off this time'—we had a constant lament of that. It is okay to wait. We all learned that. It's part of everybody's wonderful memory. You got into the rhythm of the weather. You got under the eye of heaven. Its song was the song that you were going to be the chorus of. You did not make the song. All of these were humbling lessons. It's about getting back into the rhythm of the *holo moana*—not the rhythm of the world we live in today."

Every day, for almost two weeks, Nainoa came down from his room and briefed his crew. "We are not going today," he told them. "The weather is no good. You guys do what you have to do. I will let you know when we can go." Among those waiting for the canoe's departure were the news media—both print and television. Cameras were laid out on couches in the hotel lobby—ready to shoot anything that happened. Mostly nothing did. "Newspapers. Television. I am hiding from all those guys," Nainoa recalls.

In 1978, on March 17th, Eddie Aikau had set out on his surfboard to save his crew—and the two year anniversary of that day was fast approaching. "Eddie was on my mind all the time," Nainoa recalls. "I knew we were going at the same time and that some people thought we shouldn't go at that time. It was the worst. In my mind I was going over what can and will go wrong like a broken record. I was always on edge." During one of those fretful evenings, Nainoa had a dream.

The canoe moves south toward Tahiti. She encounters the Doldrums, the zone of calms and sudden storms. He's on his navigator's platform, staring ahead. He sees a dark bar of cloud. He sees wind all across the horizon. They sail on. The clouds gather. They engulf him in darkness and stinging rain. The sea is a confused mass of white crests. Desperately he seeks wave patterns. He seeks the stars. But there are none. The canoe staggers. The wind shifts. Helplessly, he watches the steersman struggle with Hōkūle'a's massive paddle. The steersman shouts something—but it's carried away by the wind. He beseeches Nainoa for direction. But Nainoa is utterly lost. He opens his mouth to speak. What? And then he wakes up.

Nainoa tried to conjure a plan for the Doldrums. But the dream offered none. Surely it wouldn't be that bad? It was just a dream. But he couldn't shake it. He endured exile in his hotel room by going over his notes. He studied the stars he would steer by. He memorized the table of offsets he would use to calculate the effect of currents and wind on the canoe's progress. He found comfort in the neat rows of numbers stored in his brain. It was all so orderly. He was ready. But still—the dream.

There was some doubt that a western-educated person, even though of Hawaiian ancestry, could learn the ancient art of navigating without instruments. A lot of doubt, in fact. Mau had studied navigation at his grandfather's knee. At age three, he was gently held in the waters of the lagoon to feel the waves' motion. For countless hours, he had observed stars in a sky as crystalline as it gets anywhere in the world because his island, Satawal, is so far from civilization's pollutants. And he continued to train during years of voyaging, first under the watchful eyes of his grandfather, then his father, until he was ready to sail alone. Mau could not write. He had no maps to draw his course upon. These facts made his work more difficult—but it developed powers of mind and of observation that could not be replicated in a western world, enclosed as it is by walls and by perceptions requiring instruments.

Nainoa had relied on instruments to prepare for the voyage and they were a mighty help. The spinning Spitz Ball in the museum's planetarium had replicated hundreds of voyages, allowing him to step back to an era when his ancestors sailed similar sea paths. Aboard his small boat off O'ahu, he had studied the real stars. He had pored over maps, the tables of currents and winds and astronomical ephemera. Theoretically, he knew how to guide *Hōkūle'a* to Tahiti. If the sky was clear. If the wave patterns were predictable. And if all this learning in the pristine silence of the planetarium and bending over his kitchen table late into the night would actually remain in memory under the onslaught of sleepless nights, storms and the sea's unpredictable vagaries.

"Keep the vision of the island in your mind and you will find it," Mau had told him.

Nainoa thought he could see Tahiti rising there above the horizon. He had seen it a few times. But did it really exist? Or was it a kind of hallucination inspired by the presence of his teacher, this man who knew things so deeply and innately? Would the vision fade? What, after all, did such a thing really mean?

On March 14th, Nainoa drove once more out to Kumukahi. During the evening, the wind had begun to shift east. Now it was blowing east-northeast. It was not perfect, but it was good enough. The ocean swells were still steep. Nainoa knew they would not calm for another few days and the seas would be confused, but it was time to go.

THE LORD MAKANI

Chapter Thirty-Six

Saturday, March 15th, deep swells crashed against Hilo's breakwater and the wind carried tendrils of spray into the harbor. Rain slicked the lawn at the Naniloa Hotel and sheened *Hōkūle'a's* decks as a human chain passed aboard last minute gear. "People had made *lehua* blossom *lei* for us," Sam Ka'ai recalls, "and in the rain the petals were stuck on everybody's beards and faces." Steve Somsen shielded his clipboard, checking off each item that went over the gunwale. He stood out from the rest of the dark-skinned crew. He was, as one crew-member affectionately called him—"completely *haole*." Steve had been chosen quartermaster because, as another described him, he was a "linear-sequential thinker," a man who was "very clear and methodical and systematic." In 1978, *Hōkūle'a* had been loaded haphazardly. This would not happen again. Steve would see to it.

As the canoe was readied for sea, Nainoa pored over his notes in the seclusion of his hotel room. In the charged atmosphere of resurgent Hawaiian pride, he felt the weight of public scrutiny. His success—or failure—had taken on powerful dimensions.

Just before departing, crew members dropped their wristwatches into a white plastic bucket. For the next month, the sun and stars would be their only timepiece. At 11:00 a.m., they lined *Hōkūle'a's* rail and joined their voices with thronging well-wishers to sing "Hawai'i Aloha." Shortly thereafter, *Ishka* towed *Hōkūle'a* away from the Hotel's sheltered lagoon. Harry Ho waved to Laura Thompson.

"Don't worry," he yelled over the widening expanse of water.

Nainoa had told his mother how Harry had taken care of him. How he had stocked the refrigerator in the shack at Kuli'ou'ou, driven him to observation places on the Big Island, shepherded him in Tahiti. *Of all the crew,* Laura thought, *this is the man I can trust.* So she had taken Harry aside during the week of waiting at the hotel.

Nainoa and crew departing Hilo

"Take care of my son," she said.

Clearing Hilo's breakwater, *Ishka* increased speed and the two vessels moved slowly to sea, breasting ocean swells that roared down from the far horizon. Captain Gordon Pi'ianai'a divided the twelve men and two women aboard *Hōkūle'a* into two watches in a system sailors call "port and starboard." In the port watch were Steve Somsen—watch captain—along with Harry Ho, Jo-Anne Sterling, Chad Baybayan, and Pat Aiu—the ship's doctor. The starboard watch consisted of Leon Sterling—watch captain and first mate—Shorty Bertelmann, Sam Ka'ai, Buddy McGuire, Marion Lyman-Mersereau, and Tava Taupu. Nainoa, Mau, and Captain Pi'ianai'a would not stand specific watches—they would be constantly on duty. Six of the crew—Nainoa, Sam, Buddy, Marion, Leon, and Tava—were veterans of the 1978 capsizing which had occurred almost exactly two years earlier.

All hands were on deck. They secured hatches, stowed the last few items of cargo, coiled ropes—making their canoe ready for sea. Jo-Anne lit the burner in *Hōkūle'a's* galley, a simple wooden box lashed on deck, and prepared steaming mugs of coffee. At noon, the port watch took charge of the canoe. They would be on duty for six hours, until six p.m., when the starboard watch would relieve them. It was the beginning of a long seaborne routine of wakefulness and sleep.

Steve Somsen shared his *puka*, his berthing compartment, with Tava Taupu and he settled into the cramped six by three-foot space shortly after lunch. "The canoe was still under tow," he remembers. "I heard the constant sound of *Ishka's* diesel engine, the patter of rain on the canvas tent overhead and the whooshing sound of the ocean running between the hulls." Settling in, Steve found the *puka* remarkably dry and cozy. *This won't be so bad,* he thought, and was soon asleep.

Aboard *Ishka,* Alex Jakubenko and his wife Elsa, Will Kyselka and his wife Lee, John Eddy, and Michael Stroup had set up their own watch schedule. Examining *Hōkūle'a,* pitching in the swells astern, Will observed only three of her crew on deck. "A bunch of people were sick," Harry Ho remembers. "When we left Hilo, they were throwing up." "We left in a storm," Marion recalls, "as soon as we got out of the breakwater, I'm puking my guts out. They rolled me into the port hull up forward and kind of left me there. And Tava—bless his heart—was emptying my bucket and checking on me and I'm just miserable."

Late that afternoon, Nainoa ordered the towrope cast off. *Hōkūle'a* spread her sails, on a course[‡] due southeast in steady twenty-five knot winds. "Finally we came around the point and we exploded," Sam Ka'ai recalls, "we screamed along. This powerful sail—this invigoration—the Lord Makani was there. You hear it in your ears and feel it in your bones, the vibration of the deck—*ka waiwai*

[‡] Courses on this voyage are always the course "through the water" or the "apparent course" with the leeway added in.

holoholo mai—you feel it up to your knees. You lie down but it's hard to sleep. If you got sleep, you didn't remember it."

"I was afraid every day I was in Hilo waiting to go," Nainoa recalls. "I constantly rehearsed everything that could go wrong. Getting out beyond Hilo's breakwater was powerful. When I saw this whole expanse of ocean in front of me it was like freedom. Just freedom."

At sunset, *Hōkūle'a* was twenty-five miles east-northeast of the Big Island's Cape Kumukahi. The sea was slate gray, marbled with whitecaps to the rumpled horizon. The darkening sky was also gray, although a shade lighter. At sunset, sky and sea blended and *Hōkūle'a* sailed into an indistinct dark void. On this moonless and starless first night at sea, Nainoa steered by two large swells, one from the east and another from the northeast, and by the steady northeasterly wind. The course was good, southeast.

"I was glad to be at sea but I worried about staying awake," Nainoa recalls. "Mau never sleeps at sea. He can stay up for weeks on end—how in Hell was I going to do that? Not sleeping was part of Mau's magic—not part of mine."

Preparing for the voyage on land, Nainoa had conducted sleep deprivation experiments. Late at night, in his parents' house in Niu, he wrapped himself in a blanket and paced the lawn and empty streets. During the day, he continued to walk because he knew if he stopped he would fall down. Mau, watching him through the jalousie windows, laughed softly. Nainoa's record was thirty-six hours. Then he collapsed.

"I couldn't do it on land," Nainoa recalls. "So when we left Hilo I was voyaging both into an unknown ocean and into unknown regions of my own potential. It was ten thirty at night. I thought, *It's pretty late. I had better get some rest or I will be a basket case tomorrow.* I lay down and closed my eyes. I thought, *How stupid you are. You're not ready to sleep. You cannot sleep.* So I got up and went back on watch."

The sky had cleared, revealing a bowl of stars and the raging ocean from horizon to horizon. Maui's fishhook, Eddie Aikau's constellation, was rising.

"I jumped back on deck and there was Eddie—right in front of the canoe. It was so exciting—liberating."

"That day there were two liberations," Nainoa continues, "One was just getting beyond Hilo's breakwater. If I didn't leave the breakwater there was the chance that I wouldn't have to go. Then I could not fail. That was my internal battle, go—don't go, but once we were out of the breakwater it was beautiful to have this whole giant ocean in front of us. The other liberation was that moment when I didn't feel tired. From then on, I slept only three or four hours a day. When I became so exhausted that I couldn't think, I lay down and slept until I dreamed. I slept maybe twenty minutes at a time and my mind was refreshed. I learned to do that for a month. It was a whole new reality."

It was a reality that scientists today call "the zone" or "flow state." Psychologist Mihaly Csikszentmihalyi, working at the University of Chicago, first coined the term in 1988. Flow state, he says, is "…being completely involved in an activity for its own sake. The ego falls away. Time flies. Every action, movement, and thought follows inevitably from the previous one, like playing jazz. Your whole being is involved, and you're using your skills to the utmost." Csikszentmihalyi thinks that two conditions are necessary for a person to enter the zone: a high level of challenge and a high level of skill. You must overcome your fear to accept the challenge—but you must also have fully prepared yourself to succeed.

"I didn't even know that there was a zone," says Nainoa looking back on that first day at sea. "I didn't know there was a different way in which you exist between your normal life and the life of a navigator. Everything that happened before the voyage—the physical training, the mental training, the experience with Mau, all the analytical stuff and going to Mauna Kea—were steps in my preparation for this. That preparation was everything. When you add it all up, it goes back to Yoshi, to my dad, to my grandmother, to all my teachers. You're going down a path. Something inside you says that as a person who is native to this land it's a path you must take. Without knowing why. Then it culminates in this powerful focus on Hōkūle'a and on finding land for Eddie. If the zone is like a door that you walk through, I don't think you can even *find* the door unless you have prepared for it."

Sunday, March 16. Day Two.

At sunrise on Sunday, Hōkūle'a battled heavy seas. The crew kept vigil over the water in her bilges. Just before noon, Mau scanned the clouds for signs of wind.

"Take down sails," he ordered.

The wind had increased to forty knots from the east. Under bare poles, the canoe drifted west at one knot. "We got caught in that storm and we hove to," Nainoa recalls, "and I thought—Shit, this is way beyond me. We were getting a licking. The sails were down. We were out of control. And we hadn't even left Hawaiian waters."

Aboard *Ishka*, Will Kyselka felt the pain of this first day at sea. "*Ishka* creaks as it rolls," he wrote in his book—*An Ocean in Mind*. "Halyards slap at the mast and strange chafing noises persist, like the sound of someone cutting heavy paper with scissors. Once in a while I go topside for a look and quickly return to collapse on the bunk. I think of almost nothing but getting an airplane here to pick me up. Otherwise, I'll get dehydrated, I'll go into shock, and they'll have to bury me here at sea not far from Hilo."

At sunset, the canoe continued drifting west. Observing *Hōkūpaʻa*, the North Star, Nainoa thought *Hōkūleʻa* was between seventeen and eighteen degrees north latitude. It's not an auspicious beginning.

"It is wet, wet, wet," Jo-Anne wrote in her diary. "Cold seas, rough, winds are strong—thirty to forty knots. Everyone has been very quiet, just doing their work, probably concerned if the canoe can take the seas. Tava, Pat, Harry, Marion, Sam and me have been throwing up. Marion is down. Mau is suffering from his right shoulder, results of an old injury. Kaʻai claims his diet will be sugar cane for three days to prevent seasickness. …Seas gushing in. Impossible to sleep comfortably, clothes all wet."

The aft-most compartment, the last one on the port side of the canoe, was open to the elements except for the shelter provided by the navigator's platform overhead. It's the canoe's bathroom. Nainoa eased into it to take a salt water bath, towel and tooth brush in hand. "Waves were hitting the *ʻiako*," he recalls. "I hung a flashlight on the navigator's platform and I put my toothbrush down and a wave takes it and I see it go out the scupper. It's the first night. Shit, that's the only one I got."

"Harry," Nainoa said, "you got an extra toothbrush?"

Harry was prepared for this. "When Nainoa is concentrating, everything goes by the wayside, he tends to get absent-minded about mundane stuff." Harry went below and returned with a Tupperware box. Inside were six identical tooth brushes—each a different color.

"Pick a color," he said.

"After that, I knew I was in good hands," Nainoa recalls. "Harry didn't say a word, he just pulled out this Tupperware box that perfectly fit six tooth brushes."

The storm continued through the night. "The driving of the rain," Jo-Anne wrote. "The heaving of the ocean. The roaring of the water between the hulls. It's amazing, since leaving Honolulu, how much the canoe has endured. Hope to God she holds up. ...My constant prayers for all are for strength, wisdom and compassion."

Monday, March 17. Day Three.

Dawn on Monday. The sky was veined with clouds of all descriptions—as if Mother Nature had dug deep into her laundry bin to hang out every cloud she owned. *Hōkūle'a* continued hove to. The wind drove the rain in horizontal sheets.

Nainoa dropped into the number seven compartment, aft, on the port side. He squatted and examined the ocean churning between the hulls. "I was trying to figure out how fast we were drifting downwind. I saw vortices of water churning off the hulls, like little cyclones of water, making trails to windward. We're drifting fast. And we're drifting exactly where we don't want to go—west."

Mau sat on deck peering through a slit between the rail and the canvas tent that covered his compartment. "He kept looking through that crack," Nainoa recalls, "looking at the ocean. He was looking into the wind and he was looking for change. When is this thing going to change?"

"It felt like we were in a cosmic cloud," says Sam Ka'ai. "You are in the eye of the storm, what we call *maka i'a*—the fish eye. It's like saying 'god's eye is on you.' You had this feeling you were being watched, that your best conduct and most noble thoughts and best prayers were required. The Lord Makani was giving you a challenge. He was whispering his finest songs. You were filled with that kind of consciousness—everything was *now* and *present* and *real*. All our *'aumākua* were watching because so much hung on our good conduct for future generations. But at that moment you did not think about future generations. You thought *'maoli 'oe, kēia ka maoli*, this is *real.*' "

It was too rough for even minor housekeeping so the crew became inured to chaos in their *puka*. Many did not bother to change their clothes and they appeared on deck disheveled and wrinkled. All except Harry Ho, who disliked disorder of any kind. During training cruises, he invented a way of cold pressing his clothing by folding and placing them under heavy gear. Now he appeared on deck as if he'd just stepped out of his architect's office, ready for a meeting with clients. "Harry was neat and tidy out there," Chad recalls. "He rolled out on deck pressed and ironed." Harry could control his appearance, but he couldn't control the weather. He took it personally. The crew began to call particularly large assaults of spray "Harry splashes" because of his grumbling.

Just about everyone aboard the two vessels was queasy, but Marion was truly seasick, rolling painfully from side to side in her *puka*. "Marion has been in port two since we left," wrote Jo-Anne. "Feel bad for her. Christ she looks like death warmed over."

"The one I remember the most during this time was Tava," says Marion. "I'm throwing up. I'm peeing in a bucket. He was cleaning up after me and bringing me tea crammed with sugar, trying to get something into me. At one point, he told me that he was afraid I was going to die."

"She was in a waterproof sleeping bag," Nainoa recalls, "and they put her on deck to get her out of the compartment hoping she would be less seasick. She couldn't move. It was a big black bag. When they zipped her up I thought, *Damn—just like a body bag.*"

If things were bad aboard *Hōkūle'a* they were infinitely worse on *Ishka*. *Hōkūle'a's* twin hulls provide stability so she took the swells with grace, maintaining a relatively level attitude. *Ishka* is a monohull. In heavy seas, she rolled. Under a press of canvas, she leaned. Her crew lived in a heaving world slanted thirty degrees from horizontal. And while *Hōkūle'a's* slim *manu* sliced cleanly through the swells, *Ishka's* bluff bow smacked them hard. *Hōkūle'a* glided. *Ishka* pounded. At some point during all this turmoil, *Ishka's* mainsail tore. Her crew, most of them not feeling all that well, struggled to remove it from the mast hank by hank. They sent it below where Captain Jakubenko began the laborious job of sewing a patch—his vessel plunging and bobbing all the while. "Alex and the canvas fill the galley," Will wrote. "He sits on the sail, bracing his feet against the other side of the galley to steady himself. For hours he works on the sail, diligently using a boson's palm to push a heavy needle through a double-thick canvas patch."

Aboard *Hōkūle'a*, Snake lit the galley to prepare breakfast. Sam Ka'ai watched him fussing over the frying pan in the steady rain. "I saw the rain dripping off his face into the frying pan—that was a new kind of gourmet cooking with the salt from the nose."

At 6:00 a.m., the wind died a little. Nainoa gave the order to hoist sails and the feeling of being underway buoyed the crew. The wind continued out of the east, forcing Nainoa to sail south southeast—one and a half compass points, or houses, to the west of his desired course[‡]. Steve Somsen, clutching log sheets in one hand and a tape recorder in the other, approached Nainoa. Steve was the voyage documenter. It was his job to consult Nainoa at sunrise and sunset and to record the voyage.

"It's been difficult to tell how far we've sailed with this wind," Nainoa told him. "Sometimes we're sailing with one sail, then with the sails triced, then bare poles. I can't see the sun or stars—nothing."

Nainoa dealt with the fluking wind by trimming the canoe's sails. When the wind blew more than thirty-five knots, he ordered them "triced up," hauled tight against the masts. If the wind increased still more, the sails flailed against their constraints—risking damage—so he ordered them lowered to the deck. Under less strenuous conditions, he might order only one of the sails triced, proceeding with the other sheeted in to prevent it from flogging. In this manner, *Hōkūle'a* proceeded from sunrise until noon, when she encountered a line of dark squalls and the sails were dropped once again.

[‡] The courses that Nainoa gives to Steve during sunset and sunrise observations, and the courses he uses for his dead reckoning, are always the canoe's course through the water, or the apparent course (the heading) with leeway added in. The reference course is the course through the water with the additional effect of the current added in. On this leg, Nainoa's course through the water is 140 degrees true and the reference course is 144 degrees true. Theoretically, if he is able to hold 140 degrees true through the water he will be sailing on his reference course. There is one large caveat to this assumption, however, the effect of the current is dependent on the amount of time the canoe spends in the current. Nainoa assumes that it will take 6 days to complete this leg, during which the current will push her west 13 miles a day, or 78 miles total. If it requires one day longer, however, he will be 13 miles further to the west then anticipated when he completes the leg. Nainoa has no way of knowing as he sails each leg how long the journey will take, so his reported positions east or west of the reference course are only provisional—good enough until, reaching the end of the leg, he can add in the final effect of the current on the canoe.

Jo-Anne took to crawling when moving around on deck. Her knees cramped up. Going below, she curled in a tight ball, accommodating to the confines of her *puka* and bundles of wet clothes. Her legs began to cramp. "I couldn't move, let alone eat," she wrote in her log. "It was horrible when we left. Really, really bad."

"When you sail, you give your emotions to nature," says Nainoa. "If it's a calm evening with the stars out to tell you where you are and the winds allow you to go where you want to, it's just the most peaceful feeling. But now the wind was from the east and we're smoking—going in exactly the wrong direction. Nature was overwhelming us and we couldn't do anything about it. I was asking 'When is this going to end?' And I couldn't see the end."

"We don't see the sky," Tava recalls. "We don't see the sun—only black. We tired, tired."

The human body adapts to difficult situations by closing up shop. Many on board were constipated. Going to the bathroom on *Hōkūle'a* was difficult even in calm water. You stood on a narrow catwalk outside the hulls, hung on and squatted. It's important to be vigilant because large swells pick up the bow and set down the stern accompanied by a wash of green water. "You strip off your foul weather pants and hang on," Jo-Anne recalls. "And naturally you tense up—so there goes the urge. Water splashes your butt. I had visions of falling over without my pants on." She noticed Sam, who had been constipated for three days, standing on the catwalk hanging on for dear life. A little later he worked his way forward, a broad smile under his full mustache.

One moment *Hōkūle'a* lay deep in a trough, enclosed in a mountainous world of water. Another moment she broke free and climbed high atop a swell. From her deck, the view was framed by wind-blown ocean and torn clouds. There was potential for terror in this scene—except for the countervailing image of Nainoa perched on his navigator's platform deep in contemplation.

If he can do this, so can we, went the communal thought.

For Harry Ho, the thought was: *He can do it—if we help him.*

Harry brought food to Nainoa. He brought him water. He fretted over his foul weather gear. He watched him for signs of fatigue. "It boggled the mind," Marion remembers. "Harry Ho was like Nainoa's butler. Nainoa was always in this kind of other world and Harry was giving him his toothbrush, washing his clothes. He was so take-caring." *This is a man doing a job,* Harry seemed to be thinking, *and I'm just going to make sure that everything else gets done.*

Harry and Nainoa shared the compartment called starboard six. Calling it a compartment is optimistic. The crew called them *puka*—which translated to English means "hole." Each *puka* is a tiny space in the hulls about six feet long by three wide. During heavy weather, the crew slept in their rain gear, sliding from side to side as the canoe rocked. They were protected from the elements by a canvas tent rising from the gunwales and attached to the railing above. Spray tried to enter from the bottom and sides, rain from the top. It was a contest in which water was always victorious. Rain seeped through the tent and dripped on them, but the real discomfort came from spray which often achieved the velocity—and the effect—of a garden hose being squirted directly into the compartment. Harry was ingenious in arranging the accommodations he shared with Nainoa. He waterproofed the tent with duct tape. He hung a clothesline. He brought aboard two reclining chairs like the kind seen on the beach at Waikīkī. To make a bed, he broke the legs off one of them and laid it across two large Igloo coolers which also served as waterproof storage. Atop the chair, he placed a precisely cut piece of foam. When Nainoa first went below after many days on deck, he was astounded.

"Jesus Christ, Harry—it's a palace down here."

❖ ❖ ❖ ❖ ❖

In Hilo, Nainoa had waited patiently, scanning the horizon and meteorological charts for good weather. Now, he wondered, why hadn't he waited longer? Certainly there were pressures—but when to depart was his choice alone. And this first decision had been a mistake. Now, another decision lingered in the blasting winds. Should he continue drifting west or turn around and sail back to Hilo to begin the voyage anew—from a known point? A mariner's instinct is always to make ground toward his destination. Like a fire-walker proceeding across burning coals, turning around is anathema. Yet Nainoa considered it. The canoe was moving south—toward Tahiti—but she was also being forced west. Tahiti was 2280 miles south and 360 miles east of Hilo, so it was critical for Nainoa to guide his canoe constantly east. Otherwise, when he reached Tahiti's latitude, he would find himself west of it—and downwind. But exactly how far downwind of the course to Tahiti had the storm set them?

Nainoa knew that traditional navigators embraced vast quantities of data in stories, chants and memory devices like the stick chart employed by Marshall Islands navigators, but he had no such cultural tools to rely on. He needed modern memory devices, suited to the way his own mind worked. He discovered them in mathematics. As he became more secure in his ability to find latitude by the stars, he grappled with the problem of finding his longitude[†] by dead reckoning. A few months before the voyage, he had unrolled a chart on his kitchen table and plotted his four reference courses to Tahiti. The first extended southeasterly from Hawai'i to the beginning of the Doldrums at nine degrees north. The second turned westerly through the Doldrums to five degrees north. The third turned westerly again and went on to the equator, where the fourth turned easterly to landfall in the middle of the Tuamotus at Takapoto atoll. To plot longitude, he would dead reckon how far he had strayed east or west from each of these course lines. That was not easy. It involved constant vigilance. From Hawai'i to nine north, for example, he needed to sail a course through the water of 140 degrees. Whenever he strayed from this course, he must memorize the course sailed, the speed, and how long he had sailed it; then he must mentally plot the result twice a day, at sunrise and at sunset. At sea. Without a chart. It involved many calculations and they all had to be made without pencil or paper. Pondering this for a few months, he recalled a lesson in a long-ago math class—any deviation from a straight line, such as the reference course, can be described graphically by an x and y axis.

So, one night in Honolulu, he opened a clean notebook and drew a line across it horizontally—the x axis. Using a protractor, he drew another line downward and perpendicular to the first—the y axis. With a scale, he measured 100 miles, a convenient average day of sailing in trade winds, and with a compass he drew a circle enclosing the two axes. The resulting figure resembled a large slice of pie. Finally, he drew lines radiating out every 11 ¼ degrees (or one house on his star compass) from the horizontal to the vertical—defining eight rays. He surveyed the results, speaking quietly to himself.

[†] I use the term longtitude throughout the book because it is so easily understood by western navigators, but Nainoa thinks of his position east or west on the globe in relationship to his reference course.

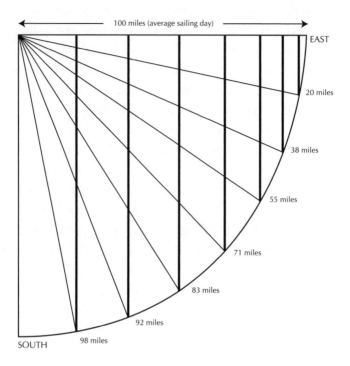

"Okay, the x axis represents my course through the water—due east let's say. What happens if the wind doesn't let me sail east? How much off course will I be if I sail one house away toward the south?"

He drew a new line perpendicular to the x axis—the desired course line— down to where the new course, one house to the south, intersected the 100 mile circle. Then he measured the line's distance: 19 1/2 miles. He rounded it off to 20.

"So, if my course through the water is due east and I have to sail one house to the south for an average sailing day, 100 miles, I will be 20 miles to the south of it."

He continued on, measuring the distances that various courses would cause him to deviate from his reference course. Two houses resulted in 38 miles. Three resulted in 55, four in 71, five in 83, six in 92, seven in 98, and eight houses of deviation would mean that he was sailing due south and would have proceeded a total of 100 miles away from the reference course.

There it is, he thought.

It was an elegantly simple solution. By memorizing this simple pie-shaped graphic and eight sets of numbers, he could mentally figure his course deviation, at sea, even when exhausted. If he sailed one house south for one sailing day of 100 miles he would be 20 miles south of his reference course. If he sailed two houses south, he would be 38 miles south and so on. Though he didn't think of it at the time, he was composing a kind of mathematical chant. A navigator's mantra.

Now, surrounded by the scream of wind, Nainoa entered this neat geometric world and began to plot the path of his canoe. When they had been able to sail, the canoe traveled southeast for a time, then southeast by south, then southeast again—following the veering winds. From 11 a.m. on Sunday to 6 a.m. on Monday—she lay hove to—drifting west. Nainoa calculated how far west from the reference course she drifted under bare poles and how far she traveled east when the wind allowed them to raise the sails. At sunrise on the 17th, he figured the canoe was 175 miles south of Hilo and eight houses—100 miles—to the west of his reference course.

To make up the eight houses that *Hōkūle'a* had traveled west, Nainoa must sail east the same number of houses. If he continued on the present course, he must make his easting bit by bit during the twenty-four hundred mile voyage. He must calculate—every day—how much he gained by sailing various courses as the wind allowed. Errors would accumulate. Starting at a known point on Earth—from Hilo—was difficult enough. But now he would be sailing from an uncertain beginning. *We're too damn far west,* Nainoa thought. *This is unacceptable.*

During the 1976 voyage, Mau had been driven west by unfavorable winds but he did not tack. He decided to sail to the latitude of Tahiti and only then, if the unfavorable winds held, to turn east and search for the island upwind. "I would not have done that," Nainoa recalls, "in my mind there's a point where you have to tack. Otherwise it will set you too far in the wrong direction. Clearly I knew Mau wanted to continue on. But it was just tearing me up to have to go so far west."

"I'm scared," Nainoa told Mau, "because the canoe is too far west."

"If we tack up we waste time," Mau replied. "I like we keep going south."

"I had to call it," Nainoa remembers. "I was very uncomfortable because I was basically telling Mau I'm going against his advice."

But Mau was sensitive to his student's mental state. This was Nainoa's first voyage and he must find his own way.

"Okay," Mau finally agreed, "we go back up."

At 1:00 p.m., with the winds shifting to east-southeast, Nainoa ordered the canoe over to the starboard tack. They sailed north-northeast, back towards Hilo.

"I remember Nainoa and Mau feeling their way as student and teacher," says Chad Baybayan. "Nainoa was saying 'I'm taking over now.' He had the courage to assume command. Mau stepped back and was comfortable with Nainoa's role. That was a turning point."

At sunset, Nainoa figured they were now a hundred and thirty miles to the south-southeast of Hilo. The canoe sailed north-northeast at about five and a half knots in fresh winds.

Everyone had been affected by those first three days of dark skies, contrary winds, and heavy seas. Jo-Anne sought a place to be alone and she fought off depression by focusing on *Hōkūle'a*. "I have a lot of respect for this canoe," she told Steve Somsen. "I talk to her. Down in my hole she seems so massive. The winds are high but she feels like she's a hundred and twenty feet long rather than sixty."

Aboard the escort boat, Alex was still repairing his mainsail. "The work is difficult because *Ishka* is taking a beating," wrote Will. "All night *Ishka's* engines turn at full speed as we move into the wind and keep pace with *Hōkūle'a*. At times we travel smoothly, then we gently rock. Sometimes we cut through a wave and expect to fall into a trench. Instead we do a roll and are thrown from side to side. A combination of wind and engine roar generates a sound like that of boxcars colliding and creates an impression of speed much greater than the four knots we are making."

Aboard *Hōkūle'a*, Marion could not sleep. Encased from head to foot in foul weather gear, she was wet and cold and miserably seasick.

"God, please get me off this canoe," she prayed.

Tuesday, March 18. Day Four.

The weather had sapped everyone. They all looked forward to climbing into their bunks after their watch was over. All except Nainoa. "I could have gone into the compartment where it was dry—at least dry. But I put my cap on and pulled it down and zipped up my foul weather gear, and I slept on deck. I never once went below. I think going below would have been a personal sign of weakness and lack of commitment. My job was to be on deck."

At sunrise, Nainoa tacked the canoe back south toward Tahiti. The wind was from the east-southeast at twenty knots. At this time of year, it should have been steady from the northeast. The canoe's course was now almost due south, but the course Nainoa wanted to sail was three and a half houses more to the east—so for every hundred miles they continued sailing this course, they would lose three and a half houses to the west. He considered tacking back north again but decided not to. *Tacking back will ruin the crew's morale,* he thought. Nainoa ordered weight moved forward to help the canoe point higher into the wind. Even so, she continued to be forced west. Would the wind shift? The story revealed by the swells was not good. The northeast swell was dying, indicating little hope for wind from that direction. The biggest swell was now from the east, but the swell from the southeast was more consistent and growing. It appeared the unfavorable wind would hold—even increase. "This is lousy wind." Nainoa told Steve, "We're just playing around out here. If we have to tack to Tahiti, it will take a century. We can't do anything unless the wind changes."

"There was a cosmic eye watching over us," Sam Ka'ai says about this time of trial, and there was indeed such a heavenly observer—a number of them in fact—Argos satellites monitoring the chirp of a transmitter aboard the canoe. In 1980, this was as high tech as it got, a collaboration between the Centre National d'Etudes Spatiales in France and the National Aeronautics and Space Administration in the United States. Depending on various conditions, Argos can locate any object carrying a transmitter to within a hundred and fifty meters.

Argos relayed *Hōkūle'a's* position to a lab at the University of Hawai'i, where it was plotted—and the track it presented was a doozey. At about noon on the second day of the voyage, March 16th, when *Hōkūle'a* lowered her sails and began to drift, the satellite showed her progressing steadily west until sunrise on March 17th when Nainoa raised sails again. The track then proceeded south for a few hours. During this time Nainoa and Mau were having their conversation about turning back. Nainoa's decision was revealed when the Argos track reversed and headed north-northeast at a rapid rate until, just after sunrise on the 4th day, March 18th, it reversed once more and headed south. The high-tech picture painted by the orbiting satellites was, in large measure, very similar to the one that Nainoa plotted in his mind.

❖ ❖ ❖ ❖ ❖

Early in the morning, the sun appeared between leaden clouds, elevating the spirits of all on board. "Good breakfast," Jo-Anne wrote, "fresh fruit, beverage, bread and crackers. The sun is out. Tava is washing everybody's clothes."

Lures trailed in *Hōkūle'a's* wake. In the afternoon, they caught a ten pound *mahimahi*. Jo-Anne soaked the fish in soy sauce and ginger and garnished it with red pepper and onions. To top it off she added soup, rice and coconut flakes. The sun lingered. The crew lounged in bathing suits. Rigging sprouted wet clothing. *Hōkūle'a* resembled a vessel inhabited by an army of rag pickers.

"Nainoa is more at ease," Jo-Anne wrote in her log, "he smiles and is learning to put up with our jokes."

Pat Aiu, *Hōkūle'a's* doctor, worried about Marion. Tava had diligently fed her soup and water to prevent dehydration but she had not eaten anything solid for four days. Pat moved unsteadily over *Hōkūle'a's* pitching deck and pulled back the curtain to her compartment. He found her listless—in an apparent state of near delirium. In addition to her obvious physical suffering, Marion was concerned that her condition might affect *Hōkūle'a's* mission. She had worked for five years to be on this voyage. She helped build the canoe. She trained aboard her and she endured the capsizing and the loss of Eddie Aikau. And now she was too sick to stand watches or help her crew-mates. She felt near death—but more than that—she was deeply embarrassed. When the canoe tacked north, Marion worried they were turning back to get in range of a helicopter.

"So," she said to Pat, "are you guys going to medevac me?"

"What the hell are you talking about?" he replied.

"I kind of snapped and came to right then," Marion remembers, "and that was when I started getting better."

CELESTIAL STEPPING STONES

Chapter Thirty-Seven

Wednesday, March 19. Day Five.

The wind shifted almost due east in the early morning. *Hōkūle'a* steered up—gaining a little ground on her westward set. Her course was now south southeast, a little better but still one and a half houses west of where Nainoa wanted to go. Once again the sky was veiled in cloud.

Two long feathered *lei*, called *lei hulu*, flew from the tips of *Hōkūle'a's* spars. Sam had made them to honor the ancestors who had sailed this same route. "They are the spirits of the old navigators dancing above us—*ka holoholo*."

At sunset, the wind blew hard in gusts. The crew managed to trice up the foresail, but when they lowered the boom it swayed wildly. There was a sharp crack. The boom had broken. Again the canoe drifted west. Mau, Tava and Leon lashed a splint to the boom. "Dangerous work in the dark," Marion wrote in her log. A few hours later, when the gusts moderated, the sails were raised once again.

"Too many clouds. No stars," Nainoa joked with Steve. "The wind is too strong from the east. We're always putting the sails down. We're drifting all over the Pacific. It's raining all the time. I'm cold. I want to go home."

"Other than that," Steve said, "what do you think of being out here?"

"Oh, it's great. I'm enjoying it. I recommend this for everybody. You ought to try it."

Nainoa paused, thinking of the days of storm and contrary winds.

"But wait until you get southeast winds, it's a lot more fun."

❖ ❖ ❖ ❖ ❖

Nainoa had made his first voyage on *Hōkūle'a* less than four years ago. In about the time a college undergraduate earns a bachelor's degree, he had passed from apprentice seaman to navigator—a far climb up the ranks. On his first visit to Tahiti, he had seen the effect of moving 34 degrees south—stars setting together that set more than two hours apart when seen from Honolulu. Traveling north aboard *Hōkūle'a* in 1976, he had observed the northern stars rise higher in the sky ahead, the southern stars sinking behind. He had studied these relationships in the serenity of the planetarium and the relative comfort of dry land and they were the basis for two unique ways of finding latitude—simultaneously setting and equally distant star pairs.

For the last five days, the sky had been overcast—affording few glimpses of these clues to latitude. On this evening, the sky finally cleared and, for the first time as navigator on an actual voyage, Nainoa saw the Little Dipper rotate up from the horizon, anchored at its handle by Polaris. He waited patiently until the constellation was upright, the Dipper's cup spilling imaginary water, and he saw Kochab aligned directly above Polaris. These two stars are equally distant pairs. When the distance between them is equal to the distance between Polaris and the horizon, as they appeared to be now, the canoe would be at 16 degrees north.

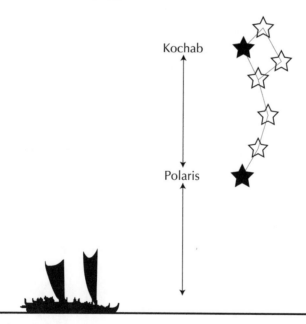

When the distance between Kochab and Polaris is equal to the distance between Polaris and the horizon - the canoe is at 16 degrees North latitude

"We're at 16 degrees north latitude," Nainoa told Steve. "This is the first clue we've had in what seems like seven hundred years."

"What about the reference course?" Steve asked.

"I think we're three houses to the west."

In the evening of the fifth day, Marion slithered out of her *puka* and staggered around on deck. She began, for the first time, to eat solid food.

Thursday, March 20. Day Six.

During the evening of March 19th and the early morning of the 20th, the wind abated. Then it pulsed—a giant heartbeat. The night thickened. The stars blinked out. A dark line appeared at the horizon and beneath it, the sea was frothed white.

Squalls.

Nainoa stood at the canoe's rail, one hand on the shrouds, examining the squall's intent.

"Stand by the sails."

The crew gathered at their stations—some forward to douse the main sail, others aft at the mizzen. The squalls were capricious. Some rushed ahead of the canoe as if to harmlessly cross its bow, only to stall and lurk in its path, others passed harmlessly astern. This one charged down on the canoe, gathering mass as it came.

"Take in sails."

Tricing lines were hauled tight. Brailing lines snugged the booms and sails to the mast. Now the wind arrived, accompanied by a deep moaning. A sharp rattling followed as the rain, now driven almost horizontally, slapped the canoe's canvas tents. A half hour later, the squall passed. The sails were raised.

"You have to watch carefully," Nainoa told Steve, "if you see a squall coming you try to sail in front of it because a squall creates a kind of vacuum behind it and there may be no wind for hours. But if you can't make it—get the sails in quickly, because the wind will tear up the rig and endanger the crew."

The order to "stand by the sails" signified a squall was near. The crew would hear that command countless times as they sailed into a zone of changing weather.

Orion and the Dog are among the most brilliant of constellations and for the last six evenings Nainoa had been observing them settle into the western horizon. Looking to the right, or more northerly, he saw the Bull with its bright red eye, Aldebaran, and the Charioteer with its brilliant, slightly yellow star, Capella. Above the Bull and Orion were the Twins, easy to find by their trademark stars, Castor and Pollux. Taken together, these five constellations filled the western horizon and they have drawn the eyes of sailors for as long as man has taken to the sea. But at this point in his journey, Nainoa's eyes were attracted to two particular stars, Mirzam in the Dog's hind leg and Betelgeuse in Orion's right shoulder—simultaneously setting pairs. When the canoe departed Hilo at latitude twenty-one north, Mirzam beat Betelgeuse to the horizon by about twelve minutes. Moving south though, the horizon tilted with each passing day and Betelgeuse began to catch up. At eighteen north, Mirzam was six minutes ahead but at sixteen north, its lead had diminished to about two minutes. Now Nainoa watched them set together, a sure sign of the canoe's address—fifteen degrees north latitude.

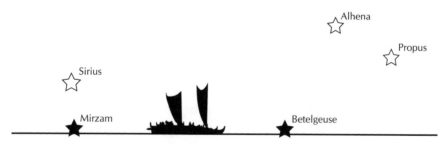

Mirzam and Betelgeuse set simultaneously at 15 degrees North latitude

Rarely did Nainoa have the opportunity to confirm his position by observing both equally distant and simultaneously setting star pairs. But now, looking south, he saw Alpha Centauri crossing the meridian with another star directly above it, Alpha Lupus. These two Alphas are equally distant pairs— when the distance between them and the distance between Alpha Centauri and the horizon are equal, as they appeared to be now, it was another celestial signpost for fifteen degrees north. Speaking into Steve's tape recorder at sunrise,

Nainoa's voice registered confidence: "I estimate we are at fifteen degrees north, three hundred and thirty miles away from Hilo, and three houses west of the line (reference course)."

Having endured their trial by storm, the crew was now accustomed to shipboard routine. "Once you enter that rhythm you're in a new world," Sam Ka'ai recalls. "It takes time to break off from the land. We were blessed that we were very busy. We were turning to—handling rigging—the line stretched tight. That's one thing about strong winds and storms. You just *ho'omaika'i i ke akua*—thank the gods for providing this trial and ask that we may be ready for the next one."

Making his rounds, Doctor Aiu found some of the crew were bruised from the beating they took in the storm and some were suffering from rashes. "The salt spray will do it to you," Jo-Anne recalls. "My butt and inner thighs were covered with rash. I was really uncomfortable."

The wind shifted northerly and piped up. In the early morning, the canoe turned up to southeast by east, one and a half houses to the east of Nainoa's planned course through the water. Yesterday, the canoe was three houses to the west of her reference course so for every 100 miles he can hold this course, one and a half houses can be subtracted from the western deficit.

At dawn, the sun rose off *Hōkūle'a's* port bow. "So good to see the rays," Jo-Anne wrote.

Nainoa studied the swells. *The dominant swell is continuing from the east,* he thought. *But now there's a minor swell building from the northeast.* This nascent swell defined his hope for the future. If it grew larger, it would signal the coming of the northeast trade winds—just what he needed to sail to Tahiti without tacking. At sunset, Nainoa saw cumulus clouds. There was little vertical development, signaling a stable weather pattern and trade winds. "The wind is clean and it's predictable, a steady stream of air," he told Steve. He judged the wind's speed by its feel against his skin and by streaks on the ocean's face— twenty knots.

By sunset *Hōkūle'a* had reached fourteen degrees north. The canoe was heading one house east of her desired course at six knots. The wind was from the northeast at twenty. The northeast swell was now larger while the southeast swell had declined. The favorable winds should hold.

Friday, March 21. Day Seven.

Hōkūle'a proceeded on course during an uneventful day.

That night, looking south, Nainoa observed the Southern Cross rise to the meridian. As the top and bottom star—Gacrux and Acrux—aligned upright, he drew an imaginary line straight down to a flickering star called Alpha Musca. The distance between these three stars is six degrees and they form the rungs of a celestial ladder that provides clues to an observer's latitude. When the distance between each rung of the ladder is the same as the distance between the bottom rung—Alpha Musca—and the horizon, the observer is at 15 degrees north. Now, the distance was a little greater, so Nainoa judged the canoe had traveled further

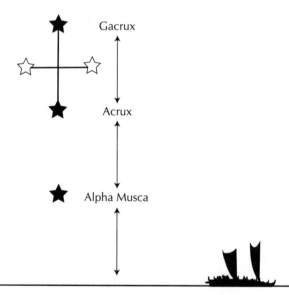

When the distance between Gacrux, Acrux, Alpha Musca and the horizon is equal, the canoe is at 15 degrees North latitude

south to 13 ½ degrees north latitude.

Nainoa's theory that pairs of stars might guide a navigator across trackless oceans had been derived from observations made beneath the planetarium's artificial sky dome, and confirmed at a few remote locations on Earth—but they had never been tested at sea. Now, for the first time, as he voyaged from one celestial stepping stone to another, the sky provided gifts that had not been used for centuries, "treasures without measure," as Sam Ka'ai had put it, given freely by *akua*—the gods. Treasures that have always been there, just awaiting a Polynesian navigator to look up once again and behold them.

❖ ❖ ❖ ❖ ❖

For the last few days, *Hōkūle'a's* steering paddle had been tied up and the canoe had been steering herself. But now, as darkness fell, she began to pitch and roll in a deep ocean swell. She corkscrewed. Her bow described an arc a house or two on either side of Nainoa's desired course.

"Man the sweep," Nainoa ordered.

Chad Baybayan grasped the polished handle of the large steering paddle. He loosened the rope lashing that secured it and inserted the blade into *Hōkūle'a's* swirling wake. Feeling pressure in his palms, he hugged the paddle to his body with both arms, legs splayed. Placing the paddle's blade into the water, the canoe responded by falling off the wind. Lifting the blade, the canoe turned into the wind. Timing it just right, he dampened *Hōkūle'a's* tendency to corkscrew. Her bow steadied on course.

"Steer by the Southern Cross," Nainoa ordered.

Chad steadied up on the constellation rising just off the port *manu*, near where the foresail shroud met the handrail.

"Good, right there."

In this kind of weather, a helmsman can retain his focus for about forty-five minutes so the task was rotated. Chad was relieved by Harry. The night slowly wore on. Pat Aiu stepped in, then Steve Somsen. At midnight, the next watch was called on deck. Chad slipped gratefully into the warmth of his *puka*.

Chad's *puka* was located near where the steering paddle passed through the deck. As the canoe rocked, Chad heard the paddle slap against the hull. Accustomed to the sound, he drifted to sleep. A few moments later, he was awakened by a sharp bang—then a muttered curse and scampering feet. Through the opening in his *puka*, Chad saw the crew wrestling the sweep out of the water and tying it down. "We rolled on a wave," the steersman, Buddy McGuire, remembers, "the canoe pitched one way, then the other way and I rolled into the paddle. When the canoe rolled back I leaned back on it hard and it snapped." The crew worked to unlash and clear the broken paddle.

"All hands on deck."

"Lights flitted about like swarming fireflies as crewmembers scurried for tools. "There was a lot of wind," Jo-Anne recalls. "People were working in the dark. The canoe was traveling at great speed. At times like this you need all hands on deck."

Leon and his watch labored through the night. By daybreak, another paddle was in place and when Chad came on deck for the morning watch, the canoe had steadied on its course to the southeast.

Saturday, March 22. Day Eight.

At sunrise, Nainoa estimated the canoe was now about twelve degrees forty minutes north. He had sailed constantly east of his predicted course through the water. Two days ago, *Hōkūleʻa* was three houses west of the reference course. Now she was back on it. In Honolulu, the Argos satellite pretty much agreed with him. The steady east-northeast trade winds allowed *Hōkūleʻa* to sail southeast at about five knots. The swells had clarified some, with an eastern swell now dominating. Above and behind the canoe, the sky was clear. But ahead Nainoa discerned a faint trace of layered clouds. Steve wondered if the clouds suggested they were approaching the Intertropical Convergence Zone—the Doldrums.

"What latitude would you expect to find the Doldrums?" he asked.

"I think about seven and a half or eight," Nainoa replied.

The Doldrums were now only three hundred miles away, about three sailing days.

At twilight, the canoe continued to sail southeast, now slowing to about four knots. Nainoa ordered the crew to continue steering so that he could hold his southeasterly course. Having sailed back up to the reference course, he wanted to stay on it—or slightly east of it—to reduce dead reckoning errors. During the day, clouds accumulated.

Sunday, March 23. Day Nine.

"Night watch. Winds up. Cold," Jo-Anne confided to her log. "Haven't been sleeping. Just concerned over the canoe's condition. Hard to write." About midnight, *Hōkūle'a* sailed easily under partly cloudy skies.

"Change the watch."

The midnight to six watch took the deck. Someone lit the propane stove and put a kettle on. There was the murmur of voices. Mugs were laid out. The off-duty crew went below. The sea all around presented a simple blackness— nothing to arouse concern. Those on watch adjusted to the darkness, sought out familiar constellations, and enjoyed the delicious suspension that a long sea voyage engenders. Suddenly the foresail began to writhe. In the darkness, the problem was not obvious. Gordon ordered the sail lowered. The crew disentangled the boom from the mess of canvas and laid it on deck. The boom had cracked. Mau emerged from his *puka* and leaned over it. He was joined by Leon and Tava.

Mau had brought aboard a collection of adzes. He chose one he had used to carve the booms for his own canoe on Satawal. The handle was shaped from the crook of a Satawalese tree. The blade was made from an automobile leaf spring sharpened to a fare-thee-well and lashed to the handle with coconut rope. His stroke was loose yet precise. The blade lifted shavings so thin you could see through them. The sound of the adze was like a metronome, a steady beat that carried above the whistle of the wind.

"He cut a scarph joint into the boom so we could join the two pieces together," Buddy recalls. "He did it all freehand. His accuracy was stunning."

From time to time, Mau stopped to examine the work, turning the wood to judge its fit, and then he began again—thock, thock. His eyes, under the glasses that Harry purchased for him, followed the blade intently. The planes of his face were composed in silent concentration.

"Watching Mau was like seeing my ancestors," Gordon recalls. "He showed us an ancient survival skill. He made the adze sing a song on the canoe."

"He completed the work an hour before dawn," Marion remembers. "As the sun came up, the boom and gaff were stepped and up the sail went. We briefly admired their handiwork when—crack—it broke again."

Mau showed no emotion. The boom was lowered and Mau measured strips of mahogany to brace the repair. Under bare poles, *Hōkūle'a* drifted west. A piece of *hau* was brought up from the port hull and Mau set to work once more. He fashioned two scarphs in the *hau*—long slanting longitudinal cuts—and then two others in the boom to match. He inserted the *hau*, flanked the repair with the mahogany strips and began the slow process of lashing. Late in the afternoon, the sail was raised once again and carefully set.

"In spite of their fatigue," Jo-Anne wrote, "everybody felt the accomplishment of using whatever was on board—and that the canoe was sailing again. Crew was on a high. Nainoa and Leon expressed the desire to have a beer."

"But we had to be real gentle with the boom all the way down to Tahiti," Chad remembers.

"When that boom broke again," Nainoa recalls, "it made me wonder—just how difficult is this voyage going to be? What is it going to take?"

In his evening report, Nainoa estimated they were between twelve and eleven degrees north. "It's pretty difficult to determine my position," he told Steve. "What with all this stopping and drifting, I'm having a hard time dead-reckoning direction and distance because I have nothing consistent."

At sunset their course continued southeast—a little east of his planned course through the water—at about five and a half knots. He saw a large swell from the northeast and single level cumulus clouds—both harbingers of steady trade winds.

NA'AU

Chapter Thirty-Eight

Monday, March 24. Day Ten.

In the evening of the tenth day, puffy cumulus clouds glowed in the moonlight like a ghost fleet of immense galleons. The first quarter moon was nearly overhead—painting the sails.

Looking south a little before dawn, Nainoa observed a star that astronomers call Eta Ara, in the foot of the constellation Ara. Nainoa calls it the "Alex Star" in honor of *Ishka's* captain. Crossing the meridian with the Alex star, ten degrees below it, was Atria in the Southern Triangle. At eleven degrees north, the distance between the two stars would be equal to the distance between Atria and the

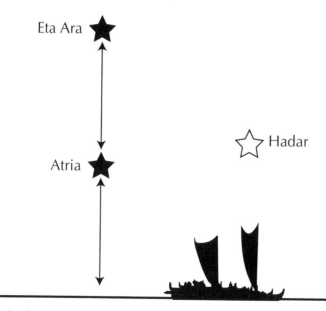

When the distance between Eta Ara and Atria is equal to the distance between Atria and the horizon, the canoe is at 11 degrees North latitude

horizon. Observing them carefully, Nainoa judged the distance between Atria and the horizon to be greater so the canoe had sailed a little further south. *Close to ten degrees north,* he thought. Observations of the Southern Cross and Polaris confirmed this position. "We're getting into the latitude of the Doldrums," he told Steve.

◇ ◇ ◇ ◇ ◇

Seated at his tiny kitchen table during long nights of study prior to departure, Nainoa had examined a series of charts in a book entitled *Atlas of Pilot Charts* which showed the flow of winds, month by month, throughout the Pacific. These charts are based on *Wind and Current Charts* published in 1848 by Matthew Fontaine Maury—a man memorialized as "the Pathfinder of the Seas."

Maury was born in Virginia in 1806 to a prominent seafaring family. Like many mariners, his father forbade him to go to sea—but Maury, thankfully, disobeyed—leaving home at age nineteen to join the U.S. Navy. By 1842, at the age of thirty-six, he had ascended to the position of superintendent of the United States Naval Observatory. Here he began an arduous study of old charts and logbooks with the goal of mapping the world's winds and currents. He also instructed American naval vessels to regularly send him current and wind observations during their voyages. This work took on something like a God-given mission: "There is no employment more worthy of the human mind," he wrote, "than that which is afforded by tracing the evidences of design and purpose, which are visible in any parts of the creation. Hence, to the right-minded mariner, and to him who studies the physical relations of Earth, sea, and air, the atmosphere is something more than a shoreless ocean, at the bottom of which his barque is wafted or driven along. It is an envelope or covering for the dispersion of light and heat over the surface of the Earth..." [10]

In 1686, Edmund Halley—the famous astronomer—had produced one of the first systematic studies of Earth's atmosphere and identified solar heating as the principal cause of the planet's wind systems. Maury refined Halley's theory and his work has largely withstood the test of time. Even today, to convey the basics of planetary wind flows, most teachers of climatology begin as Maury did—by asking their students to imagine an Earth at rest—affected only by the unequal heating of its surface due to the sun striking it more fully at the equator. Hot air rises from Earth's midriff and flows aloft toward the poles, where it cools and descends to flow back to the equator. In this idealized case, there would be only two constant surface winds—one flowing from north to south in the Northern Hemisphere and one from south to north in the southern. Where the winds meet—at the equator—they would join the rising air to flow back to the poles.

Adding Earth's motion creates a more complex picture. Hot air rising at the equator flows north and south but as Earth rotates it causes the apparent flow to bend right in the northern hemisphere and left in the southern. The right-bending north-flowing air reaches a point at about thirty degrees north latitude where it's traveling almost directly from west to east to become what's called the subtropical jet stream. Here the flowing air encounters an atmospheric traffic jam and some of it begins to settle back to Earth. This settling is abetted by the fact that air cools as it moves north, becoming denser and heavier. Reaching the surface, some of it returns to the equator. In the Northern Hemisphere this air is bent to the right and becomes the northeast trades. In the Southern Hemisphere, it is bent to the left to become the southeast trades. The two belts of wind collide near the equator. Scientists call this place of collision the Intertropical Convergence Zone (ITCZ). Sailors refer to it more poetically as the Doldrums. It's a place of rising warm and moist air, low air pressure, cloudiness, high humidity and light variable winds punctuated by squalls and thunderstorms.

Tahiti-bound air passengers—even though flying six miles or so above the ITCZ—feel a strange buffeting caused by this vast zone of ascending air. Air in the Doldrums is indeed moving, but it's doing so vertically. Sailors, of course, rely on horizontal flow. Sir Francis Chichester, the famous British circumnavigator, wrote that in the Doldrums the "calms were the very devil." French sailors call this region of still and silent seas le pot-au-noir—black like the inside of a pot of boot polish. Samuel Taylor Coleridge, in his poem "Rhyme of the Ancient Mariner," pictures the Doldrums as a kind of hell:

Down dropt the breeze, the sails dropt down,
'Twas sad as sad could be;
And we did speak only to break
The silence of the sea!

All in a hot and copper sky,
The bloody Sun, at noon,
Right up above the mast did stand,
No bigger than the Moon.

Day after day, day after day,
We stuck, nor breath nor motion;
As idle as a painted ship
Upon a painted ocean.

Water, water, every where,
And all the boards did shrink;
Water, water, every where,
Nor any drop to drink.

The ITCZ moves with the seasons, north in summer and south in winter. Voyaging in March, Nainoa could expect to encounter the Doldrums anywhere between five and ten degrees north. He anticipated long periods of calm followed by buffeting squalls, heavy clouds then windless days once more—a navigator's nightmare. "I dreaded the Doldrums," Nainoa recalls. "I had no confidence that I could get through it. My navigation depended on seeing the stars or moon. When I got into the Doldrums there would be a hundred-percent cloud cover. I would be blind."

✦ ✦ ✦ ✦ ✦

All mariners who become masters of their trade develop a bond with their vessels. Nainoa occasionally felt this deep connection as a member of *Hōkūle'a's* crew, but now, as navigator, he joined his senses with the canoe in a new way. "I began to feel the canoe all around me and I sensed the stars in relation to the canoe without really thinking about it. I could *feel* when we were on course and when we were off. I became attuned to her motion."

During the early morning hours of March 24th, Nainoa felt *Hōkūle'a* shudder. It was a subtle motion, what you might feel on a city sidewalk when a subway train, a hundred feet below, rumbled past. It was not constant. It was choppy, but it was there alright. At dawn, he noticed a zone of disturbed sea surrounding the canoe, like water in a glass tumbler that was being gently shaken.

"Look at the ocean," he told Steve during the morning report. "There's ripples that appear to break but instead of rolling forward they remain stationary." Both Nainoa and Steve had seen this phenomenon before. When the wind blows against a current, it causes the sea to stand up—the waves seem to march in place.

"I think we're entering the Equatorial Counter Current," Nainoa said.

The Equatorial Counter Current was handmaiden to the ITCZ. The northeast and southeast trade winds pushed against the ocean to create two vast belts of current that flowed from east to west. The sea level rose in the west, creating a discontinuity of immense proportions. The Equatorial Countercurrent was a kind of relief valve—a belt of easterly flowing water in a zone that roughly coincided with the ITCZ. So the choppy motion that Nainoa felt may be a clue that *Hōkūle'a* was at last crossing the northern frontier of the Doldrums.

At mid-day, Alex received a message from Honolulu on *Ishka's* single sideband radio: "Kainalu Bertelmann born March 24th, 1980, 11:51 a.m., six pounds five ounces. Length nineteen and a half inches." Shorty had a son. The *Hōkūle'a* singers cranked into action—Marion Lyman-Mersereau composer, Dr. Pat Aiu lyricist.

Kainalu, Kainalu the ocean wave
Kainalu, Kainalu grows strong and brave
His Daddy is near, though he's far away
He's not gonna stray, he's on an ocean wave
The morning dawned gray, when we heard you were here
Mālolo soared far, the day became clear
For Kainalu, Kainalu, the ocean wave
Kainalu, Kainalu grows strong and brave
The stars guide his path, he'll be home real soon
The heavens shined bright, your first night was half-moon

"During the day Shorty sat on the navigator's platform staring out to the horizon with his thoughts of home and his wife," Jo-Anne wrote.

The wind continued to shift as the day advanced, eventually blowing from due east at twenty knots. *Hōkūleʻa* followed it to a new course of south-southeast. The canoe surfed a big northeast swell, picking up speed. At sunset, Nainoa summoned Steve for the evening report. "We've averaged four knots for fifteen hours from this morning," Nainoa told him. "So now we're at about nine and a half degrees north." The canoe drifted west when the boom broke and she had sailed south-southeast for about sixty miles, one and a half houses west of the desired course, so Nainoa estimated they were now three houses west of the reference course.

"I don't like that, but we can't do anything about it in these winds. We tack now and it's going to be a bad mistake."

Ahead, the high clouds increased.

At sunset, the southern sky faded from a wan blue to a darker cerulean. Argo Navis appeared—the ship—named after the famous vessel in which Jason sailed to find the Golden Fleece. The constellation sprawled across so much celestial real estate that the International Astronomical Union eventually divided it into four parts: Carina (the keel), Vela (the sail), Puppis (the poop), and Pyxis (the compass). By about eight o'clock, when it was dark enough to see the stars well, Nainoa found the sail to the south-southeast with the compass riding high above it, the stern to the right and the keel lying lowest of all—marked by Canopus and Miaplacidus. Miaplacidus is important in Nainoa's system of navigation because it was bright and because in northern latitudes it crossed the meridian low in the sky, and it rose steadily as the canoe moved south. Above Miaplacidus, also

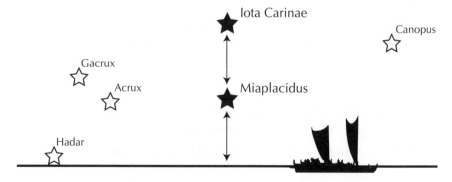

When the distance between Iota Carinae and Miaplacidus is equal to the distance between Miaplacidus and the horizon, the canoe is at 9 degrees North latitude

in the keel, is a star called Iota Carinae. This star and Miaplacidus are another of Nainoa's equally distant pairs. As they crossed the meridian together a few days earlier, it was obvious that the distance between the two stars was quite a bit more than the distance between Miaplacidus and the horizon. Now they were exactly the same—*Hōkūle'a* had reached nine degrees north latitude.

Tuesday, March 25. Day Eleven. Leg Two.

A little after midnight, when Steve came on deck for his watch, he observed the upright Southern Cross rising to the meridian almost directly in front of the canoe. Nainoa had changed course to begin the second leg of his journey, a course through the water of 170 degrees true, about south by east.

At daybreak, the intertropical convergence zone revealed itself—a wall of clouds, ascending to forty thousand feet ahead of the canoe. "We saw it in the early morning," Nainoa recalls, "like a curtain, and we kept sailing toward that curtain. It was like a wall—and so clearly distinct—multiple layers of cloud. It was beautiful but also terrifying. I didn't want to go into it. I thought, *Let's just turn around and wait until this thing goes away.* But we sailed on."

At twilight on Tuesday, it began to rain lightly, then with deliberation. The crew rigged tarps and collected thirty gallons of fresh water. Chad Baybayan watched the sky ahead: "I remember a big gray cloud. I remember trying to steer around the cloud and ending up inside of it. And then being trapped in there."

With the evening came the squalls. The wind accelerated. Heavy swells puckered the ocean. "The wind was shifting," Nainoa recalls. "The waves were shifting. The stars were gone. The rain was stinging cold because it came from so high."

Hōkūle'a leaned against her lee hull and plunged forward. All around the darkening horizon, too far away to hear the accompanying thunder, lightning licked at swirling knots of cloud that blotted out the moon and concealed squalls that rushed the canoe. A little before midnight, terrific gusts shook the canoe, driving rain violently across her deck. Swells crashed aboard.

"Trice in the back sail," Nainoa ordered. "Sheet in the foresail."

The canoe fell off the wind. Nainoa tried to steer by the big swell from the east that caused the port hull to lift first—then the starboard. The canoe proceeded due south under a starless sky.

"When we arrived in the Doldrums," Nainoa recalls, "The sky went black. It was solid rain. The wind was strong and it was switching around. It was stronger in the squalls. We were moving fast. That's the worst thing that can happen— you're going fast and you don't know where you're going."

As the wind gyred around the compass, Nainoa lost all hope of steering by it. "I couldn't tell the steersmen where to steer. I was very, very tense. I knew that I had to avoid fatigue so I couldn't allow myself to get physically tense. But I couldn't help it. I just couldn't stop myself."

The wind backed around from south to west and continued backing. The seas mounted and clashed. Nainoa lost all sense of the swells.

"Big seas," Harry remembers, "a lot of wind. And dark—oh man, was it dark."

"I was watching Nainoa being so focused and so single minded and so careful," says Marion. "I mean he had to—the responsibility, especially after Eddie—knowing that our lives were in his hands."

"When we were in the Doldrums, Nainoa appeared to be very calm—at least outwardly," Buddy remembers.

But Nainoa was far from calm. He was fighting off panic. All the normal steering clues were lost. The swirling wind was no help. The canoe pitched wildly, without any detectable rhythm. Buddy struggled with the big sweep to hold the canoe on course, but what was the course?

"Nainoa, where do you want me to go?"

"That single cry went right through me," Nainoa recalls. "I had no answer. I was out of control. I had no idea what to do. I was mentally and physically exhausted. I could barely hold myself up. I spread my legs. I grabbed the rail and locked my elbows so I wouldn't fall down. I closed my eyes." *I can't do this,* I thought. *This is finally it—I'm going to fail.*

"Then something strange happened," Nainoa continues. "I gave up fighting to find a clue and I settled down. Then, a warmth came over me. I felt the moon on my right shoulder. All of a sudden, I *knew* where the moon was. I couldn't see the moon—it was so black—but I *knew* where it was."

During the initial moments of Nainoa's confusion, the canoe had followed the swirling wind and was now heading north—back to Hilo. What happened next was clearly fixed in the memory of everyone on deck.

"The canoe got turned around," says Buddy. "We couldn't see the stars. Nainoa ordered us to change direction. Then there was a break in the clouds."

"The moonlight shone through and Nainoa used that to navigate," says Chad Baybayan.

"I *felt* the moon before I saw it," says Nainoa. "I had an *image* of the moon in my mind so I knew where to go. I turned the canoe around and headed south again and then, just for a moment, there was a hole in the clouds and the light of the moon shone through—just where I expected it to be."

"I can't explain it," Nainoa continues, "there was a connection between something in my abilities and my senses that went beyond the analytical, beyond seeing with my eyes. It was something very deep inside. Before that happened, I relied on math and science because it was so much easier to understand things that way. I didn't know how to trust my instincts. My instincts were not trained enough to be trusted. That night, I learned there are levels of navigation that are realms of the spirit. Hawaiians call it *na'au*—knowing through your instincts, your feelings, rather than your mind or your intellect. It's like new doors of knowledge open and you learn something new. But before the doors open you don't even know that such knowledge exists."

DOLDRUMS

Chapter Thirty-Nine

Wednesday, March 26. Day Twelve.

The storm continued through the night. Gusts of wind carried the rain like pellets shot from a gun and with almost equal strength. When the rain encountered the sails or the crew's foul weather gear it made a sharp cracking sound. It was the tropics, so it was not overly cold, but hypothermia depends not so much on temperature but on how long a person is exposed to the elements. Good gear will delay it but the slickers worn by *Hōkūle'a's* crew were pretty basic. Water seeped in around the throat, the wrists, along the big zipper in front. And the rain had fallen from high altitudes so it was cold. By morning, when the wind diminished, Nainoa had been awake for almost eighteen hours and before that—for the last twelve days—he had slept fitfully. He was exhausted and wet. "I started to shiver and I couldn't stop. I was tired and fatigued and I couldn't get warm."

Tava Taupu had been on deck all night. It was his custom to be on hand when things became marginal and his presence on such occasions signified to the crew that the situation was dire but—not to worry—they would persevere. Tava watched out for his crewmates. Now, seeing Nainoa shivering uncontrollably, he wraped his arms around him in a Marquesan bear hug.

"Tava didn't ask," Nainoa recalls. "Typically it wouldn't be a manly thing to do—but he just came over and gave me his warmth."

⬥ ⬥ ⬥ ⬥ ⬥

Sunrise revealed a dull and sullen ocean, as if all the energy had been drained from it, except for a big swell marching from north to south in a steady pulsing rhythm.

Hōkūle'a in the Doldrums

"It was like a wave from home," Nainoa remembers. "It was very comforting. I could tell direction from it no matter what. The swells were at least ten feet high. They were so big it was like an elevator lifting us and dropping us, and when the canoe dropped back into the trough it would create its own wind and we would move a few inches. There wasn't any wind, so I could have just let the canoe go—don't steer. But people were on the sweep all the time. Even though it was another sixteen hundred miles to Tahiti, every inch counted."

A wall of cloud surrounded *Hōkūle'a*, enclosing her in a tube with a radius of about a mile. Jo-Anne Sterling pushed aside the canvas flap of her *puka* and peeked out. "It was heavy overcast," she recalls, "no wind, drifting, very still and eerie. It played on your nerves."

"We're totally becalmed now—just wallowing," Marion wrote in her log. "A helpless feeling. The swells slosh at the hulls and the wind slaps the sails this way and that. The Doldrums."

To the east, the surrounding cloud wall was the color of slate and it had rain in it. Nainoa saw the rain falling in straight vertical lines. To the west, the cloud appeared lighter and orange in color. As the canoe moved, the tube of cloud moved with it.

"Because I had that wave, I knew we were headed south—but when the sun came up, it appeared to be on the wrong side of the canoe. On the west side it was more orange and light—so visually it made me think that west was east. It was like the sun was rising in the west. That's how confusing it was. To get oriented, I walked up and stood on the bow. I held onto the headstay and scanned around the canoe. I was borderline hallucinating. But I remember that day as one of the most beautiful days I ever had on any voyage. I was in the Doldrums. One hundred-percent cloud cover, surrounded by a wall of clouds—my worst nightmare. And at the same time I knew where we were going. I had conditioned myself to be afraid of the Doldrums, but now the fear was gone and I was in one of the most beautiful places on Earth. It felt like I had gone through a door into another way of seeing the world."

There was no way, Nainoa figured, that he could replicate Mau's experience and his instinctual understanding of the ocean, so he had prepared his intellect by using the tools available to him—math, science and the wonderful planetarium. Yet clearly, as he voyaged south, that preparation had conditioned him to open his mind to new ways of knowing. "Science and math gave me some grounding to go out and understand the world. But now, as I got more experience, I became more trusting of my instinct. It's always there, but I didn't trust it at first. And in the world I grew up in you are taught not to trust it."

❖ ❖ ❖ ❖ ❖

Early in the afternoon, Alex shut down *Ishka's* diesel to change a fuel filter. He squirmed into the hot engine compartment, drenched in sweat, his vessel rolling slowly in the uneasy calm. He removed the old filter and replaced it. He ascended to the deck, wiping his brow in a wrinkled handkerchief. There was a stirring of wavelets—a breath of air. A few hundred yards ahead, *Hōkūle'a* began to move. Alex pushed the starter button. Nothing happened.

"He removes the deck plates and goes below to see what the problem is," Will wrote. "Nothing obvious. Once more he touches the starter button. Bzzz. Blue smoke billows through the chart room and three carbon dioxide extinguishers converge from three different directions. Fortunately we don't have to use them, but we are given to a moment's reflection upon the vulnerability of a vessel on fire at sea and, in this case, the irony of it all if the escort crew should have to continue to Tahiti aboard its charge. Alex inspects the engine and finds a warm, burned-out starter. He then does a thorough step-by-step examination of the engine, checking and cleaning electrical contacts with emery cloth. During shutdown, and due to an unusual distribution of weight on the boat, water may have entered the engine."

That was a problem. Under sail alone *Ishka* cannot keep up with *Hōkūle'a*. The canoe was a catamaran and she sliced cleanly through the water, while *Ishka* was a stout monohull and must push the water aside. Her sails were relatively small so she depended on her engine for speed. At about 1:00 p.m., *Hōkūle'a* resumed sailing, now on a starboard tack, heading east. *Ishka* followed as best she could, wallowing in the swell, Alex in the bilge tinkering with his engine.

"*Hōkūle'a*, this is *Ishka*." Alex was on the radio.

"Go ahead, *Ishka*."

"Can you send Leon over to help with the engine?"

Hōkūle'a hove to. Alex picked up Leon in *Ishka's* rowboat and conveyed him to the stricken escort. *Ishka's* engine was critical. If they can't fix it, the voyage would take longer to complete. Food and water supplies had been calculated to last forty days and that may not be enough.

Thursday, March 27. Day Thirteen. Leg Three.

The Doldrums were short-lived. Early in the morning, the wind picked up and *Hōkūle'a* accelerated, sailing a course to the east of Nainoa's planned course through the water. After the capsizing two years ago, the Polynesian Voyaging Society had imposed a strict radio schedule, *Ishka* would contact Honolulu in the morning and evening. But without the engine to charge his batteries, Alex informed PVS that *Ishka* would listen only—twice a day at 7:15 a.m. and 4:15 p.m.. If the batteries were to die completely the escort could not call for help in an emergency.

"Sun is out," Jo-Anne wrote in her diary, "*Ishka* still without power." Off watch, Jo-Anne searched for a shady place to rest. The sails cast a shadow near the galley so she lay down in it, luxuriating in the coolness. Soon she became aware of a figure peering down at her. "It was Sam Ka'ai," she recalls, "telling me with his eyes that I had invaded his space. I left. We were getting pretty territorial. It's humorous when you consider the little things that annoy a person, especially when it's hot."

At sunset, Nainoa estimated they were at four degrees north and *Hōkūle'a* was one house east of her reference course. The canoe now began the third leg of her journey. Nainoa figured *Hōkūle'a* would travel about 75 miles a day on this leg on an apparent heading of 155 degrees true. The lee drift would be 15 degrees west, so her course through the water would be 170 degrees true; and the current would carry her another 10 degrees west so her course over the ground—the reference course—would be 180 degrees, due south. The wind picked up to eighteen knots from the east-northeast. *Hōkūle'a* sailed one house east of Nainoa's planned course through the water. He guided her by the big ocean swell from the northeast. At sunset, the sky cleared. Regulus, Jupiter, and Mars danced around the rising moon. *Ishka* had lagged behind the canoe. She was a small speck in *Hōkūle'a's* wake.

Friday, March 28. Day Fourteen.

The sun rose, arced through a clear sky and passed almost directly overhead. The wind began another dance around the compass, shifting from east to southeast to south. *Hōkūle'a*, on the port tack, accommodated by sailing south, then southwest, then west. Nainoa responded by tacking at 2:00 p.m. and heading east by south. For two days, the lagging escort vessel had held *Hōkūle'a* back, and now the wind was forcing her off her course toward Tahiti. During the day, the wind continued southerly, right from the direction they wanted to sail, at twelve knots, accompanied by a southerly swell. "If that swell gets larger tomorrow, the wind will hold," Nainoa said.

"Take in sail."

At twilight, Gordon hove to so that *Ishka* could rejoin them. First mate Leon Sterling swam back to the canoe. He had had no luck with the engine. Shortly thereafter, the canoe hoisted sail again and continued east at three knots in a freshening wind.

Saturday, March 29. Day Fifteen.

Friday shaded into Saturday. There was lightning low in the west. The canoe's decks were slick with spray, cool under bare feet.

"You see that?" Mau said to Steve when he came on deck for the early morning watch, "You see that moon?"

Steve saw a halo around the moon.

"We call that a moon dog," Mau said. "Means more wind—maybe rain."

"Well, let's hope it's an east wind so we can turn south and get the hell out of these equatorial latitudes," Steve said.

But the wind continued southerly, preventing *Hōkūle'a* from turning down toward the Tuamotus during the night. A pod of porpoise frolicked for a time at the canoe's bow, scattering sprays of phosphorescence, sprinkling the ocean with tiny dots of light. At sunrise, the wind shifted dramatically—northeast by north—and, as Mau had predicted, picked up to twenty knots.

"Prepare to tack."

Just before breakfast, Gordon gave the order to come about. The crew brought

Hōkūle'a into the wind, she stalled for a moment, then swung around on the port tack. Nainoa steered south-southeast. Finally, after a full day of capricious winds, the canoe was back on course, making six knots in a freshening wind.

The winds had delayed the canoe's progress to the south, forcing her to sail a zig-zag course, first west, then east. How far had she strayed from her reference course? To figure that out, Nainoa sat on his navigator's platform and deployed his deviation triangles and mathematics.

At sunrise yesterday, we sailed mainly west, he thought, *until 2:00 p.m., when we tacked and headed back east.*

On this leg of the voyage, the canoe's desired course was south by east but between 6:00 a.m. and 2:00 p.m., she had sailed five houses west of that course.

We traveled 24 miles or about one quarter of a 100-mile sailing day.

If the canoe had traveled west for a full sailing day, she would have gone five houses to the west, but she travelled only one quarter of a sailing day. One quarter multiplied by five is one and a quarter houses west.

When we turned west, we were one house to the east of our reference course so by 2:00 p.m. we were one house minus one and a quarter houses or one quarter of a house to the west of it.

In the same way, Nainoa calculated the deviations caused by sailing six houses east of her desired course at 2 knots from 2:00 p.m. until 9:00 p.m., and then seven houses east at 3 knots until 6:00 a.m. today when he tacked south.

So when we tacked back down toward Tahiti, Nainoa thought, *we were about three houses to the east of the reference course.*

In Honolulu, the Argos satellites showed his estimated position was quite accurate, but aboard *Hōkūle'a* Nainoa had no way to know that. "To navigate you have to *believe* in your calculations," Nainoa says. "You have got to *decide* where you are and then base the rest of the trip on that decision—right or wrong." If Nainoa were to second-guess himself, he would be truly lost.

During the day, the northerly wind continued steady and strong so *Ishka's* crew set a large genoa jib and struggled to keep up with the canoe.

Shortly after dinner, Nainoa briefed the crew: "I'm concerned about our food supply. We've been forced east in the last few days and we want to sail south toward Tahiti, so we've made little progress. If this keeps up, we may have to ration food."

◇ ◇ ◇ ◇ ◇

The clouds dissipated and the wind felt dry. In the afternoon, the sea presented well-formed swells from the southeast. "We're moving out of the ITCZ," Nainoa told Steve.

In the evening, gossamer clouds moved like vapors across the moon, sheening the ocean and intensifying the contrast between sea and sky so that Nainoa could easily lay his fingers on the horizon and measure the altitude of Polaris. About four degrees.

"Trice up the sails."

Ishka had lagged behind.

Sunday, March 30. Day Sixteen.

"Sunday—such a peaceful and easy slow forward motion," Jo-Anne wrote. "I slept on deck under the full moon, the Southern Cross getting higher and higher. Antares glowing ever so bright—a twinkling star, a glowing yellow

Halfway to Tahiti

hue. I awoke refreshed." To port, *mānai-a-ka-lani*, Maui's fishhook—Eddie's constellation—rose into the sky. The canoe proceeded south by east. Nainoa saw high cirrus clouds. *Where are the trade wind cumulus?* he wondered, hoping for the steady southeast winds that would speed the canoe to landfall.

"Fish on the line."

Sam and Buddy scurried aft. Soon, three *aku*—small tuna—were flapping on deck. Sam and Buddy cut the flesh into thin strips which they served immediately—sashimi—along with soy sauce. Later they would sauté some of the fish in a skillet. They would dry the rest or chop it into cubes and add Hawaiian salt, ground *kukui* nut, onions, sesame oil and soy sauce—a dish called *poke*. Buddy once worked as a cook at The Willows—one of Hawai'i's most revered "old style" restaurants. He had brought aboard a selection of seasonings and he was growing sprouts in a wet napkin.

In the afternoon, the wind dropped. *Hōkūle'a* continued a little east of her course, now barely making headway in a light breeze. "We're a little less than three degrees north," Nainoa told Steve, "about half way between Tahiti and Hawai'i."

Monday, March 31. Day Seventeen.

"A beautiful dawning, but it was a very slow morning," Marion wrote. "We didn't move more than a half knot from the time we came on watch at midnight until about noon today when the breeze freshened up."

For the last seventeen days, Dr. Pat Aiu had monitored the crew's health. The most common ailments were Staphylococcus infections. Staph bacteria dwell in the skin and hair, and quickly migrate to cuts and abrasions where they thrive as rashes and boils. "Right at the beginning people began to break out in sores," Jo-Anne recalls. *Hōkūle'a* offered scant protection from the elements and her crew spent most of their time on deck so they were seldom dry, creating a Staphylococcus heaven. "We got rashes on our butts from our wet clothes and our hands looked like dried prunes or something worse." During the last few days, Tava had adopted a strange costume. "He was wearing a two-ply Hefty garbage bag as a skirt," Jo-Anne recalls, "to air out his groin and buttocks to reduce a rash." Buddy was suffering from gout,

Chad Baybayan

probably caused by the abrupt change in diet.

The need to be constantly observant and to mentally calculate course and speed was extremely tiring, so from time to time Nainoa freed his mind by daydreaming and observing the crew. Generally, he liked what he saw. After two years of training, they had learned to care for each other and their canoe. Chad Baybayan seemed to be everywhere. When extra hands were needed, his were usually among them, and when Nainoa and Steve huddled over the navigation reports, Chad was often within earshot. He never interrupted, but he was clearly taking in it all in. Nainoa recognized a kindred spirit.

"I could see that Nainoa was always looking for signs—the swells, the stars, the wind—and I tried to see what he was seeing," Chad recalls. "I knew that he was in a different world from the rest of us and I was curious about what kind of world that might be. Just watching him, I began to dream that someday I could be a navigator. I knew it was a far-fetched dream but that was my opportunity so I decided to learn as much as I could."

Chad held Nainoa in high esteem, but he regarded Mau as a man apart. It wasn't only that Mau could find land over long distances and survive at sea—he embodied ancestral values. He was a natural leader—yet he was quiet, humble and generous, freely giving his knowledge to anyone who showed a desire to learn. "He was so unselfish," Chad recalls, "you just had to ask the right questions." Chad also admired Mau's imperviousness to racial distinctions. The fracture between Hawaiians and *haole* had been a major irritant on the 1976 voyage, and the discord had eventually driven Mau back to Satawal. Yet here he was again, willing to give it another try. "Here's a man who said, 'Let's not dwell on things that are different between people. Let's concentrate on what we have in common,' " Chad says. "We love our ocean. We love our islands. And so does he. He identifies with that, not with what race they may be or where they came from. His teaching united us."

In the afternoon, Nainoa observed cumulus clouds and predicted trade winds would fill in. At sunset, he saw red smoke on the horizon. Wind stirs moisture into the atmosphere that refracts sunlight, creating shades from light pink to crimson depending on the wind's strength—the darker the color, the stronger the wind. "It will be windy tonight. Everyone be careful," Nainoa told the crew during the evening briefing.

TRADE WINDS

Chapter Forty

Tuesday, April 1. Day Eighteen.

A crystalline night, heading south. As Nainoa had predicted, the easterly wind increased to fifteen knots. Astern, the North Star twinkled on the horizon. Nainoa raised his hand to it, the top finger extended along the horizon. *One, maybe one and a half degrees,* he thought. The equator was now only about a hundred miles away.

Dawn arrived behind a veil of cloud, overwhelming the second and third magnitude stars, leaving only the brightest glowing bravely against the light. Then they too were gone. From a vanishing point on the eastern horizon, trains of cumulus stirred in long serrated columns. The clouds were aligned in what Mau calls "the road of the wind"—a sign the winds would be constant. They scudded over the canoe, their tops crimson in the rays of the rising sun. Nainoa looked into the sun, studying the space between the horizon and the cloud base. "I don't see much smoke," he told Steve, "there's not much red in the clouds so the wind won't be strong, but there are no signs it will change—no swell lines, no high buildups. I think the trade winds are here to stay." *Hōkūle'a's* course was still south by east at four and a half knots. The wind was from the east at fifteen knots. "This course is right on the money," Nainoa said. "We should cross the equator tonight five houses east of the reference course."

They continued on in the rising heat of the eighteenth day. Jo-Anne was in her *puka,* writing in her journal. "We relish the privacy of our bunks—writing, reading, or just being by ourselves. But on hot days it is impossible to enter the compartment, it's like a sauna bath."

The watches changed in an orderly rhythm every six hours. The sun crossed over the mast, then began to descend. Nainoa reclined on the navigator's platform for a catnap. Two hours later, he awoke with a start. "I

Leon Sterling in his *puka*

went to sleep," he told Steve. "I don't have the intensity. Today it was so hot, I was just lullabying all day."

At sunset, *Hōkūle'a* headed south-southeast toward the rising Southern Cross. The wind continued northeast by east and increased to eighteen knots.

Wednesday, April 2. Day Nineteen. Leg Four.

During the early morning, *Hōkūle'a* passed Earth's midriff. Nainoa now sailed on the last leg of his voyage straight toward Takapoto atoll in the Tuamotus. His apparent course would be 155 degrees true, but his leeway will be 10 degrees to the west so his course through the water would be 165 degrees. Adding in the effect of the current, his reference course (or course over the ground) would be 175 degrees—between south by east and due south. Ahead of the canoe, the Tuamotus formed a line of atolls 1000 miles long from east to west—directly

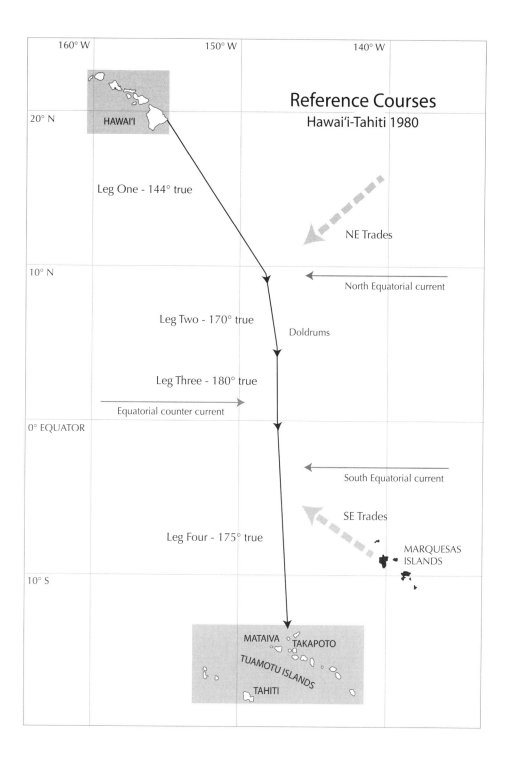

Reference Courses
Hawai'i-Tahiti 1980

160° W 150° W 140° W

20° N
HAWAI'I

Leg One - 144° true

NE Trades

10° N

North Equatorial current

Leg Two - 170° true

Doldrums

Leg Three - 180° true

Equatorial counter current

0° EQUATOR

South Equatorial current

SE Trades

Leg Four - 175° true

MARQUESAS
ISLANDS

10° S

MATAIVA TAKAPOTO
TUAMOTU ISLANDS
TAHITI

across the canoe's track. He had plotted this course to intercept Takapoto about two hundred miles to the east of the last atoll in the chain, Mataiva. The currents and winds would push him west, so by aiming for Takapoto he allowed for a large margin of error.

◇ ◇ ◇ ◇ ◇

Early in the voyage, a few days after Nainoa had turned back toward Hawai'i to rejoin his imaginary reference course, Mau had paid him a large compliment — by not paying much attention to him at all. *You're the navigator and you're doing pretty well,* he seemed to be saying. He often napped in his compartment and when on deck he sat immersed creating a model of a Micronesian *wa'a serak,* accompanied by the soft thud of his adze, the planes of his face composed in an expression resembling a complacent Buddha. When *Hōkūle'a* was stalled in the Doldrums, the sound of the adze was all there was — a gentle metronome that soothed the crew. They watched the shavings pile up. *If Mau isn't worried about our progress, why should we be?* seemed to be the general thought.

Hōkūle'a sailed south by east at five knots in a twenty-two knot easterly wind, following Nainoa's course toward Takapoto. As night fell, the crew steered by Gacrux and Acrux almost directly ahead and the northern pointers astern. Just before midnight, Nainoa figured they had reached two degrees ten minutes south. Buddy McGuire and Pat Aiu broke out their guitars. Their voices blended with the wind whistling in the shrouds.

Thursday, April 3. Day Twenty.

The Pacific is the largest ocean in the world, larger than all of Earth's land masses combined, and *Hōkūle'a's* course took her far from active shipping lanes. For almost three weeks, the horizon had been devoid of life. The crew had entered a paradoxical world of unlimited frontiers and confined space. As the horizons expanded, their vessel seemed to shrink. When searching for words to describe this unusual environment, Dave Lyman spoke of "time-space compression" where simple disagreements often flare into discord and even violence, as they had on the first voyage to Tahiti. Yet now all was peaceful. Their training had taught this crew to be sensitive to one another. "The crew becomes as one more and more each day," Marion wrote in her journal, "each respecting the other's right to their moods and being beautifully courteous and helpful at all times. The bond between us will never be broken."

At mid-day, Nainoa figured *Hōkūle'a* had reached three degrees thirty minutes south. He sailed a little west of his planned course to Takapoto because he was four houses east of his reference course. "The southeast swell is getting bigger, the swells from the east, northeast and east northeast are getting smaller. The southeast trades have set in. We will lose about a house a day but it's no problem because we have so many to give up."

Friday, April 4. Day Twenty-One.

At about 10 a.m., the canoe continued hard on the wind, heading due south at about four knots. Nainoa figured they had lost one house yesterday and

Deck view of *Hōkūle'a* looking forward

should now be three houses east of the reference course.

"Fish on the line."

Buddy and Sam hauled in two *aku*, one of them weighing more than twenty pounds. Sam filleted them and sliced the red flesh into thin strips which he laid out on a bed of alfalfa sprouts from Buddy's paper towel garden.

Fishermen the world over see things that are invisible to landsmen. A slight glitter on the ocean's surface may be a momentary brush of wind, or perhaps the tracings of bait fish fleeing predators. Big fish may be feeding there. And those terns—do they fly straight, commuting from one fishing ground to another, or do they wheel—having seen something from their airy perch? Do they dive? And if so, do they rise with the sparkle of tiny bodies in their beaks? Fishermen love to discuss technique and tackle into the wee hours. If they hunt the deep oceans, they talk of hundred pound leaders, fifty pound mono-filament line and titanium reels that set them back a week's salary. If they stalk mountain streams, they discuss line as fine as spiders' webs and lures shaped cunningly to resemble motes of insect life. But if a fisherman were to speak with Sam Ka'ai, he would find himself in unfamiliar territory. It's not that Sam's knowledge was more profound, or that the fish he stalks were different—it's the equipment Sam employs. Sam fashioned his lures from bone and shell, and decorated them with feathers from birds trapped in the wildness of remote Hawaiian valleys. He tied his hooks to line woven from coconut husks and weighted them with stream-smoothed pebbles. In hunting the depths, Sam was seeking not just fish, but the secrets of his ancestors.

Ancient Hawaiians shaped hooks of human bone because it contained *mana*—the spiritual power—of its owner. Sam used cattle bone to make hooks he calls *makau iwi*. Hooks made of mother-of-pearl were called *makau pā* and those of hawkbill turtle were called *makau honu 'ea*. He shaped the bone using stone files. "I found sandstone on Maui that makes beautiful files," Sam says. "They slice the bone good. I also use a file made of *'a'ā*—lava. A metal file does not change its shape so you get perfect cuts but when you make hooks with a stone file it keeps changing, it wears away real quick." Sam used his grandfather's pump drill to make holes in his hooks and although his grandfather used a metal drill, Sam fashioned his from coral. "I use candle coral. It looks like an eraser. You put it on the bone and it worries itself right through." He made small hooks for bottom fishing from a single piece of bone. Ancient Hawaiians also used a larger hook fashioned from two pieces of bone so Sam made some of his hooks that way, tying the pieces together with line made from the *'olonā* plant. "You cut the leaf, scrape it, roll it and soak it, and later on you scrape off the outside and you pull out the fiber and make the thread." He shaped a whale's tooth—a *niho palaoa*—to resemble a torpedo and fastened it to a leader. Then he tied on yellow feathers which attracted the fish and red feathers to resemble the streak of gills, and he wrapped the lure with *mahimahi* skin. Sam prepared the skin by peeling its colored outer layer from the inner translucent one while the *mahimahi* was still fresh. Then he tied the skin so that it flowed backwards over the lure. For fishing on dark days, he used white feathers from the Hawaiian goose, or *nēnē*. For bright sunny days, he dressed the tooth in black chicken feathers. One time Mau took one of Sam's hooks and adorned it with strips torn from a white plastic bag. The irony was not lost on Sam who was working hard to use only natural materials in the old way. "It was magical," Sam recalled, "the last of the navigators trained in the ancient way will use whatever he can find to catch fish."

Sam had about fifty different hooks and lures, from tiny ones of turtle shell for bottom fishing to ones of bone and wood larger than his hand for shark. Aboard *Hōkūle'a*, he had brought only his trolling lures. Before the voyage, he took them to an ancient fishing shrine, a *kū'ula*, to pray over them. For Sam, making the hooks and the line and casting them into the sea was a spiritual act—a metaphor within a metaphor. The words Sam used to describe fishing have *kaona*—hidden meaning. His fishing line, for example, was the "*aka* cord" that connects past and present. Fish are not taken by fisherman, Sam believes, they are given by the gods. "Gifts have been given without restriction for thousands and thousands of years to my kind. They are called *i'a*—fish—and from this we sustain our life. Kanaloa gives this gift readily. It has always been given by Kanaloa." When Sam throws a line overboard, he recalls the creation of Polynesian islands by Maui who raised them from the ocean floor with his magic fish hook. And Sam envisions Nainoa and Mau fishing up islands—literally raising them from the sea by following the same stars that guided their ancestors.

◇ ◇ ◇ ◇ ◇

For the last four days, Nainoa had steered the canoe to the west of his desired course through the water, slowly losing his eastern credit of houses. "By tomorrow we'll be two houses to the east of the reference course. I want to eliminate the two houses by the time we get to nine degrees south. Then turn down for landfall."

That evening, Nainoa estimated his latitude to be five degrees ten minutes south. The southeast swell was strong and trade wind cumulus dominated the horizon—the wind would continue to speed *Hōkūleʻa* south. Nainoa estimated landfall in five to six days.

Saturday, April 5. Day Twenty-Two.

At sunset on this twenty-second day at sea, the canoe had traveled more than sixteen hundred miles south from Hawaiʻi, so the sky had changed dramatically from the one Nainoa beheld from his grandmother's cow pasture. Gacrux and Acrux, in the Southern Cross, had now risen too high to be easily measured by

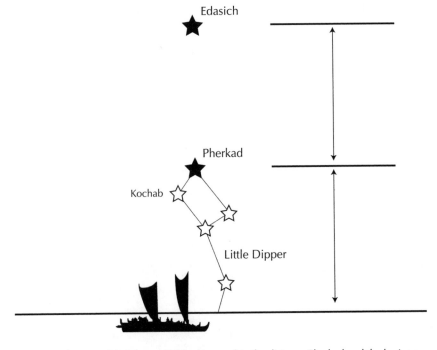

The distance between Edasich and Pherkad is equal to the distance Pherkad and the horizon at 5 degrees South latitude

an outstretched hand and Polaris was lost beneath the northern horizon. But as Polaris sank, all the northern stars sank with it. Pherkad, for example, at the bottom of Little Dipper's cup, rose to an altitude of 39 degrees when observed from the cow pasture, crossing the meridian with Edasich thirteen degrees above it. At the equator, 21 degrees further south, Pherkad crossed the meridian at 18 degrees of altitude, and at 5 degrees south it would cross at 13, and the distance between it and Edasich would finally be equal to the distance between Pherkad and the horizon. The distance between them now appeared greater so Nainoa decided they had gone further south—to about six degrees twenty minutes.

That night, first mate Leon Sterling patrolled the canoe—inspecting her masts, sails, rigging, decking and 'iako—and he found Hōkūle'a suffering from fatigue. Eight cross-beams of laminated white oak—the 'iako—joined the canoe's twin hulls and supported the deck. The forward-most 'iako also supported the foremast and it was subject to great stress when the canoe encountered rough weather. Now, it was delaminating—the result of a flaw that Leon had inherited from the drafting board. Leon consulted with Harry, a professional architect familiar with load bearing surfaces. They decided the 'iako should last until they get to Tahiti where they could repair it.

"I don't want to mention the 'iako situation to Nainoa," Leon said. "I don't want to worry him. He has enough on his head right now."

BECALMED

Chapter Forty-One

Sunday, April 6. Day Twenty-Three, Easter.

Seven degrees south latitude. The canoe proceeded south for most of the day, until about 6:00 p.m. when the winds sputtered and died.

"We are becalmed," Jo-Ann wrote. "The ocean without a ripple. Very glassy and very hot. Water consumption has gone up. It's Easter Sunday and we are twenty-three days out."

It's also Tava's birthday. He was thirty-five.

"Marion and I blew up balloons," Jo-Anne recalls. "We scrambled eggs topped with Spam and brown bread, and brewed coffee and cocoa. We opened a can of New England fruit cake and lit candles and his eyes lit up."

Pat Aiu dressed for the occasion. "He put on shoes," Jo-Anne recalls. "He had a hat. He was hanging on to the rigging and he was singing. It felt like we were in our own little world."

The canoe moved slowly. The wind, what little there was, had now shifted northerly and it carried heat and moisture from the vast baking equatorial belt four hundred miles behind them. It was humid and sticky.

"Nainoa," said Mau, "you got two Doldrums."

"We got out of the first Doldrum," Chad recalls, "and we got into nice weather and then we hit a big empty area—no wind. It was like the Doldrums again. Your head hurt because the sun was so hot." The crew filled their water bottles from five-gallon jugs. Water may soon be a problem.

"Scattered around us are isolated puffs of cumulus clouds," Will Kyselka wrote aboard *Ishka*, "but there are no lines of clouds anywhere to raise our hopes for a return of the winds. Slight swells rock our vessel as sails flip-flop from one side of the mast to the other... The sharp interface of the sea and sky is everywhere around. A vapid view."

Nainoa reading aboard *Hōkūle'a* in the "second Doldrums"

The crew read in shade pools cast by the limp sails or dozed in their bunks, the canvas flaps of their half tents tied open to encourage errant wind drafts below. The air was thick. The sea was satin.

At sunset, the wind gyred—spinning the canoe in lugubrious circles. High clouds were moving very slowly to the southwest. The previous four days of steady easterly winds had allowed Nainoa to steer generally south for about four hundred miles, following his desired course of south by east for one day, and then turning almost due south for three days, losing three houses to the west. When Nainoa began this long straight shot, he had been five houses east of the reference course. Now he was down to two.

Darkness enveloped the canoe. In this uneasy calm, the ocean mirrored the stars as they descended to the horizon. Nainoa watched Rigel approach its mirrored twin. The two stars slid toward each other—like a giant kaleidoscope—joined, then disappeared below the horizon. *The stars are eating each other,* he thought. Bellatrix consumed its twin. Then the stars in Orion's belt—Mintaka, Alnilam, Alnitak. Earth orbited toward daylight spawning cannibal stars.

Monday, April 7. Day Twenty-Four.

When he got off watch, Tava lingered on deck, watching the stars slide overhead, listening to the gentle wash of the wake. Finally entering his *puka,* he quickly fell into a deep sleep and began to dream. "I saw the face of my dad in the dream," he recalls. "He looked just like when I was home in the Marquesas." The dream recalled the day Tava left Taiohae on the island of Nuku Hiva, many years ago. "When I left from Marquesas Islands my father said to me, 'You go all over. Don't turn back. You go forward always.' My father was hugging me and his face was turned away. 'It's time that you leave now—like the wind—like Makani,' he told me. That is the old way, that is how they think."

Tava's father was a Marquesan jack-of-all-trades. He tended cattle in the mountains above his home. He built canoes for fishing and sailing between the islands. He crewed on inter-island schooners and rose to the rank of captain. He traveled widely and he knew the pain of homesickness. When it came time for his son to strike out on his own, he took Tava aside and blessed him. Then, turning his head aside so Tava would not see the tears, he said, "Do what you love. Don't turn your face and come back. Go like Makani."

When Tava awoke the next morning, he knew his father's spirit was trying to tell him something, but what? It was not until the canoe reached Tahiti that he would learn that his father had passed away, possibly on that very evening. "My father came in my dream," Tava recalls. "When we got to Tahiti my uncle asked me, 'You want to go home to the Marquesas? See your family?' I said no because the dream told me I am supposed to be on the canoe. Like Makani. Like the wind. No turn your face back—go like the wind."

The morning dawned hot. The ocean was glassy to the horizon. *Hōkūle'a* bobbed in a gentle swell. "Just keep busy," Gordon told his crew, "read, write in your journal, do something so you can pass the time."

Mau labored over his canoe model. The gentle percussion of his adze carried in the silence surrounding the stalled canoe. He carved the bow, turned the model over and lifted his eyeglasses to regard it critically. Then he began to carve some more. He had inspired Tava, Buddy and Sam, who took up pieces of wood and began to fashion whatever came to mind. Sam and Tava were accomplished sculptors, Buddy was a game amateur. Mau watched him as he worked on a piece of wood, leaving a large pile of shavings without producing a recognizable artifact.

"Oh, look at Buddy," Mau said to the other carvers, "too much rubbish he make. Big piece wood, cut, cut, cut. Lot of rubbish—but nothing come out."

Buddy was aroused from his reverie by their laughter.

"What did he say?"

"He says you start with a big piece of wood and now all you got is this rubbish over here."

Before the canoe departed Hilo, Steve Somsen had carefully calculated the crew's water needs, taking into account that should they run out, *Ishka* could resupply them from its on-board desalinator. But without the engine to power it, the desalinator was useless. Would the water last? Steve sat on deck, paper and pencil in hand. When the canoe left Hilo there were two hundred and thirty gallons aboard. During the first seventeen days, the crew consumed an average of seven gallons a day. But in the heat of this past week, daily water consumption had jumped to more than nine gallons. Only fifty-eight remained, enough for six days. The Tuamotus were now about four hundred and eighty miles away and the canoe was motionless. Steve recommended rationing.

"We had two glasses of water a day," says Chad, "one in the morning and one in the evening. I poured my water into a glass and I would just watch it. I wouldn't drink it. I would just look at it for the longest time." "Water became gold," Marion remembers. "We used it to make bets, whether a squall was coming or not, and to this day Leon owes me a gallon of water."

The sun baked the crew. A slight breeze riffled the ocean. *Hōkūle'a* moved slowly south, but *Ishka* wallowed. At noon, Gordon lowered the sails to wait for the escort. Progress had been dismal, maybe a mile an hour in the last twenty-

Steve Somsen cooling off

Nainoa and Harry rig a sunshade

four. "The wind seems to be decreasing," Nainoa told Steve. "Maybe tonight no wind."

The sea had turned azure. Looking over the side on the first day of drifting, the crew imagined they saw into the ocean's deepest heart—a vast blue desert completely devoid of life. But now, shade cast by the canoe and the algae growing on her hulls had attracted baitfish. They flitted about—tiny silver specks. At night, they disturbed swarms of plankton that glowed like darting fireflies. Sam Ka'ai watched this gentle fireworks display with great interest. "We saw this gray-green fluorescence and it went blue and sometimes it went yellow. It was big. It stretched from the bow, right across the bottom of the canoe to the back."

In the shape, Sam perceived a *mo'o*—a lizard. The lizard's backbone conjured the *lei* of bones—the genealogy of Sam's ancestors stretching back in time to the founding of his line. It recalled the great ancestral voyages. It was, Sam believed, an affirmation that the voyage was *pono*—in harmony.

Tava Taupu also noticed the glowing thing below the canoe, but he regarded it more pragmatically. Before the voyage, he had fashioned an ironwood harpoon tipped with six metal spikes. Now, harpoon in hand, Tava stalked Sam's *mo'o* as it moved from one side of the canoe to the other. He knew that baitfish had attracted larger game. He was fishing for *mahimahi*. The crew watched him with wonder. "He stalked the fish with complete attention," Nainoa recalls, "for a whole night he never threw that harpoon." "He was so patient," says Marion, "every day he would wait for the *mahimahi* to come alongside and he would try to spear it." "It was moving fast," says Nainoa. "He had to account for the refraction of the water, the fish was not where it appeared to be. He picked the exact moment and threw that harpoon." "He pulled up one *mahimahi*," says Sam. "There were hundreds of *mahimahi* swimming—like one green *mo'o* under the sea." "That was a big event for us," says Marion. "Tava gave the head to Mau for his soup. That was a good gesture."

"Next fish I get I make for you," Mau told Tava.

That night, Nainoa estimated their position to be seven and a half degrees south. They had traveled only 30 miles in the last day. The canoe should have entered the zone of southeast trades, but the wind switched west, then northwest. "I don't understand it at all," he thought, "totally flat, then north and west winds. What happened to the east winds?"

Tuesday, April 8. Day Twenty-Five.

Nainoa observed clouds moving all around the compass. Some flowed east, others west, still others moved north. *They're crazy,* he thought. The surface winds were even more puzzling—they shifted from north to east then south-southeast. For a while it seemed the southeast trades might come up, but then the winds shifted back north. The swells were from the north, northeast and east. He searched for southern swells that might indicate trade winds, but there were none. The canoe continued south, barely making a knot in a whisper of wind.

During the night. *Ishka's* mast light became a twinkle low on the horizon.

Once again, she had fallen behind. They waited. "We were escorting the escort boat," Marion says. "Think how hard it was for Nainoa to figure out how long we just sat there." Yesterday *Hōkūle'a* had stopped for three hours. Today they waited for another three. Waiting dulled Nainoa's concentration. "It kills my fight to get speed out of the canoe," he told Steve, "or maintain a perfect course, because it doesn't matter. I know we'll have to trice up and wait. It kills my intensity."

"Nainoa was struggling to stay awake," Chad remembers. "I said, 'Shit, this guy is going to kill himself.' His face got burnt real bad because he was out in the sun. He was mentally so focused on navigating that physically he didn't look after himself. His eyes were all red."

"It seemed like he was always on—always awake," Marion recalls.

The science of sleep deprivation is a relatively new field, but even in 1980 it was known that going without sleep produced a wide variety of symptoms—irritability, memory lapses, confusion, depression, high blood pressure, and hallucinations. A person who gets less than six hours a night will lose coordination and judgment. Long haul truckers who drive more than seventeen hours a day act more like drunks than those who are legally intoxicated. In the United States, over a hundred thousand traffic accidents each year are caused by fatigue.

Dr. Claudio Stampi, the head of the Chronobiology Research Institute in Newton, Massachusetts, is known as "Doctor Sleep." His clients include NASA, police departments, and famous solo ocean racers such as Ellen MacArthur who in 2005 set the single-handed, non-stop, round-the-world sailing record of a little more than seventy-one days. Stampi has competed in such races. In 1975, he sailed in the Clipper Race from England to Australia, monitored the performance of his crewmates, and published the results as his Ph.D. thesis. From his research, he distinguishes between monophasic sleep—the normal kind we all get, large chunks of sleep—and polyphasic sleep—short chunks or frequent napping. He administered laboratory tests to subjects who were allowed to sleep only three hours a day and found that those who slept the three hours in one chunk (monophasic sleep) suffered a 30% loss of cognitive performance while those who slept for a half hour every four hours (polyphasic sleep) lost only 12%. He found that naps produced what he calls slow wave sleep which is more effective in rejuvenating mind and body than REM sleep, a deep sleep in which we are most likely to dream. Stampi set a regimen of half hour catnaps for sailor Ellen MacArthur, at about four hour intervals, which she claims allowed her to set the world record because she could stay awake longer to wring the maximum performance from her speeding yacht. When Nainoa set to sea from Hilo, all this knowledge was way in the future. He was improvising but as he did so, his discoveries mirrored those of Dr. Sleep.

About four times a day, Nainoa lay down on the navigator's platform, next to the steering paddle, and took a catnap. "I rested for about fifteen or twenty minutes," he says, "and I would sleep and dream of fire, and when the fire came, I would jump up. I would be wide awake. I slept only two and a half hours a day. I can't do that on land. I think it's the sheer anxiety of navigating that allows me to do it on the ocean. I catnapped just enough for my mind to clear. You don't

Gordon Pi'ianai'a

want to sleep more than an hour at a time. Never. Once you get up, you've got to get back to studying where the canoe has gone while you slept."

A navigator not only abstains from sleep but, following Mau's teaching, he also abstains from physical exertion. So Gordon and Nainoa had decided on a clear division of labor—Nainoa would be in charge of finding land and Gordon would make sure that he could conserve his energy to do that. "You've got to discipline yourself," Nainoa says. "You don't run around the canoe doing things. You want to stay still and calm so you don't get tired. You don't want to have highs and lows during the day. It becomes a kind of meditation. You want to stay level so if there's a navigational clue that you have to be ready for, you're not wasted. It's an issue of endurance—you have to go until the island comes out of the sea."

Wednesday, April 9. Day Twenty-Six.

Eight degrees forty-five minutes south latitude. The wind was a whisper from the north. Towering cumulus clouds dominated the horizon. Nainoa estimated the Tuamotus were about three hundred and seventy miles away.

"Trice the sails."

Ishka had once again dropped behind the canoe.

Nainoa's briefings with Steve occasionally revealed exhaustion. He misspoke, corrected himself, misspoke again. He might say east when he meant west and his math was shaky. The trial by storm off Hawai'i had taken a toll and when he turned back toward Hawai'i, he had to make complex calculations about course, speed and westward set of wind and current. In the Doldrums, the southern wind had forced him to sail east when he wanted to go south. And now he must wait for *Ishka*.

Mau appeared unfazed by the delay. On the first voyage in 1976, they had waited a week for wind. But as he took up his adze to work on his model canoe, a look of sadness, inspired by thoughts of his home island, flickered across his face.

For more than a hundred generations, Satawal had been beyond the reach of Western civilization. The island had no natural resources to exploit and it lay outside traveled sea lanes. Visitors were few. Life was an eternal round of gardening and fishing. But following World War II, the Carolines had become a United States protectorate and with that came well-intentioned plans to bring modern education to the remotest of them. Many of Mau's sons and daughters left Satawal for school on nearby Woleai atoll, and some of them went on to Guam or the United States and never returned. All the islands were losing their brightest kids.

A government vessel called at Satawal every few months to deliver supplies. Canned goods replaced fresh garden produce and fish in the island's diet. Cinder block replaced thatch, bathing suits replaced the traditional *lavalava* and, most alarming to Mau, outboard motors began to replace sails and paddles. For the first time in the island's history, forty-gallon drums of gasoline appeared out of the hold of the visiting ship and made their way into the island's canoe houses. Even worse, few young men approached Mau to learn navigation. Only one of his sons, Sesario Sewralur, appeared to have an interest and Mau was determined to pass on his knowledge to him. But even that was uncertain. Traditional navigation was no longer a viable career because trained instinct was rapidly being replaced by western instruments. Mau's son, Peter, was first mate on the government ship. Mau worried about losing "the talk of the sea"—a rich body of traditional wisdom that had not only been essential to island life but was a thing of beauty in itself. In many ways, navigation and sailing had defined what it meant to be a man on Satawal. It was the heart of the island's culture. What would take its place? There were more practical reasons to worry as well. Gasoline depended on the whims of outsiders and it cost money. The wind was free and omnipresent. If no one knew how to harness the wind and find the fishing grounds, how would the islanders survive? Mau had spoken of these concerns to Harry and Nainoa, but not to the others on the crew. If any of them noticed the fleeting look of sadness on Mau's face, they had no way of knowing why it was there.

Thursday, April 10. Day Twenty-Seven.

A brilliant light streaked high above the canoe's stern and arced over her bow, streaming a wake of fire that burned for a moment then snuffed out.

"Look at that," yelled Sam. "Look. Look."

The fireball arced from north to south, matching *Hōkūle'a's* course. It split into three pieces, obliterating the stars.

"It just exploded," says Sam. "It was a *hōkūlele*—a flying star—and it broke into pieces and went right over the horizon."

It was probably a meteor—at least that was the opinion of most—and, as far as Western logic went, Sam agreed. But why a meteor just then?

"You had this feeling when we first set out of being in a storm with the eyes of the ancestors upon you," Sam recalls, "and you thought that Makani was giving you a challenge to see if you would be *maoli*, if you were real. Then there was the *mo'o* under the canoe and now you had this *hōkūlele* mark your path—go down the same path we were going. Maybe they got so happy—that heavenly host—that they got on their own canoe and went so fast that it was like fire showing us the way."

When Sam settled into his *puka* that night, he was certain that the voyage continued to be *pono*—in balance. The wind would come and they would speed south, *Hōkūle'a* following the path of the *hōkūlele*—the ancestral spirits.

Nainoa also felt the presence of spirits sailing with him—his grandmother,

Hōkūle'a's sails

Gardie, who had given him pride of Hawaiian identity; Eddie Aikau who showed him the meaning of courage; Yoshi Kawano who introduced him to the ocean's beauty; and his father who had made explicit the values that would sustain him.

"I was not sailing by myself," Nainoa remembers. "They were with me. As I was pulling the island out of the sea, in my mind and heart, I was sailing for them. They were my strength. Maybe that would be my own personal definition of *'aumākua*."

Friday, April 11. Day Twenty-Eight.

Ten degrees south latitude. At dawn, Nainoa saw cumulus clouds forming wind streets. "The southeast trades are coming," he told Steve. A little after sunrise, the canoe's sails stirred then filled. *Hōkūle'a* proceeded south at three knots.

At Polynesian Voyaging Society headquarters in Honolulu, a large chart was posted. The canoe's reference course, four different legs from Hilo to landfall in the Tuamotus, were drawn on the chart, and neat circles accompanied by a date, showed the canoe's location as revealed by the Argos satellite. Triangles indicated Nainoa's estimated positions and for some time they had been consistently about one hundred miles too far to the east. The cause of this discrepancy was the South Equatorial current.

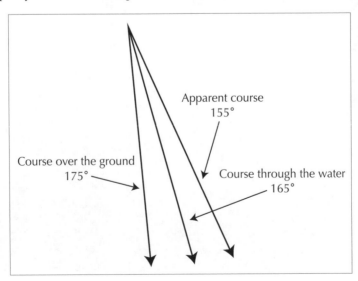

The mental map that Nainoa sailed resolves the complexities of what appeared to be true from his vantage point at sea and what is actually true when wind and current are taken into account. This can be diagrammed by three lines: the course the canoe seems to be taking (the apparent course); the course she is sailing due to the wind pushing her to leeward (course through the water); and the invisible effect of the current (course over the ground). The diagram appears to be a simple two-dimensional graphic, but it in reality it contains an invisible third dimension—time.

When Nainoa plotted the four reference courses, he made assumptions about how long it would take to sail each of the legs. The first would require six days, the second three and a half, the third four, and the fourth nine. These assumptions were close enough for the first three legs, but on this last leg the canoe had languished in the second Doldrums and was often forced to stop and wait for *Ishka* to catch up. As a result, it had taken six more days than he predicted to reach ten degrees south latitude. The South Equatorial Current flows from east to west at an average speed of 20 miles a day, so for six days the canoe had been forced west a total of one hundred and twenty miles. She was now six houses west of her reference course.

Nainoa had decided not to account for this current effect until the trade winds filled in and the canoe began to move once more. Now he did so, and the result, when plotted in Honolulu brought his triangle for April 11th to within 30 miles of the satellites' circle. When the folks in Honolulu regarded this new plot, they took a collective breath of relief.

Nainoa had planned this last leg to end at Takapoto Atoll because it was 200 miles to the east of Mataiva, the last island in the Tuamotu chain, and it provided a comfortable margin of error after voyaging 2400 miles from Hawai'i. But during the day, the wind increased and shifted southerly, forcing the canoe off course to the west. Following the wind would allow *Hōkūle'a* to make better speed. *Let me go,* the canoe seemed to say, *I know where land is.* Mataiva was the last outpost in the Tuamotu chain before the open ocean so if he turned toward it and he was farther west than he thought, he would sail right by the island and into the open sea. And turning west was a break with his sail plan—all that intellectual preparation bending over charts with dividers and scales in hand. *Go with your instinct,* the canoe told him, *trust your gut—your* na'au.

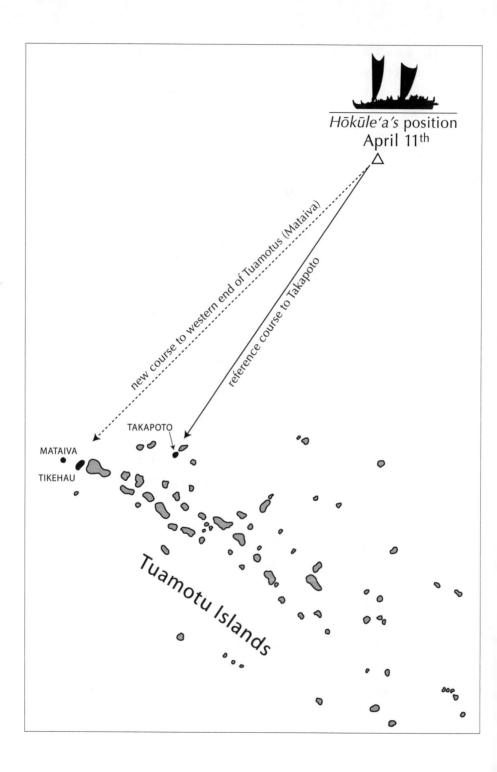

Hōkūle'a's position
April 11th

new course to western end of Tuamotus (Mataiva)

reference course to Takapoto

TAKAPOTO

MATAIVA

TIKEHAU

Tuamotu Islands

A little after noon, Nainoa held a meeting with his crew. "We're not going to Takapoto, we're going directly for Mataiva," Nainoa told them. "I think we can make it. I'm pretty confident of my navigation."

As the canoe steadied on her new course, the wind—as if on cue—increased to ten knots. *Hōkūle'a* picked up speed, *Ishka* in her wake. The eastern swell clarified and clouds on the horizon were forming wind streets—stronger winds were coming.

❖ ❖ ❖ ❖ ❖

Islands announce their presence long before they rise out of the sea. In the morning, birds fly as far as a hundred miles over open ocean searching for food, and at night they return—signaling to navigators where their nests lie over the horizon. A circle around an island with a hundred-mile radius defines the zone in which a sailor can assume he will see birds. In addition to this, islands shed detritus—palm fronds, coconuts, plastic garbage bags—a cornucopia of junk that floats to sea until it becomes waterlogged and sinks. The physics of water absorption, with the exception of plastic, means that a mariner encountering such junk can assume that land was within a few hundred miles. So at noon when *Hōkūle'a's* crew spotted a leaf and seaweed of the kind that grew only on coral reefs, they knew that land was near. Just before midnight, Nainoa estimated their latitude was eleven degrees thirty minutes south. If Mataiva was ahead of them—it was now only about two hundred miles away.

"It was exhilarating to be moving again—and fast—but also frightening," Nainoa recalls. "When I turned west, I was not sure that Mataiva was where I thought it was. I was going to find out if I was right or wrong—and soon. My stomach was churning. I was confident because of all my training but I was also fighting a lifetime of fearing failure. I couldn't shake it—that fear in the back of my mind—and now, soon, I would find out if I had succeeded or failed."

HAWAIKI RISING

Chapter Forty-Two

Saturday, April 12. Day Twenty-Nine.

During the evening, the southeast trades established themselves, blowing steadily at eighteen knots. *Hōkūle'a* accelerated. Squalls dotted the horizon but they did not deflect the wind, indicating it had momentum. A few days earlier, the wind had been warm, a sign that it came down from the equatorial zone to the north. Now it was cool—just what you would expect if it were blowing across a long stretch of cool ocean from the east-southeast. The clouds were what Nainoa calls "dry cumulus," unlike those that rose in towering parapets in the equatorial zone, they had settled into a single layer. At sunrise, Nainoa saw red smoke under them. "We're in the trade wind belt and it isn't going to change. All I see is good weather from here on down," he told Steve. "If we keep going like this we'll be only ninety miles from landfall at sunset and about seven houses west of the reference course."

Nainoa saw swells from the northeast, east and southwest but there were no swells from the southeast—the direction of the prevailing trade winds.

"Do you think that the Tuamotus might be blocking them?" Steve asked.

"It could be," Nainoa said. "This is my first time doing this, but I think that islands may be blocking the swells ahead of us."

The Tuamotus are the tops of mountains that sank into the ocean over millions of years. Many of them are only fourteen feet above sea level but they are a significant barrier to deep ocean swells nevertheless. The atolls lay sprawled across *Hōkūle'a's* path, so the diminishing swells confirmed they must be near.

"Steering a good course is now critical because land is near," Nainoa told his crew. "Steer up in gusts but come off the wind right away when it dies. Keep her fast, but keep her on course." To help with the steering, Nainoa stood behind the helmsman, gently coaching him.

"Come up," he said, directing him to turn upwind.

Except for Nainoa, no one spoke. There was only the sound of the wind and the waves slapping the hull. Nainoa leaned against the lee rail, humming softly.

"Good," he told the helmsman.

Nainoa was concerned about encountering the atolls at night. Land birds provide an early warning system, but the most common of them, the *noio*, fly only about forty miles to sea during the day, returning to their nests at sunset. Between sunset and sunrise, *Hōkūle'a* would sail sixty miles, so it was possible they might miss the birds altogether and make landfall abruptly on a coral reef. "If I think we're close tomorrow and we haven't seen any birds by sunset," Nainoa told Steve, "we'll go only another thirty miles and then we'll heave to and wait for morning."

Composed of seventy-eight atolls, the Tuamotus are difficult to see from the deck of a ship, so it's not surprising that it required more than three centuries for European navigators—beginning with Magellan in 1521 and ending with the American Commodore, Charles Wilkes, in 1845—to produce a map of all of them. Because of the danger they pose for ships, they have earned a variety of disreputable names: "The Dangerous Archipelago," "The Rough Waters," "The Labyrinth," "The Low Archipelago," and "The Rough Sea Archipelago."

"If we get close to a reef at night we are not going to know it." Nainoa told the crew. "I think we'll see land in the next thirty hours. I think we're close to Mataiva."

Sunday, April 13. Day Thirty.

At about three in the morning, Nainoa estimated the canoe was at thirteen degrees forty minutes south and nine houses west of the reference course. If he was right, Mataiva and Tikihau should be about eighty miles away. "We should see land tomorrow night," he said. "I don't see the southwest swell or the southeast swell. They're blocked. The water looks pretty calm."

The canoe continued cautiously south. The sun arced over a scrim of cloud. Shorty climbed the forward mast to look for land.

"Bird," said Mau.

"Where?"

Mau pointed to a flight of *noio* flying on a line from south to north.

"Mau taught me that the seabirds are a navigator's best friend," Nainoa says, "and sure enough, there they were just like they were supposed to be. I was exhilarated because I knew that land was close by."

"They're heading for the feeding grounds," Nainoa told Steve, "I think land is maybe forty miles south. The signs are pretty good."

The crew watched as the birds wheeled and beat their wings to hover over a promising spot of ocean, then swooped and dove, spearing tiny baitfish with sharp bills.

"When it's time to go back to their nests, when the sun gets low, you watch which way the birds fly," Nainoa told the crew. "They will lift off the water, fly higher, and then fly straight to the island."

"Sure enough," Nainoa recalls, "when the sun went down, the birds flew south-southeast. I lined up the direction of their flight with the star compass and I said, 'Okay that's where the island is.' We were all excited. We didn't know what island it was, but at least it was land. We sailed south-southeast. I climbed the mast at sunset to see what I could. Nothing. Still, I knew it must be close. The moon came up late so we sailed on in the darkness. It was scary."

Nainoa assembled the crew: "The voyage is almost over," he told them, "now we look for land. Be alert tonight. Get organized in teams. Tava and Chad will be forward on lookout. The rest of you must steer a good course. Concentrate on it. I will be in charge of steering tonight."

In 1888, Robert Louis Stevenson made a similar approach to the Tuamotus aboard his yacht, the *Casco*. "In no quarter are the atolls so thickly congregated," he wrote as they probed cautiously for land, "in none are they so varied in size from the greatest to the least, and in none is navigation so beset with perils, as in that archipelago that we are now to thread. The huge system of the trades is, for some reason, quite confounded by this multiplicity of reefs; the wind intermits, squalls are frequent from the west and southwest, hurricanes are known. The currents are, besides, inextricably intermixed; dead reckoning becomes a farce; the charts are not to be trusted; and such is the number and similarity of these islands that, even when you have picked one up, you may be none the wiser. The reputation of the place is consequently infamous..."[11]

Monday, April 14. Day Thirty-One.

When he laid out his reference course from the equator to Takapoto, Nainoa took note of the distance—in terms of houses—that Mataiva and Tikihau should lie to the west of it. Tikihau is at fifteen degrees seven minutes south latitude and nine houses west. Mataiva is at fourteen degrees fifty-three minutes south latitude and eleven houses west. As the canoe approached landfall, she both moved south and was set west by the current, moving over Earth as an airplane would do when landing in a stiff cross wind. On Saturday, two days ago, she was seven houses west; on Sunday, she was nine houses west; and now, as landfall was imminent, she was ten west. By steering away so much from his reference course, Nainoa had thrown the dice. If his calculations were correct, Mataiva should lie just over the horizon. If they were not, *Hōkūle'a* would be sailing into open ocean.

"April 14ᵗʰ, crew on strict lookout for sight of land," Jo-Anne wrote in her log. Maui's fishhook—Eddie Aikau's constellation—was dead ahead, high above the sails, over the place where the Tuamotus should rise. "This particular watch finds the crew more alert than they have been since we left Hilo nearly a month ago," Steve noted in his log.

Gordon stationed Tava and Chad on the bow of the canoe. "Keep a sharp lookout," he told them. "Use all your senses. Watch for lights, listen for surf on a reef. You may even smell land before you see it."

As the canoe neared landfall, no one aboard was more aware of it than Mau. He had voyaged under these stars all of his life. He had seen the land signs in the drifting reef weed and only four years earlier he had sensed the calm waters in the lee of these same islands. "I am sure that Mau knew the island was there long before any of us," Nainoa recalls, "but he kept his silence."

"Mau, you see the island?" Harry asked.

"Me, I smell copra," Mau joked.

The canoe proceeded south at about five knots in a brisk trade wind. "An occasional wave breaks against the port hull," Steve wrote in his log, "dousing people on deck. Tava and Chad, the appointed watch keepers, maintain a vigil to port and starboard. They cling to the rigging as they peer ahead into the darkness. There is a surprising amount of light all around us just from the stars. There is no moon. There is a wonderful, a marvelous anticipation of the coming of land.

Surely it is near. We are in the latitude of the Tuamotus—at least in a portion of them. The question is—where will we make landfall within that archipelago that stretches for so great a distance from east to west? The whole complexion of the trip has changed now as we anticipate landfall. We look for a dark line on the horizon. We look for lights. We look for land birds. We listen for the surf, although discerning that sound above the noise from our vessel will be difficult."

Jo-Anne stood near the aft shrouds. Steve and Pat Aiu were near the galley to starboard. Nainoa was perched on the railing forward of the navigator's platform with one hand on the shrouds. Behind him were Mau and Captain Pi'ianai'a. Harry was aft keeping an eye on the escort vessel trailing in *Hōkūle'a's* wake. If the crew on *Ishka* saw land first, they would signal by light. So far, there had been no signal.

"Since my watch came on duty at midnight, Nainoa has taken only two or three five-minute catnaps," Steve wrote. "He told me that he intended to stay awake until landfall. And so, for his sake, I hope that landfall is soon. Everyone on board realizes that when we make landfall it will never be the same again for this small group of fourteen people. We are a family. There's no doubt we have our minor problems. We try to air our grievances. …For the most part, we are a harmonious group. We eat and sleep and sing together and share the joys and frustrations of voyaging. When landfall comes—even though we will still have a ways to sail to Tahiti—the voyage will in a big way be over."

Leon checked the canoe's ground tackle—the anchors, swivels, chain, and rope that would be needed in case of an emergency. Buddy helped lay the anchors on deck, a primary anchor in the bow and a secondary in the stern. They flaked the rope in long lines, neatly curved upon each other to run free if needed.

Written in 1894, the *Instructions for Mariners* contains numerous guidelines for making landfall in the Tuamotus, as good today as they were a hundred years ago. "In normal weather the groups and fringes of coconut palms can be seen from twelve to fifteen miles from the mast of a schooner (50 feet high) and from five to six miles from the deck," the *Instructions* caution. "The bare reefs are marked by breakers. In calm weather, when the sea does not break, they cannot be seen until one is right on top of them…The breakers, if the light is good, can be seen from three to four miles. In a calm or light land breeze and especially at night when all is calm on board, the roaring of the breakers can sometimes be heard over a long distance if a strong swell is breaking on the reef. This is a valuable indication but must not be relied on too much, since there are numerous reasons for its disappearance." Another section of the *Instructions* lists several specific steps to be taken by all prudent mariners:

> Do not try to make landfall at night except under exceptionally favorable conditions from every point of view.
> Keep a very thorough lookout by setting up a regular watch when the ship is estimated to be twenty miles from land.
> Keep the vessel in a constant state of readiness to change course.

Though they had not read the *Instructions,* Gordon and Nainoa were making a textbook approach to the Dangerous Archipelago.

"Nainoa has been on the alert—directing our vessel ever since we left Hilo," Steve wrote. "Now that we have traveled twenty-five hundred miles from Hilo, the voyage almost at an end, he is more alert than ever…We know land is there. He may feel some apprehension in spite of all his preparation. This is the first time that he has attempted such a feat. What a feat it is. To bring the canoe all the way from Hilo to this landfall in the South Pacific, from twenty degrees above the equator to fourteen degrees below it. To deal with all the changes in course. It is a remarkable feat. And I speak of it as though we are practically at the dock— which we are not. Yet I personally feel very confident that Nainoa's navigation is very good."

A little after midnight, Nainoa ordered the sails triced. The canoe slowed, came to a stop, rolling gently in the swells. The crew lined her rails, peering intently into the night. A few hundred yards astern, *Ishka* doused her sails.

"About four o'clock, just before dawn, I asked the whole crew to form a circle around the rail of the canoe to look for birds," Nainoa recalls. "There was no talking. I remember hearing the waves lapping against the canoe. The wind was clean—a dark, cool wind that made a humming sound in the rigging. The canoe rolled softly. We were all tense. Ahead of us was a horizon full of islands. We could all feel it."

"Dawn comes," Nainoa continues. "No birds. Not a single *noio*. I'm getting anxious and puzzled. Everything had worked like clock-work up to now. But no birds. No clue. No place to go. We waited, and we waited. Mau just sat back and did not say a word."

Jo-Anne lit the propane stove and began to fry Salisbury steaks and boil rice. Cans of fruit cocktail were opened. *Ishka* maneuvered alongside and delivered muffins and coffee cake. Elsie had been in her galley baking.

"The ring of people looking at the horizon started to collapse," Nainoa recalls. "They were getting tired. We had to start breakfast. It was another day at sea. But it was traumatic. I didn't know where to guide the canoe because now we're no longer following the stars, we're following birds. And there were no birds. The sun rose higher. It was about eight o'clock or so. The sun was blazing. No birds."

"Hoist the sails," Nainoa ordered.

"We continued heading south, but I was uncomfortable and I felt empty about it because I was really not sure which way to go. The ring of bird watchers had collapsed but Harry Ho, always the good crewman, was still in the stern looking for birds."

"We waited till morning," Harry recalls. "We sat there and the sun came out and all of a sudden I looked back and I saw a bird coming."

"Mau, look at that bird," Harry said.

"That one he feed the baby," said Mau, "he goes home."

Nainoa did not hear Mau's comment. In the morning, birds generally fly away from land—out to sea—looking for food. In the evening, they return home. Nainoa expected to see the morning birds heading north to the fishing grounds, but this one was heading south.

"Out of the north comes this *noio* flying straight over the canoe," he remembers. "He's traveling south, exactly the opposite of what I expected. None of this is making sense. I'm getting panicky. Maybe it was fatigue, maybe it was anxiety—but all I could think of was that somehow we drifted *past* the island and now it's to the *north* of us. How could we have done that with the sails down?"

"Turn the canoe around," Nainoa ordered.

"We steered north. I was really anxious, on the borderline of panic. Mau had taught me to compare the height of the sun to when you see the bird to get some idea of how far away the island is. The higher the sun, the farther away the island, because the bird had to fly farther. That assumes that he leaves at sunrise. When we turned the canoe around, we saw more birds coming from the north.

I'm thinking that we drifted a long way because the birds are appearing so late. None of it made sense. How could I go past the island at night when we were just drifting? I was not thinking it through. I was desperately hanging onto the rules Mau had taught me. I wasn't using my imagination. I had a fixed idea and I hoped that it would work. We sailed north. I was tense and uptight."

"Nainoa, turn the canoe around," Mau said. "You go follow the bird."

"I was thinking, 'Wait a minute. It's not sunset. That's not part of the rules,'" Nainoa recalls, "but of course I'm going to do what he told me. I was confused and a little upset that he came and changed the course. I was not upset at him, I was upset at myself."

"In one hour we see the island," Mau told him.

"Mau was real calm," Nainoa recalls. "He seemed almost indifferent. He had made hundreds of landfalls. In his mind he had already arrived. He knew where the island was but I didn't and I was losing confidence rather quickly. Mau sat on the navigator's platform as relaxed as could be. Then I remember it so clearly—everybody does—all of a sudden he stands up, holding the shroud, and he says 'The island is right there.'"

"I was standing almost next to him," Chad recalls, "he pointed and there was a pile of birds—all kinds of birds—and then he jumped up and said 'Island.'"

"Plenty birds came from the island," Mau recalls. "When I stood up, I saw the island is close."

"Now we were climbing the mast," says Nainoa. "We were running all over the place. Total anxiety. We don't see anything. Nothing. We are straining and we don't see it. Mau sat down and he never said another word."

"They climbed up on the mast and they look, look," Mau recalls. "They say, 'We don't see the island.' But it's there."

"Mau knows how to look for that little disturbance on the horizon when the tips of coconut trees rise above the water," Nainoa says. "My eyes were physically stronger than his, I was younger, but I couldn't see it for twenty minutes. On a calm day it's easy to see, but when there are swells it's hard because the tips of the trees bounce in and out of the horizon when they're far away. Finally, I climbed the mast. There it was. The first time I had seen an atoll coming out of the ocean. It was so powerful. We were home. It has got to be the Tuamotus."

"The tops of the coconut trees looked like little brushes on the horizon,"

Chad remembers. "Like a grove of mangrove trees. It just grew and grew."

"It was like these tiny cockroach legs on the horizon," Marion recalls. "It took me the longest time to see it."

"*Ishka* this is *Hōkūle'a*," Leon was calling on the VHF radio.

"Go ahead *Hōkūle'a*."

"We've got two guys up on the rig. Nainoa is on the aft mast and Shorty is on the foremast—and both of them are looking at land right now."

"Congratulations to Gordon and your splendid navigator and to all the crew," Alex radioed back. "I am more excited than you are. I was just dancing and my wife told me off."

Mau disregarded the hubbub around him but a smile creased his weathered face. "Mau is not the kind of person to say 'Congratulations, you did well,' " Nainoa says. "But I could see, without saying a word, that he was very, very content."

Later, when the excitement had worn off, Mau called Nainoa over to him.

"Why I know the bird was flying back to the island was because he has a fish in his beak," Mau told Nainoa. "These birds they nesting. They feed the babies. So they come out in morning, get fish, and fly back to nest. Not same as when I tell you they fly out for fishing in morning. That was why I say turn canoe around."

✧ ✧ ✧ ✧ ✧

Professional seaman observe thousands of arrivals and you might think the experience becomes mundane, but even the most jaded is drawn to the rail when the horizon is creased by the rumpled shape of land. For *Hōkūle'a's* crew, there was something deeper. Hawaiki Rising. "The navigator spun the *aka* cord over his head, in the stars, and he threw out the magic fishhook," says Sam Ka'ai, "and he pulled up an island."

Chad Baybayan sensed time racing backward. He relived ancestral voyages. He felt spirits joining him at the canoe's rail. "My *'aumākua*," he remembers, "were with me."

Sam raised his *pū* and blew a long warbling note. He blew again. And again. The last two notes rose in pitch and echoed back from the island. "When the canoe capsized, my *pū* went into the depths of the third dimension, the *moana*, the ocean. But it came back to me. It was blown when the canoe was launched and when she

Nainoa on aft mast

arrived in Tahiti on the first trip. Now she announced once again Hawaiki rising. But this time, after so many centuries, the fisherman was Hawaiian."

On this voyage, Maui's fishhook had risen thirty-one times from the sea to point the way south. Everyone knew this was Eddie's constellation. Six of the crew had been aboard when *Hōkūle'a* capsized and many times during the voyage they had sensed Eddie's presence—but now his spirit seemed to walk among them. "All of a sudden I had this flash of Eddie Aikau," Marion recalls, "I saw his smiling face. I just imagined him running around on deck and asking Sam if he could blow the conch."

"There was celebration on the canoe," Nainoa says, "but there was no high-fiving and jumping up and down. It was deeper than that. Mau said 'There's the island'—and no one could see it. Then everyone began to see it—one at a time. We were excited to see the tree tops, but once everyone saw the island there was a kind of uncomfortable quietness about the crew. I think everybody was struck by the same thought. What do I do now? There was a hollow emptiness because the voyage was over. It was a time that intrigued me. I saw people trying to be busy. I saw Snake washing things that had already been washed."

Hōkūle'a turned west and sailed in the island's lee on an ocean that was now flat and deep blue.

"I climbed up the mast and I looked over the trees and into the lagoon. The reefs were extensive and beautiful, and they had these sand pockets that were turquoise in the calm of the lagoon. And nobody. No people. It was just nature. I thought, 'God, we are passing it.' I wanted to go and feel and touch this island, but I knew we needed to go. We didn't know how to get into the lagoon. We didn't know if it would be safe. We turned to follow the coast. The trees kept coming up and coming up. We had no idea where it would end. We were no more than a quarter of a mile away. The island seemed so untouched and so pure. I had not really slept for a month, but I had a very strong urge to see the island. I said to myself—'Someday, I have got to come back here.' "

After thirty-one days on an empty sea, the sight of land was surreal. The island seemed huge. It filled the horizon to port. Coconut palms seemed to leap into the sky.

But what island was it? At about 10:30, Steve Somsen approached Nainoa with his notebook and tape recorder. Last night, Nainoa thought the canoe was approaching the Tuamotus, about nine houses west of their reference course. For the next twelve hours or so, they had traveled about a half a sailing day on a course two houses to the west of the desired course.

"Right now I would put us ten houses to the west of our reference course," Nainoa says, "that should be close to Mataiva."

"What do you feel is the latitude?" Steve asked.

"I would say about 15 degrees 20 minutes south."

By Nainoa's calculations, the canoe was approaching the western end of the Tuamotus which was anchored by the last island in the chain, Mataiva.

"But it's not Mataiva," he said. "Mataiva is not an atoll like this. It's horseshoe shaped. It's much smaller than this one. I think we are to the east of Mataiva."

Aboard *Ishka*, Alex leaned against the mast, taking a noon sextant sight of the sun. A half hour later the radio crackled. The island was Tikehau, about 40 miles to the east of Mataiva.

Later, when he had time to consider it, Nainoa thought that Mau might have been a little startled by how close his student's navigation had been. "I think he was surprised it was Tikehau. It's so close to Mataiva. So close."

The final destination, Tahiti, lay about a hundred and sixty miles to the south, but for all intents the voyage was over. After a hiatus of a thousand years, a Hawaiian navigator had found land in the old way.

The men and women standing at *Hōkūle'a's* rail had been raised in two seemingly irreconcilable worlds—Hawaiian and *haole*. But Pinky Thompson had seen values that were shared by both: vision, discipline, preparation, planning, and the binding power of *aloha*. Having trained together and having endured the rigors of the voyage, this crew had joined across potential barriers of race, ethnicity, and income. The vision of an island rising from the distant horizon had united them. It was a powerful moment, but it was tinged with sadness.

"I felt hollow," Jo-Anne remembers. "We had joined together as a crew and now, soon, we would all go our own ways. We might not even see each other again. It started to get into the evening and it was very quiet. I watched Marion who was silhouetted against the setting sun and I thought, 'It's over. Everything is over.'"

Quiet by temperament and his respect for the powerful ocean world he had inhabited all his life, Mau's outward recognition of this landfall was subtle. Yet it was a powerful moment nonetheless. One of his students had followed the ancestral seapath to raise an island from the sea. Later, back in Hawai'i, Mau would tell Nainoa that this was a culmination of his life as a navigator. "I am proud and happy for you," he said, "but I am more happy for myself because I am your teacher."

The secrets that Mau received from his father and grandfather had been carried down from the earliest settlers of Satawal. Passing them on went beyond a duty—a *kuleana* as Hawaiians would call it—it meant a kind of immortality. A master navigator lived on in the sound of voices chanting in the canoe house—his students conveying his knowledge to new generations. "Mau told me," Nainoa recalls, "that a navigator is never really considered a master until he passes on his skills to his students."

❖ ❖ ❖ ❖ ❖

Nainoa had found land alone, seeking council from no one during the voyage, yet he had never been without the companioning presence of his teachers. Mau's physical presence had been a blessing, and a short distance away, aboard *Ishka*, he felt the constant support of Will Kyselka. His father— Pinky Thompson—always voyaged with him. "My father gave us our chance. He believed in us. He let me go. He understood that if *Hōkūle'a's* legacy was tragedy it would set us further back than anyone could imagine. He knew we had to heal the depression and dysfunction that our people were going through. He knew there was a cultural, spiritual connection to the ocean that had to be well, and he knew that connection was being woven by the canoe. So when we found Tikehau, we found a new dignity and pride and I knew that he was proud of his son."

"I remember Nainoa getting emotional then," Chad recalls. "He needed to be by himself."

For the first time on the voyage, Nainoa descended into the compartment that he shared with Harry and zipped closed the door.

"There was a real sense of completion when I saw the island, but then all I wanted to do was get away. I had stayed on deck the whole trip; I never went down in the hulls. When I went down into my *puka*, everybody left me alone. It was overwhelming. My most powerful image was that conversation back in Honolulu with Eddie when he said, "I want to see Hawaiki coming out of the sea." I was in the *puka* crying. I knew we couldn't bring him back to life nor could we ever do anything to justify his death. Eddie inspired us to keep going during all those days of doubt. And now, seeing that island come out of the sea meant we had accomplished the dream that we all shared."

Over twenty-four hundred miles of open ocean, through three belts of current, five days of storms off Hawai'i, stubborn south winds above the equator that forced the canoe off course, five days becalmed in the second Doldrums, enforced delays while waiting for *Ishka*, the multiple vagaries of wind and current, Nainoa had navigated *Hōkūle'a* to landfall with an error so small as to be infinitesimal—about forty miles.

"I was awake for a long time," he remembers. "I couldn't sleep. I was too excited. Then I was half awake—half meditating. It was a beautiful private time. I closed my eyes."

It was dark in the *puka*. He saw thin slits of light around the zippered entrance and listened to the sound of the canoe moving through the sheltered water in the island's lee. The sound gentled him. Half asleep, half meditating—he saw a familiar image: a door with a ghostly light behind it. It was a vision from his childhood—Yoshi's door—and behind it was the sum of all his fears. "But now I saw that the fear behind the door was myself—it was part of me. And, for the first time, I saw that it was also my best friend." His fear, he realized, had been an essential part of his success—a goad that drove his preparation. "Accepting the risk of failure is part of the process of preparing for success. When Eddie left the canoe to save his friends, he risked everything. He gave me courage to accept the challenge. 'Is the voyage worth the risk?' my father had asked me. 'If so, then have the courage to let go the lines.' Now, I expect to be afraid whenever I take on a challenge."

Nainoa slept with Harry standing protectively near the entrance to his *puka*. The canoe sailed on past Tikehau and Mataiva, with *Ishka* now in the lead, Alex navigating by compass and chart. Once clear of the atoll, the two vessels turned south toward Tahiti. The sun went down and the watch changed. It was another day at sea.

At ten o'clock, Nainoa woke and went on deck. The sea was calm. To starboard, about half way to its meridian, he saw Maui's fishhook—Eddie Aikau's constellation—poised to pull Hawaiki from the sea.

EPILOGUE

Satawal

The island was tiny. As we sailed around its southern shore, the aroma of land reached us. We saw a line of lofty canoe houses and a crowd on the beach. Their singing—soft, undulating—blended with the wind.

It was March 15th, 2007, and I was aboard *Hōkūle'a* as we made landfall on Satawal, Mau Piailug's home island. This voyage began fifty-one days ago when *Hōkūle'a* set off from Hawai'i, accompanied by another voyaging canoe—*Alingano Maisu*—a similar double-hulled vessel that had been built as a gift for Mau.

A conch shell was blown on the island and small boats came out to assist with placing our anchors. The sun, low on the horizon, glowed in surf breaking on the reef. We had finally arrived at the place where the revival of the ancient art of navigation, led by Mau, had begun.

❖ ❖ ❖ ❖

Mau's decision to sail aboard *Hōkūle'a* in 1976 and 1980 was motivated by his desire to preserve his art. If the young men of Satawal did not want to learn it, he would pass it on to those who did. But sailing aboard a Hawaiian canoe did not mean that Mau had given up on his own people.

Hōkūle'a's 1976 voyage had been filmed by a National Geographic crew and when it was broadcast on television world-wide, Mau immediately understood the value of modern media. In 1982, he agreed to appear in a film that I produced called *The Navigators—Pathfinders of the Pacific*. During an interview, I asked Mau why he decided to make the film.

"I wanted to make the film," Mau replied, "because I'm afraid that when I die there will be no more navigators. When the people see the film, they may realize how important navigation is."

In 1984, Mau agreed to a request by author Steve Thomas to live on Satawal to study navigation and write a book entitled *The Last Navigator* published in 1987. Two years later, Mau made yet another film—also entitled *The Last Navigator*—which Steve produced. From 1985 to 1987, Mau sailed aboard *Hōkūle'a* on a two-year, 16,000 mile retracing of the traditional voyaging routes—inspiring a revival of seafaring culture throughout Polynesia. In New Zealand, Hekenukumai Busby built *Te Aurere* in 1992, a large voyaging canoe of his own. In 1993, *Hawai'iloa* was launched on O'ahu with support from the Polynesian Voyaging Society, and in 1995, Shorty Bertelmann and his brother Clay launched *Makali'i*, on the Big Island of Hawai'i. In that same period, *Tahiti Nui* was built in Tahiti and *Takitumu* and *Te 'Au o Tonga* were built in Rarotonga. In 1995, all these canoes set off from the Marquesas bound for Hawai'i, the first time in a thousand years that a fleet of Polynesian canoes had journeyed together. All arrived safely and returned home again, guided by navigators trained by Mau Piailug and Nainoa Thompson.

These voyages, and Mau's mentorship of Polynesian navigators, stimulated not only the building of canoes, but the revival of Polynesian culture in general. Among Hawaiians, where the loss of culture had been particularly severe, *hālau hula* (hula schools) seemed to spring up everywhere, *heiau* were rebuilt, ancient curing practices were revived and, in 1999, the first class of high school students graduated having spoken only Hawaiian from their entry into the first grade. Reinvigorated Hawaiians stood up to demand the return of lands taken from them illegally. In 1995, President Clinton signed the Apology Decree— validating their claims—and today, many Hawaiians are working to regain their sovereignty as a native people.

In 1999, Mau carried out the most significant step in his plan to revive his

Mau Piailug, *Pwo* ceremony, 2007.

own traditions by navigating the Hawaiian canoe, *Makali'i,* to his home waters - visiting many of the major islands in Micronesia. In 2001, Mau returned to Hawai'i to help build *Alingano Maisu*—a gift to him from Shorty and Clay Bertelmann and many others for all that he had done for Hawaiians.

Now, in 2007, as *Hōkūle'a* and *Maisu* anchored off Satawal, Mau was 75 years old and suffering from a life-threatening kidney ailment. It was time, he thought, to bring together his voyaging family for an ancient initiation ceremony—*pwo*.

Eleven men from Satawal had studied sufficiently to earn the privilege of being initiated as *pwo* navigators; Selestine Retewailam, Andrew Igomal, Isidore Metewalur, Romanes Yarofaichiy, Lorenzo Sartilug, Manno Ratilou, Alfonso Reilug, Luke Yauritik, Camilo Eraegmai, John Lalogo, and Mau's son, Sesario Sewralur. In addition, five men from Hawai'i would be initiated;

Nainoa Thompson, Shorty Bertelmann, Chad Paishon, Chad Baybayan, and Bruce Blankenfeld.

❖ ❖ ❖ ❖ ❖

On Sunday, March 18th, the day of the *pwo* ceremony, the wind died and shifted easterly, casting the anchorage in a lee. Outrigger canoes were drawn up on Satawal's sheltered shore beneath lofty canoe houses, their thatch roofs glistening in the sun and their floors covered with freshly woven mats. The sixteen navigators, powdered with yellow turmeric, dressed in red loin clothes, and garlanded with headbands of colorful flowers sat patiently in the canoe house. Around their necks was a lei of ginger leaves—*yoangerhik*—a medicinal plant. The women of Satawal were gathered outside, singing rhythmically.

At about 10:00 a.m., Mau was helped to a white plastic seat cushioned by blankets. One by one, the men crawled to him and he rubbed them with a sacred medicine, first on the forehead, then on the heart, chanting as he blessed them. Joining Mau for the ceremony was a *pwo* navigator from the nearby island of Pulap, Lambert Lokopwe. "The medicines are given to the heart and to the mind for the navigator to have *seram*—light," Lambert explains, "so he voyages with the light, never darkness."

Next, Mau touched each navigator on the shoulder with a long strand of coconut fiber which he then parted and placed over their heads as a garland. Mau's face was somber, reflecting the power of this blessing. The incoming navigators were then given a special coconut to drink—*nuun-lesseram* or "coconut in the light." "The coconut will give *seram*—light—to the new navigator," Lambert said, "but the deeper meaning is perseverance. That coconut is a large one. Each navigator drinks it and never stops until it is completely gone, meaning that he has full confidence in himself—that he will pursue the course until it is finished."

The sacred calabash, the *uulong,* was then covered with woven mats. Two gods—*Luukeileng,* the center of heaven, the god that controls everything; and *Weriyeng,* the god of navigation, owned the calabash. During the final rites, Mau instructed each incoming *pwo,* one by one, to place their right hand on the covered *uulong* while he prayed to the gods to bestow *pwo* upon him.

Each new *pwo* was then given a bracelet that contained two kinds of coral.

Mau Piailug blessing Shorty Bertelmann

Hard coral signified the mental and physical toughness of the navigator, and stinging coral symbolized the strength of the navigator's command at sea. Mau chanted softly. "Mau is calling upon *Luukeileng* and *Weriyeng* to bestow all rights, everything concerning navigation, on this person," Lambert explained. Finally, the food from the sacred calabash was divided and eaten by all the initiated navigators. The *pwo* ceremony was complete.

❖ ❖ ❖ ❖ ❖

The following morning, Satawal's Hawaiian visitors packed their bags and carried them down to the beach where small boats would ferry them off to *Hōkūle'a*. *Alingano Maisu* bobbed at anchor. She was now under the command of a new captain, Mau's son—Sesario Sewralur.

"It came to that dreaded moment when it was time to say goodbye," Nainoa recalls. "There was a crowd of people in Mau's house. I wanted to see him last —to spend a quiet moment with him. Finally everyone left. Mau was tired. The prognosis that he might survive even through that year seemed doubtful. I did not know how to say goodbye. He did not know how to say goodbye. It was awkward. So we just said, 'see you later,' and I left. I walked down the beach. I was stumbling, kind of weaving. I stopped. I said to myself—'this is all wrong.' I turned around and ran back to Mau's house."

"Mau," Nainoa said, "you taught us to sail, so when we sail, do you sail with us?"

Mau nodded.

"If we teach navigation do we teach you?"

"Yes," Mau said.

"So, if we teach navigation then you will be with us forever?"

Mau smiled and nodded.

Maybe that was one reason why he gave us pwo, Nainoa thought. *To make sure that we would be together forever, through his teaching.*

"Then we embraced in a special kind of way," Nainoa recalls, "and I walked out of the house. It was a sunny day. I looked back into his room. It was all in shadows. The windows were back-lit and I just saw Mau sitting there—just his silhouette. All by himself. Alone."

A few hours later—aboard *Hōkūle'a*—Nainoa watched Satawal slip slowly below the horizon.

✧ ✧ ✧ ✧ ✧

In March of 2008, Mau presided over one last *pwo* ceremony for Maori navigator Hekenukumai Busby, the builder of *Te Aurere*.

On July 12, 2010, he passed away on Satawal.

All his life, Mau had struggled to spread the knowledge he inherited from his ancestors. Almost single-handedly he reversed two centuries of cultural decline among Hawaiians, replacing it with a resurgent pride in their great seafaring heritage. Today, *Alingano Maisu* sails among the Caroline Islands, captained by his son, Sesario Sewralur, to carry on Mau's mission of reviving his own seafaring culture. And throughout the vast Pacific, canoes are being built and sailed by a revived nation of seafarers. The *seram* — the powerful light — that Mau Piailug first carried to Hawai'i in 1973, will forever inspire the people of the Pacific and beyond to raise islands from the sea.

AFTERWORD

By Nainoa Thompson

My teacher, Mau Piailug, told me that after a *pwo* navigator has been initiated on Satawal, his first duty is to sail from his island and return with "something of value" for his people. This voyage is symbolic of a navigator's responsibility to help sustain his community in harmony and health. In our Hawaiian language we have a word—*mālama*—which means "to care for," and I think it evolved from our own heritage of long distance voyaging. Our ancestors learned that to arrive safely at their destination they must *mālama* each other and their canoe.

Hōkūle'a has now sailed more than 130,000 miles to visit most of the major islands in Polynesia. On all of our voyages, we become attuned to nature and we begin to see our canoe as a tiny island surrounded by the ocean. We have everything aboard that we need to survive—as long as we marshal those resources well.

The wisdom and values of our ancestors enabled them to *mālama* Hawai'i and her surrounding oceans for nearly 2,000 years. By carefully managing their natural resources, they were able to sustain a large, healthy population. Now, we must learn to treat our planet in the same way.

On June 8th, 2013, we will begin a voyage around the world to *mālama honua* —"care for the Earth." We will sail for approximately 36 months; travel more than 45,000 nautical miles; and visit at least 26 countries, with 62 stops. During the voyage, we will connect with communities that share our values and vision.

Returning home, we will bring with us "something of value"—lessons of hope and action as we navigate toward a safe, peaceful, and sustainable future for our children.

ENDNOTES

1. Salmond, Anne. *The Trial of the Cannibal Dog*. Penguin Books, 2004 - page 105.

2. Wyllie, R.C. *Answers to Questions Proposed by his Excellency*. Honolulu: March 27, 1848 - page 13.

3. Rhodes, Elizabeth Flemming. *On the Fringe of Fame – the Career of Richard Bland Lee II in the South and West, 1797-1875*. Castle Press, 1990.

4. Daws, Gavan. *Shoal of Time*. Honolulu: University of Hawai'i Press, 1968 - page 140.

5. Twain, Mark. *The Sandwich Islands*. New York Tribune, January 6, 1873.

6. Golson, Jack. *The Settlement of Oceania*. In Polynesian Navigation, Polynesian Society Memoir No. 34. Wellington: Polynesian Society, 1963 - page 23.

7. Thomas, Stephen. *The Last Navigator*. New York: Henry Holt and Company, 1987 - pages 163-164.

8. Banks, Joseph. In *Canoes of Oceania*, edited by A. C. Haddon and James Hornell, Honolulu: Bernice P. Bishop Museum, 1975 - page 121.

9. Coleman, Stuart Holmes. *Eddie Would Go: The Story of Eddie Aikau, Hawaiian Hero and Pioneer of Big Wave Surfing*. New York: St. Martin's Griffin, 2004 - page 174.

10. Maury, Matthew F. *Wind and Current Charts*. Washington: William A. Harris, 1858 - page 14.

11. Stevenson, Robert Louis. *His Best Pacific Writing*, Honolulu: Bess Press, 2003 - page 43.

ACKNOWLEDGMENTS

Thanks to:

Steve Somsen for his log of the 1980 voyage, without which the book could not have been written. The Aikau family for their comments and support. Keōmailani Fergerstrom for editing the Hawaiian language with the help of Sam Gon and David Eyre. Val Hart for initial copy editing of the manuscript. Christina Thompson and Keith Leber for editorial comments. Herbert K. Kane Family Trust, and David Swann for providing illustrations. Ben Young, Steve Somsen, Steve Thomas, Kamehameha Schools, and Monte Costa for photographs. Nan Bacon, Tara Kenny, and John Kramer for invaluable help designing the book. The entire staff at Island Heritage for their assistance in publishing the book.

And to those who read the book and provided valuable comments: Michael Ambrosino, Nan Bacon, Chad Baybayan, Bruce Blankenfeld, Brock Callen, Deborah Carr, Solomon Aikau, Myra Aikau, Clyde Aikau, Stuart Coleman, Dr. Ben Finney, Todd Follansbee, Wally Froiseth, Val Hart, Harry Ho, Roger Jellinek, Anetta Kinnicutt, Philip Kinnicutt, Herb Kane, Dr. Bernie Kilonsky, Dr. Patrick Kirch, John Kruse, Mike McCoy, Paul Schneider, Steve Somsen, Hardy Spoehr, Karin Swanson, Maile Swanson-Low, Laura Thompson, Nainoa Thompson, Ted Westlake, Gaylord Wilcox, Jock Williams.

And to those who gave generously of their time during interviews for the book: Snake Ah Hee, Pat Aiu, Solomon Aikau, Myra Aikau, Clyde Aikau, Chad Baybayan, Shorty Bertelmann, Bruce Blankenfeld, Dr. Ben Finney, Wally Froiseth, Harry Ho, Kiki Hugho, Kimo Hugho, Alex Jakubenko, Sam Ka'ai, Herb Kane, Captain Kawika Kapahulehua, Bernie Kilonsky, John Kruse, Will Kyselka, *Pwo* Navigator Lambert Lokopwe, Dave Lyman, Kimo Lyman, Marion Lyman-Mersereau, Buddy McGuire, Mel Paoa, Gordon Pi'ianai'a, Mau Piailug, Billy Richards, Steve Somsen, Jo-Anne Sterling, Tava Taupu, Nainoa Thompson, Laura Thompson, Pinky Thompson, Michael Tongg, Dr. Ben Young.

HAWAIIAN GLOSSARY

By David Kāwika Eyre

'a'ā · slow-moving clinker lava

'a'ama · black crab that lives on shore rocks

'ahu lā'ī · a rain cape

'āina · land, country

'Alenuihāhā · channel between the islands of Hawai'i and Maui

'ama'ama · medium-sized mullet

'aumakua · (pl. 'aumākua) ancestral spirit

'awa · a drink prepared from the kava plant

'iako · outrigger boom

'ōkolehao · strong liquor distilled from the root of the ti plant

'ōlelo · language, to speak, to say

'olonā · native shrub; inner bark used to make strong cordage

'opihi · edible shellfish, limpet

Mānai-a-ka-lani · the fish hook of the great Maui

ahu o ka moana · altar of the sea

ahupua'a · land division usually extending from sea to mountains

aka'ula · red shadow or glow, red sunset seen as a sign of rain clearing

aku · bonito, skipjack

ali'i · chief, ruler

awa · milkfish

Hakipu'u · land section on the windward side of O'ahu

hālau hula · meeting house or place where hula is taught

Hālawa Valley · land sections and valleys on several Hawaiian Islands

hale · house, building, shelter

Halema'uma'u · crater located within the larger Kīlauea Crater on
    Hawai'i Island

Hāmākua · district, northeast Hawai'i Island

Hāna · district east of Kīpahulu in East Maui

Hanauma Bay · bay on southeast side of O'ahu near Koko Crater

haole · foreign, foreigner, Caucasian

Hawai'i · largest of the Hawaiian Islands

Hawaiki · homeland of the Polynesian people

heiau · Hawaiian place of worship

ho'okele · to sail, sailing, to steer

ho'omaika'i i ke akua · to thank, bless, praise a god/the gods

ho'oponopono · to make right; a process of conflict resolution

Hōkūle'a · the zenith star Arctus; name of replica voyaging canoe

hōkūlele · shooting star, meteor, comet

Hōnaunau · land area, village, bay, South Kona, Hawai'i Island

Honolua Bay · bay in the Lahaina district of Maui Island

Hualālai · large volcano in Kailua, North Kona

hukilau · to fish with a hanging net to which are attached *ti* leaves

Humu'ula · land section and sheep station in Mauna Kea
    and Humu'ulu districts of Hawai'i Island

i'a · fish

kāhea · to call, to greet, to name,

Kaho'olawe · island in Maui county, earlier name was Kanaloa

kahuna lapa'au · healer, medical practitioner

kanaka maoli · a native Hawaiian; a person who has Hawaiian blood

Kanaloa · one of the four great Hawaiian gods

Kāne · one of the four great Hawaiian gods

Kāne'ohe · district and bay in windward O'ahu

kaona · hidden or underlying meaning as in Hawaiian poetry or song

Kaua'i · island, also known as Kaua'i o Manokalanipō after its
    celebrated chief

Kaupō · district in East Maui, west of Kīpahulu

Kēia ka maoli · This is real

Ke'ehi · lagoon and beach park on O'ahu's south shore near
    Honolulu Airport

Kealaikahiki · channel between Lāna'i and Kaho'olawe, launching place
    of voyages to foreign lands

kiawe · introduced dry-land tree; pods used for animal feed; wood used for charcoal

koko · blood

konohiki · head man of an *ahupua'a* who represented a chief

kū'ula · a fish shrine

kū'auhau · genealogy, lineage, history, historian

Kualoa · land division, point, park in the Waikāne district of O'ahu.

kuleana · right, privilege, responsibility

Kūlepeamoa · heiau and ridge near Koko Head, Island of O'ahu

Kuli'ou'ou · land division, valley and forest reserve on south shore of O'ahu

kūmū · goat fish, symbol of a woman or female qualities

Kumukahi · easternmost cape on Hawai'i Island, named after migratory hero from Kahiki

kupuna (plural: *kūpuna*) · elder, grandparent, old timer

Lahaina · district and town in West Maui

lāhui o ka lani · the heavenly hosts

Lāna'i · island in Maui County

lau hala · pandanus leaves

lehua · the flower of the *'ōhi'a* tree

lei hulu · feather *lei,* formally worn by royalty

mahimahi · dolphin, a popular food fish

maka i'a · fish eye

maka'āinana · commoner

Mākaha · land section, village, valley in Ka'ena, O'ahu

Makapu'u · beach park, point and surfing area, Koko Head, O'ahu

makau honu 'ea · hook made from shell of hawksbill turtle

makau iwi · hook made of bone

makau pā · hook made from mother-of-pearl shell

makua hānai · adoptive parent

mālama · to take care of, protect, save, preserve

mana · power, spiritual power, authority, privilege

mana'o · thought, idea, belief, opinion

mele · song, to sing

menehune · legendary race of small people who built ponds, temples, and roads at night

mo'o · lizard, water spirit, dragon

mo'okū'auhau · genealogy

mo'olelo · story, tale, myth, history

moemoe · to sleep (a rare plural)

Mōkapu · peninsula, point, land division in Kailua, O'ahu

Moloka'i · island between Maui and O'ahu

Nālehia · name of a canoe

namunamu · to grumble, complain

nēnē · Hawaiian goose

Ni'ihau · island to the northwest of Kaua'i Island

niho palaoa · carved whale's tooth, worn by royalty

noio · Hawaiian noddy tern

O'ahu · most populous of Hawaiian Islands; located between Moloka'i and Kaua'i

'ohana · family, relative, kin group

'ohana wa'a · canoe family, members of a crew

pāhoehoe · smooth, unbroken lava

paniolo · a Hawaiian cowboy

pāpio · a young *ulua* (trevally fish) under 10 pounds in weight

pū · large shell of the triton conch or helmet variety used as an instrument

Pu'ukoholā · hill and heiau built by Kamehameha I in Kawaihae area of Hawai'i Island.

pueo · owl

pule · prayer, grace, church service

pūne'e · a large, moveable couch

ulua · jack or trevally fish, symbol of a male or masculine qualities

Wai'anae · *ahupua'a* on the west side of O'ahu

Waikīkī · land division on the south side of O'ahu

Waipi'o · valley, bay, stream in north Hawai'i Island

weke · small goat fish

Wākea · first human to live in Hawai'i

PHOTOGRAPHS
AND
ILLUSTRATIONS

Photographs and Illustrations

Except where noted above, all illustrations are created by Sam Low and produced by the design department at Island Heritage Publishing.